THE ONE MINUTE MILLIONAIRE

THE ONE MINUTE MILLIONAIRE

The Story that Transforms Your Life and Makes You Rich

MARK VICTOR HANSEN
and ROBERT G. ALLEN

Vermilion
LONDON

To all the present and future Enlightened Millionaires

11 13 15 17 19 20 18 16 14 12

Published in 2002 by Vermilion, an imprint of Ebury Publishing

Ebury Publishing is a Random House Group company

The Random House Group Limited Reg. No. 954009

Addresses for companies within the Random House Group can be found at
www.rbooks.co.uk

A CIP catalogue record for this book is available from the British Library

The Random House Group Limited supports The Forest Stewardship
Council (FSC), the leading international forest certification organisation.
All our titles that are printed on Greenpeace approved FSC certified paper
carry the FSC logo. Our paper procurement policy can be found at
www.rbooks.co.uk/environment

Printed and bound in Great Britain by
Cox & Wyman Ltd, Reading, Berkshire

ISBN 9780091884635

Copies are available at special rates for bulk orders. Contact the sales
development team on 020 7840 8487 or for more information.

To buy books by your favourite authors and register for offers, visit
www.rbooks.co.uk

CONTENTS

EXPLANATION OF US FINANCIAL & LEGAL WORDS OR
CONCEPTS AS USED IN THIS BOOK

401k
an individually tailored pension fund for private individuals, which conforms to certain US fiscal requirements. The name comes from the Internal Revenue Code, Section 401(k), which established the concept in 1981.

Certificate of Deposit (CD)
an instrument which records the receipt of a deposit of funds for a fixed period; CD's are issued by banks, credit unions and savings and loan associations (SLA's) in the US and to some extent substitute what in the UK would be a term deposit with a bank or building society; for this reason a CD usually carries a higher rate of interest than a simple savings account.

Closing
the completion of a (purchase, sale or other) transaction; **Closing Costs** are the legal and other expenses of such a transaction or transactions; **Simultaneous Closing** occurs when related purchase and sale transactions occur on the same day.

Condominium
a multi-unit building, usually an apartment building, which is owned by the owners of the individual units.

Corporate Bond
a loan instrument issued by a company, which can be actively traded on securities markets; these instruments usually yield above average rates of interest.

Distressed Property
a "blighted property" in the UK, i.e. one suffering from some problem, such as sitting tenants in situ, or with a blight arising from a recent cause, such as fire or flood.

Duplex
an apartment with accommodation on two floors.

Equity
as used in this book, equity refers to the stake one has in a property after repaying all loans relating to it; **Refinancing Equity** (or "cranking") as discussed by Sam and Michelle on page 319 involves selling one property to buy a second, cheaper property with the same level of loans, thus enabling any surplus equity released from the first to be turned into cash.

Escrow
an asset (usually property) held in trust by a commercial lender.

Escrow Officer
an official working at a commercial lender's office, whose function would be similar to a mortgage officer in the UK.

Flip/Flipping
in this book, the action by a purchaser of assigning a property to another purchaser in the course of his or her purchase transaction; such a course of action would be highly unusual (and is not believed to be possible) in the UK.

Foreclosure	a legal procedure, undertaken by a lender once loan (repayment) conditions have been broken, that bars a mortgager from any rights over the property mortgaged; this usually leads quickly to eviction of the occupier.
Hard-money Lender	a provider of high ("market") rate, short-term loans under strict conditions, often against the security of an asset such as a house or other personal property.
Homes for Lease	rental properties.
HUD foreclosure	a "Homes under Distress" property in danger (or in the process) of **Foreclosure** (see above).
Infomercial	a form of (TV) marketing that attracts attention by providing (or purporting to provide) interesting factual information.
Intrapreneur	an employee working from the base of a large company (such as US manufacturer 3m) who would be remunerated by commissions rather than salary.
IPO	an "Initial Public Offering", or new share issue, by a company seeking a quote on one of the leading securities exchanges; a high risk investment.
IRA	an "Individual Retirement Account", or savings account into which a person can make tax-deductible contributions to accumulate a pension for retirement.
Leverage	the use of a lever, in the form of financial or other assistance, to gain an advantage (see pages 98 to 100 for more details of what the authors mean by this). In financial terms, leveraging refers to the use of external funding to undertake one or more transactions.
Lien	a charge by a lender upon a borrower's assets, which might include his or her property.
Listing broker	the primary estate agent.
Mutual Fund	a collective investment product bought and sold in units, similar to a UK unit trust, which can be invested in shares, bonds, certificates of deposit or other investments; a **growth mutual fund** would aim to achieve, typically, capital growth by investing in investments with a higher risk rating; an **aggressive growth mutual fund** would aim to achieve an even higher potential return by investing in even riskier investments.
NASDAQ	a New York stock exchange primarily focussed on smaller companies.

Nikkei	a reference to the Nikkei Dow Index, which records the movements of key stocks on the Tokyo stock exchange.
Note	see **Promissory Note** below.
Obligation	any contractual commitment, such as a loan guarantee or a commitment to pay for the past or future costs of hospitalisation, care, property usage, etc.
P/E Ratio	a reference to "Price/Earnings Ratio", a measure enabling comparison between different company valuations nationally and internationally.
Promissory Note	a written promise to pay a certain amount of money to a specified individual (often the bearer) who has entitlement to receive it; such notes are often used as the basis for obtaining/providing credit in the US.
Real Estate	the US term for property in the form of land and/or buildings.
Realtor	an estate agent.
Renter	a tenant.
Rezoning	commercial redevelopment (of an area).
Secured note	a **Promissory Note** (see above) with property used as security for the lender.
Simultaneous Closing	related purchase and sale transactions occurring on the same day.
Soft-money Lender	a provider of loans at sub-market interest rates; in the context intended by the authors, this could include a willing individual who wanted to dispose of his property.
Tithing	the practice of giving a tithe (i.e. a tenth) of one's income to charitable causes.
Wraparound mortgage	a mortgage "wrapped around", i.e. secured by, the **Equity** (see above) stake in a property.

INTRODUCTION

MILLIONAIRE MOUNTAIN

Imagine this: You just received a phone call from the estate of a long-lost relative. You have inherited a million dollars in cash! It's waiting for you in a safety deposit box in a Swiss bank. There is only one catch. The key to the box is in a silver container hidden at the summit of Mount McKinley in Alaska—at 20,320 feet, the tallest mountain in North America. The instructions are clear—you must personally climb the mountain (no helicopters!) and retrieve the key yourself. If you complete the task within 12 months from today, the money is yours. If not, you lose the money forever.

Let that sink in for a minute. Would you do it? Could you do it?

Mount McKinley is not an impossible climb. Thousands of climbers have made it to the summit. But it still requires some serious planning, preparation, and training.

Becoming an Enlightened Millionaire™ won't be nearly as difficult or as dangerous as climbing Mount McKinley. But some things are similar. You'll still need mentors who will guide you along your path. That's us. We'll serve as your veteran climbers to mentor you to the top.

You'll need to follow a training regimen—The Millionaire Map. We've provided you with that.

You'll need to be disciplined enough to follow through. We'll support you with this also.

Are you willing to take the first step?

Yes?

Then turn to the next page.

Enlightened Millionaire is a trademark of One Minute Millionaire, LLC.

OF COURSE, THERE IS MORE
TO LIFE THAN MONEY!

Clearly, money isn't everything. For us, it's not even in the top four—miles behind family, health, friends, and spiritual values. An abundance of these four life dimensions constitutes true wealth. J. Paul Getty—the richest person of his time—used to receive letters from his not nearly as rich brother that started with, "To the richest man in the world from the wealthiest."

We agree; one can be wealthy without being rich. Still, a lot of "good" people dismiss the concept of financial success as an "unworthy" goal—perhaps even morally suspect. And with a title like *The One Minute Millionaire*, we're certain to raise a few eyebrows.

Money, by itself, is neither good nor bad—it's neutral. Money is an energy tool. Like a hammer, money can be used to build or to destroy. We believe that understanding money—how to ethically make it, keep it, and share it—adds a positive dimension to wealth. Our lives, our relationships, and our happiness improve when we have enough money. That's why we wrote this book. Money properly earned and combined with enlightened intentions makes the world a better place.

Almost anyone can become a millionaire, but we're hoping you'll aim for enlightenment at the same time. Just follow our proven system and the odds are substantially in your favor to become an *enlightened* millionaire. All you have to do is to read this book and travel the path. If you want it, it's there for you. And it's never been easier. Never. We are not asking you to believe you can do this. Let us believe for you. We'll show you how—with just a few extra minutes a week, a little more effort, and a few extra dollars invested in the proper places—anyone and everyone can become financially successful. We believe that you'll be a better employee, a better family member, a better friend, a better member of society, when you learn and use our proven system of financial success.

Are you ready? Let's begin.

WHY WE WANT YOU TO BECOME
AN ENLIGHTENED MILLIONAIRE™

Are you willing to share the oxygen we all breathe? Do you mind if someone takes a few extra breaths? Of course you don't. Why? Because there
is more than enough oxygen to go around. When there is abundance of
anything, whatever it is, then sharing it is not an issue. A rich person is
one who has *more* than enough. We want to get you started on having more
than enough money (being rich) by providing you with the tools and a path
to make your first million dollars. When that happens to you, we believe
you will naturally share with others.

In fact, our goal is to help create 1,000,000 millionaires. Why?

The cascade effect of 1,000,000 millionaires sharing their wealth (both
in knowledge and cash) will positively change the economic future of the
world.

We are both millionaires. Throughout our careers we've inspired thousands of others to become millionaires through our bestselling books
and presentations. Along the way, we've also experienced setbacks. Each
of us has suffered through devastating periods of financial instability—
even bankruptcy. These were hard, embarrassing times. Fortunately, we
rebounded to earn even higher incomes and build even greater fortunes.
We know the road to wealth, from its annoying potholes to its extraordinary vistas. Now we will show you how we did it—and how you can,
too.

We can only provide you the tools and a path (our system) that will
make it easier for you to become a millionaire. However, you have to *use*
the tools and *travel* the path.

We believe that it is no accident that you are now reading these words.
Let's work together to fulfill your financial dreams. Join us. Set your sights
on lifting yourself to financial freedom and then spreading your prosperity to your family, to your friends, and, ultimately, to the world.

HOW THE ONE MINUTE MILLIONAIRE SYSTEM IS ORGANIZED

This is not a typical book. In fact, it's two books in one—a nonfiction book, which you're reading now, *and* a novel, which we'll get to shortly.

You may be wondering why we designed such an unusual hybrid.

After having coached tens of thousands of people to financial success, we've learned that people have different learning styles. Generally, they are either "artists" or "engineers." The artists among you are right-brain "visual" learners. You engineers are left-brain "logical" learners. By using both learning styles, we drive the message home more powerfully. Instead of just "informing" you, we want you to be "transformed."

Therefore, after these few introductory pages, the book will be divided into distinctly different left- and right-side pages. The right-side pages will tell the fictional tale of a single mother, Michelle Ericksen, who is faced with a terrible dilemma. She needs to earn a million dollars in 90 days in order to reclaim her two children.

Could you make a million if your loved ones' lives depended on it?

The right-side pages are meant to represent the "right brain" of wealth—the drama of the struggle between our dreams and our fears. We hope you will get swept up in the story of Michelle. Put yourself in her shoes—imagine what you would do in her place. How would you handle the challenges she faces? Then imagine taking the place of Michelle's wise guide, Samantha—Sam, for short—and notice what advice you would want to give Michelle. How would you help her cope with her fears? Overcome her oppressive obstacles? What wisdom would you share?

The left-side pages are organized into nonfiction Millionaire Minutes— stand-alone lessons condensed into one- or two-page digests. These form the actual step-by-step guide for becoming an Enlightened Millionaire in a short period of time. The Millionaire Minutes are divided into distinct

THE ONE MINUTE MILLIONAIRE SYSTEM

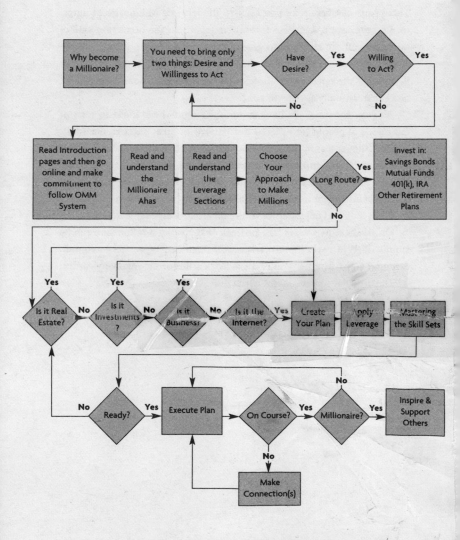

modules, which parallel the lessons that Sam imparts and the practices that Michelle comes to embrace.

You'll notice that throughout the novel on the right-side pages certain words and phrases are accompanied with page numbers in superscript. These page numbers refer you back to the left-side Millionaire Minutes. In the novel you'll see these lessons in action; on the nonfiction side of the book, you can review your grasp of these concepts or, if you read the novel first, you can learn about them for the first time. It doesn't matter if you read the novel or the nonfiction material first. Read them in the order that naturally appeals to you.

As your mentors, we have used and taught these ideas to tens of thousands of people (in different formats) with great success. Each Millionaire Minute lesson builds on the earlier ones. We also encourage you to visit **www.oneminutemillionaire.com,** our website, for a free One Minute Millionaire exercise designed to deepen your understanding of what is being taught in each stand-alone lesson.

Now, let's find out whether you're an artist or an engineer.

On the next two pages, the process of becoming a millionaire can be summarized in two different ways. Although both approaches contain essential steps whether you're an artist-learner or an engineer-learner, which particular way resonates with you?

MILLIONAIRE MOUNTAIN

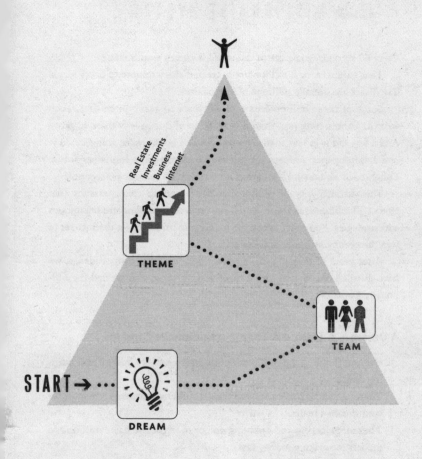

START →

DREAM

THEME

Real Estate
Investments
Business
Internet

TEAM

THE MILLIONAIRE EQUATION

Every 60 seconds, someone in the world becomes a millionaire.

That's right. A new millionaire is created every minute of every single day. There are literally millions of millionaires.

Some of these millionaires took 60 years to accumulate that much wealth. Others took less than a year. Some did it in less than 90 days. And a few did it in less than a minute. In this book, we're going to show you a step-by-step process for not only becoming a millionaire, but an Enlightened Millionaire—whether it takes you 60 years or 60 seconds.

The vast majority of millionaires share certain characteristics that almost all millionaires share. You must implement millionaire techniques and strategies. You must adopt the millionaire mind-set—a distinct set of wealth-creating attitudes and beliefs.

After years of research on ourselves and with our own students, we have distilled our system into a three-stage process that we call the Millionaire Equation:

A Dream + A Team + A Theme = Millionaire Streams

1. **Dream:** Building the Millionaire Mind-set—self-confidence and burning desire.
2. **Team:** Attracting mentors and masterminding partners to help make your dream a reality.
3. **Theme:** Selecting and applying one or more of the basic millionaire models for making money fast.

The steps in this book are designed to help you focus on these three critical stages of the wealth process. They form the combination to the vault of financial success.

THE BUTTERFLY EFFECT:
ONE MINUTE IS MORE THAN ENOUGH

Every time you wink the stars move.

EMERSON

Edward Lorenz started it all four decades ago. As a research meteorologist at MIT he created a computer program designed to model the weather. Lorenz had reduced weather into a series of formulas that behaved in recognizable weather patterns.

In his superb book *Chaos*, James Gleick recounts a winter day in 1961 when Lorenz wanted to shortcut a weather printout by starting midway through. To give the machine the initial conditions, he typed the numbers straight from the earlier printout.

Something unexpected happened. What he noticed was his simulated new weather pattern had diverged dramatically from the previous printout.

At first he thought his computer had malfunctioned. Then it suddenly hit him. There was no computer malfunction. The answer was in the numbers he had put into the computer. In the original programming he had used six decimal places: .506127. In the second run he had rounded off the numbers to .506. He assumed that the difference—one part in a thousand—would have no real impact. He was wrong. This slight change had made a HUGE difference. This *tiny* change in input had quickly created an overwhelmingly different output!

The formal name for this phenomenon is "sensitive dependence on initial conditions." Its informal and more popular name is the Butterfly Effect. Simply stated, it means that the tiny changes brought about by a butterfly moving its wings in San Francisco have the power to transform the weather conditions in Shanghai.

W. Edwards Deming came up with a very similar conclusion. Deming is the American statistician who established the Total Quality Movement, first in Japan, then in the rest of the world. Deming's contribution is historically so important that *U.S. News & World Report* called him one of the "nine hidden turning points in history" (along with the birth control pill and the Apostle Paul).

After over 50 years of statistical study, Deming pointed out that in every process there is a beginning and an end. When you focus on the first 15% of that process and get it correct (its initial conditions), you ensure at least 85% of your desired outcome. By focusing on the first 15% of anything, the remaining 85% will effortlessly follow.

This is what *The One Minute Millionaire* is designed to do. It is a system that creates tiny movements in your thoughts and actions—one minute at a time. It is the first 15% of the process. Get this as close to perfect as possible. Once you do, these tiny one minute corrections will speed up the process of your becoming an Enlightened Millionaire.

ON THE WINGS OF
THE ENLIGHTENED MILLIONAIRE™

According to the Butterfly Effect, as we explained, the tiny flutter of a butterfly's wings as it bounces gently on the breeze can create enormous changes halfway around the world. Drawing on this respected scientific theory, we believe you can accomplish amazing things with your life—even become a millionaire—using a carefully designed system of focused actions delivered in 60-second increments. We call each of these million-dollar flutters a Millionaire Minute. Now invest but a few minutes as you start to flutter *your* wings and prepare to take flight.

Flutter #1. The Enlightened Millionaire Decision

Everywhere you look, even in these economic times of uncertainty, growing numbers of people are feasting on incredible banquets of prosperity—while most of the rest settle for the crumbs that fall from the table. The journey to financial freedom starts the MINUTE you decide that you were destined for prosperity, not scarcity—for abundance, not lack. Isn't there a part of you that has always known this? Can you see yourself living a bounteous life—a life of "more than enough"?

It only takes a MINUTE to decide. Decide now.

Flutter #2. The Enlightened Millionaire Idea

Have you ever had an idea for a new product or service? Then, a short time later, you discover that someone else has beaten you to it. They're making millions from "your" idea! Realize that almost every day you have a new million-dollar idea. What million-dollar idea is floating around your head this very moment that you simply need to become aware of? The minute you become aware of it, you're a One Minute Millionaire. But awareness is not enough. You need to act on it.

Flutter #3. The Enlightened Millionaire Pattern

How many times will you spend money today? Three? Four? Five times? Rich people look at these *money transactions* differently than most people. Millionaires have a special pattern—a unique way they spend money. During each money transaction, they invest an extra minute. This extra minute makes them rich. That's why we call it a Millionaire Minute. Would you invest an extra minute during each of your money transactions today if you knew it could make you a millionaire?

Flutter #4. The Enlightened Millionaire Technique

The entire process of becoming a millionaire can be broken down into bite-sized, one minute techniques. In this book, we will teach you more than a hundred of them. Yes, you can become a millionaire one minute at a time.

Flutter #5. The Enlightened Millionaire Moment

A moment occurs in every millionaire's career when everything hangs in the balance—when the temptation exists to turn back. For many, this moment occurs after a devastating defeat or extraordinary failure. Will you be ready for your millionaire moment? When it happens, take a minute. Draw a deep breath. Take another step forward.

Flutter #6. The Enlightened Millionaire Threshold

All great contests come down to the final minute—the last step you take as you cross the finish line—the final dollar that puts you over the top. Won't that minute be exciting?

THE ENLIGHTENED MILLIONAIRE™ MANIFESTO

What is so important about making money the "enlightened way"? When millions are made the enlightened way, the *process* of obtaining the money makes the world a better place.

One of the Enlightened Millionaire's goals is to make money. In many ways he or she is acting like the honeybee. The honeybee's primary objective is to obtain nectar to make honey. While in the process of going after the nectar, the honeybee is actually involved in a much larger purpose. At 90 degrees to the direction of the honeybee's flight path, pollen is being dusted on its wings. As it goes on its search for more nectar the honeybee is cross-pollinating the rooted botanicals. This cross-pollination is a far more important outcome than making honey, for it results in a beautiful, bountiful garden.

Enlightened Millionaires are honey-money-seeking bees. By focusing on adding as much value as possible in pursuit of making millions, the Enlightened Millionaire is actually increasing the standard of living on the planet. This increase in the standard of living is at 90 degrees to the direction of the Enlightened Millionaire's flight path.

This 90 degree phenomenon has been defined scientifically by Dr. R. Buckminster Fuller as *precession*. When something is in motion moving toward a specific objective, what happens precessionally, at 90 degrees, is far more important.

Enlightened Millionaires understand this. They know that they must create wealth where everyone wins (creating a win/win situation). When they focus on adding value, what happens precessionally will be positive. They may not fully understand or appreciate all the precessional events as they occur. They just know that unexpected positive things will happen as long as they focus on adding as much value as possible. (See DNA illustration on page xv.)

In contrast, an endarkened Millionaire focuses on going for the money without seeking to add value (resulting in a win/lose outcome). When this happens, the precessional events are negative. Thus, the unenlightened Millionaire's path will not provide a continuous stream of riches over the long term. Eventually the failure to add value stops the flow of money.

Simply put: The more Enlightened Millionaires there are, the better the world is. By adding 1,000,000 new millionaires in the next decade we know that the *precessional cascade* of these new Enlightened Millionaires, as they share their wealth both in knowledge and cash, will change the economic future of the world.

This is our mission: to positively change the world by providing the tools and a path (our system) to those who commit to become Enlightened Millionaires. When this happens, it will generate billions of dollars focused on the well-being of humankind.

THE DNA OF
THE ENLIGHTENED MILLIONAIRE™

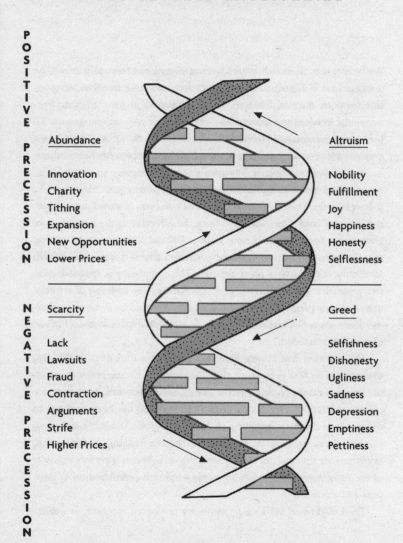

P
O
S
I
T
I
V
E

P
R
E
C
E
S
S
I
O
N

Abundance

Innovation
Charity
Tithing
Expansion
New Opportunities
Lower Prices

Altruism

Nobility
Fulfillment
Joy
Happiness
Honesty
Selflessness

N
E
G
A
T
I
V
E

P
R
E
C
E
S
S
I
O
N

Scarcity

Lack
Lawsuits
Fraud
Contraction
Arguments
Strife
Higher Prices

Greed

Selfishness
Dishonesty
Ugliness
Sadness
Depression
Emptiness
Pettiness

PRINCIPLES OF
THE ENLIGHTENED MILLIONAIRE™

We believe that all wealth comes with privileges and responsibilities. The privileges are well documented: money freedom, time freedom, relationship freedom, spiritual freedom, physical freedom, and the ultimate freedom—the freedom to discover and develop your own unique genius. To become an Enlightened Millionaire is to be free to be, do, and have whatever you desire as long as it hurts no one and simultaneously helps others.

An excellent example is Newman's Own, a company started in 1982 by actor Paul Newman and his longtime friend author A. E. Hotchner. As it states on their website, www.newmansown.com, *It started out as a joke and got out of hand.* The idea came from the Newman family's tradition of giving away bottles of their now famous Oil and Vinegar Salad Dressing as a Christmas gift. Then someone suggested that if it was good enough for family, it might be a great product. The company was founded upon two principles: (1) top-quality products without the addition of artificial ingredients or preservatives and (2) all profits would be donated to charity. Their tongue-in-cheek motto is, "Shameless Exploitation in Pursuit of the Common Good."

The company was immediately successful, donating over $1,000,000 to charity in its first year. Since then the company has expanded its product line into salad dressings, pasta sauces, salsas, popcorn, lemonade, ice cream, and steak sauce. More than $125,000,000 has been donated to thousands of charities, including children's programs, disaster relief, environmental causes, medical research, affordable housing, hunger relief, organizations that aid the elderly, and the arts. This is a perfect example of the Enlightened Millionaire in action—the noble combination of business and philanthropy.

The Enlightened Millionaire pursues a principled approach to wealth:

First, do no harm. Borrowing from the Hippocratic oath that many doctors take as they graduate from medical school, the Enlightened Millionaire commits to avoid any wealth-building activities that harm or impoverish other people. Create only abundance, never scarcity. This means creating wealth in an ethical, honest, and win/win manner.

Second, do much good. The Enlightened Millionaire enjoys creating wealth that improves the lives of many people. The goal is to enrich oneself while enriching others.

Third, operate out of stewardship. Enlightened Millionaires are stewards over their financial blessings—enjoying the privileges of financial success while creating an ongoing legacy to bless others. Many Enlightened Millionaires feel a personal "calling" to provide support to one or more specific causes (such as Jerry Lewis and muscular dystrophy). The goal is not to amass personal wealth for its own sake, but to ultimately create a perpetual giving fund to support worthy causes. In other words, your wealth is not just for you (selfish), but for blessing the lives of many people (selfless). The first proof of your commitment to make money to bless other people is to give at least the first 10% away.

We want to inspire a million millionaires to give 10% of all they earn each year back to their communities—to improve the lives of others around them. When this happens, it will generate BILLIONS of dollars focused on improving the well-being of humankind. For years, both of us have been dedicating 10% of all our earnings back to our communities. Please visit our website at www.oneminutemillionaire.com for details.

THE ENLIGHTENED MILLIONAIRE™ COMMITMENT: THE FIRST STEP

Take the first step in faith. You don't have to see the whole staircase. Just take the first step.

MARTIN LUTHER KING JR.

No matter your present circumstances, the first step to making your first million is the commitment to become a millionaire.

At some level we are all familiar with what commitment means. Yet many of us do not understand the essential elements needed to make it real, to capture its magic.

To have a genuine commitment requires two things. The first is *desire*. The very fact that you have read this far is proof that you have desire. The second is *faith*. You need to commit on faith. We have the tools and the system that will allow you to become a millionaire. You need to have the faith in the process.

With your desire and your willingness to have faith in our proven system, commitment will emerge. It will strengthen as you take each enlightened One Minute Millionaire step.

Hans Selye, the pioneer in the understanding of human stress, was often asked the following question: "What is the most stressful condition a person can face?" His unexpected response: "Not having something to believe in."

The good news is, you don't have to believe that you can be an Enlightened Millionaire. Let us believe that for you. We know our system works. What you need is the desire and enough faith to follow the steps we present in this book. When you do this, you will be on your way to becoming an Enlightened Millionaire.

Now choose to be an Enlightened Millionaire by signing on the next page:

Enlightened Millionaire™ Commitment

I hereby decide to become an Enlightened Millionaire so I can eliminate my money pressures, enjoy a life of complete financial freedom, and share my abundance with others.

Signed this _____ day of _____ 200___.

_____

Your signature

As a further demonstration of your commitment, please go to www.oneminutemillionaire.com and sign up. It's free. We will e-mail you a certificate of commitment memorializing your critical first step. Or write us at One Minute Millionaire, P. O. Box 7665, Newport Beach, CA 92677 or call 1-888-ONE-MILL (1-888-663-6455) and tell us you're committed.

THE ENLIGHTENED MILLIONAIRE™ COMMITMENT: THE SECOND STEP

God does not give a lick of an ice cream cone without wanting you to have the whole cone.

MARSHALL THURBER

Congratulations! If you have gotten this far you have taken the first step—the first lick of the ice cream cone—and you are on your way to becoming an Enlightened Millionaire in the shortest possible time.

This second essential element of the magic of commitment is action. Besides having a strong belief, commitment boils down to behavior.

All of us have multiple commitments: self, family, career, friends, and community. Each day you take multiple actions that line up with these commitments. That is, you take committed action.

To earn a million dollars quickly, you must be willing to take similar committed actions directed toward becoming an Enlightened Millionaire. You must be willing to travel a path that reflects "Enlightened Millionaire congruence," where there is integrity between desire and action. When this happens, the magic of commitment starts to unfold.

If you have not yet done so, go to www.oneminutemillionaire.com and sign up. By sharing your commitment with us, you are taking a major step (you are taking action) that will dramatically improve your probability of becoming a millionaire quickly.

As a One Minute Millionaire member you get *free* **website trainings.** On our website you will find a series of exercises designed to support you in becoming a One Minute Millionaire. In addition, as part of your free membership, you will receive a series of daily One Minute Millionaire Minute e-mails. Each daily e-mail is designed to inspire you to continue climbing your Millionaire Mountain.

DO YOU HAVE WHAT IT TAKES TO BE
AN ENLIGHTENED MILLIONAIRE™?

How would you like to compare yourself to the habits and traits of actual modern-day millionaires? As you read the pages of this book, you might find it interesting to take a simple online test to help you determine whether or not you have the "right stuff" to become a millionaire. Please go to **www.oneminutemillionaire.com** and log on to *Do you have what it takes to be an Enlightened Millionaire?* diagnostic and follow the instructions. This statistically valid study is based on the habits and traits of actual millionaires.

Please answer the questions honestly. Once you have answered the questions you will have your answer instantly. This diagnostic will give you an excellent idea of the probability of your becoming an Enlightened One Minute Millionaire.

THE ONE MINUTE MILLIONAIRE

MICHELLE'S STORY:
THE ENLIGHTENED WAY TO WEALTH

TWO WAYS TO MILLIONIZE YOUR LIFE

There are two routes for climbing the Millionaire Mountain: the long route and the short route.

First, let's talk about the long route. The long route is the safest and easiest. You can literally become a millionaire by investing as little as a dollar a day ($30 a month). Study the following chart.

HOW THE INVESTMENT OF ONLY ONE DOLLAR PER DAY GROWS INTO $1,000,000

% Interest	Number of Years to Grow into a Million Dollars
3%	147 years
5%	100 years
10%	56 years
15%	40 years
20%	32 years

To become a millionaire in your lifetime, all that is required is (1) the ability to find investments that yield at least 10% annually after taxes (as in your tax-deferred retirement account) and (2) the discipline to keep up the process, year in and year out.

The following chart tells the story of what can happen if individuals save a dollar a day from the day they are born until they reach retirement age.

Michelle was always grateful that her children weren't in the house when she noticed the red light blinking on the answering machine. It was her husband, Gideon, calling from his car to tell her he'd be a little late getting home. Nicky and Hannah never heard how their father's cheerful rendition of "Puff the Magic Dragon," intended for them, was interrupted by the jarring screech of his brakes, of metal against metal, of cars colliding. Michelle, alone in the kitchen while the kids scampered happily around the backyard with their small menagerie of pets, played the message over and over, hoping it would end differently.

She learned later from a grim-faced state trooper, clutching his hat in his hand, that her husband had been the only fatality of a four-car pileup. The drunk who caused the accident spent a day in the hospital and then was released to his girlfriend.

Most of the town of Deer Creek, Colorado, came to the funeral. Michelle's friends arranged a wake at her house following the trip to the cemetery.

Michelle sat on a folding chair in the living room. On her lap, she balanced an untouched plate of spanikopita and fruit salad that her friend Summer had handed her. With her eyes lowered, all she could see were anonymous bottom halves of people milling about. Slowly she registered that a couple was approaching: a man in a black suit and a woman with dimpled knees under sheer black hosiery. Gideon's parents.

Reluctantly, Michelle looked up. Anthony Ericksen stood over six feet, his wife just a few inches shorter. Anthony's strawberry blond

A DOLLAR A DAY INVESTED
AT VARIOUS INTEREST RATES FOR 66 YEARS

	% Interest		Amount Accumulated
(Hidden in a mattress)	0%	=	$24,000
(In a savings account)	3%	=	$77,000
(Certificates of deposit)	5%	=	$193,000
(Corporate bonds)	8%	=	$1,000,000
(Growth mutual funds)	10%	=	$2,700,000
(Aggressive growth mutual funds)	15%	=	$50,000,000
(Real estate, businesses)	20%	=	$1,000,000,000
			(That's One Billion!)

Yes, you can even become a *billionaire* on the investment of a dollar a day—given enough time and the right interest rate. But this is the long route—it certainly isn't the way most of us want it. We want it FAST! And that is definitely possible, as we will show you. But while you're creating rapid wealth, why don't you also take the long route at the same time? Put aside $50, $100, $500—as much as you can afford—every month, from now on. It's simple. It's easy. It can be automatically deducted from your bank account. Then, if you make a million the fast way, so much the better. But no matter what happens, you'll still be a millionaire—sooner or later. Agreed?

hair was only flecked with gray, and so abundant that Michelle suspected a transplant. His eyes were swimming-pool blue. Natalie, with the help of a face and eye lift, radiated an imperious beauty at 60.

The Ericksens had always disliked Michelle, and it had been difficult for her not to return the sentiment, though she had been as polite as possible for Gideon's and the kids' sake. But seeing them now she felt a stirring of pity: They had lost their only child.

They stopped in front of her. Anthony stood stiffly. Natalie looked around, as if to see who was watching them. Michelle didn't know what to say. *"I'm sorry" is always best in situations like this,* she thought. Maybe that's what they would say to her, too.

Then Natalie whispered, "You know, dear, I would have been happy to help you buy something nice for Nicky and Hannah to wear to their father's funeral."

Michelle remained speechless. She glanced over at her children. They were in a favorite spot next to the fireplace, Nicky holding Hannah's hand. She had heard him say to his sister that morning, "I'll be like your daddy now." With her free hand, Hannah held Mr. Moo-Moo up to her cheek. Mr. Moo-Moo was the yellow-and-pink blanket that Michelle had crocheted for her while she was pregnant and hoping for a girl.

Nicky was a precocious seven-year-old: a serious reader, excellent in math, and reflective to the point of being almost somber. He loved sports, especially baseball. Hannah was five and completely unaware that she was stunning, with curly auburn hair and radiant fair skin. Her appearance favored the Ericksen side. Michelle had straight brown hair, brown eyes, and an olive complexion.

Hannah was bright, like her brother, but she did struggle with shyness. That struggle was on Michelle's mind when she said weakly, "I'm a good mother."

"We can see that," Anthony observed, looking toward Nicky and a small bandage he sported on his forehead, the result of an errant line drive he'd tried to field only days ago.

A DOLLAR A DAY, A MINUTE AT A TIME

No matter your present circumstances, here are the four steps to your first million.

1. Decide that it's okay for you to become a millionaire.

Some people believe that the accumulation of wealth is an unworthy goal. Before you begin your journey to become an Enlightened Millionaire, search your attitudes to make sure you are willing to create wealth in a way that will support your inner beliefs and values.

2. Practice imagining yourself enjoying an abundant lifestyle.

All great fortunes started in someone's imagination. See yourself living in the home of your dreams, enjoying ideal relationships with friends and loved ones, contributing to the world through your own unique talents and abilities. Imagine the fortune you could create and the good it could do. Believe it and you will see it.

3. Spend less than you earn.

But how? Pay yourself first. Deduct 10% off the top of your income, and deposit it into your investment account. Convert all your credit cards except one to debit cards so it is impossible for you to go into debt. Then live on what is left over.

4. Invest the difference.

Invest your 10% surplus into investments that can earn at least 10%. A dollar a day invested at 10% interest becomes a million dollars in 56 years. In other words, anyone can become a millionaire by investing only a dollar

"He was playing baseball!" Michelle raised her voice now. She *had* felt guilty, had reproached herself that day all the way to the emergency room, would probably still be thinking about it if it hadn't been for . . .

"We'll make this brief," Anthony said crisply. "It's no secret that you weren't our first choice for a daughter-in-law."

You weren't exactly my *first choice, either,* she thought.

"I always saw Gideon as taking over Ericksen Timber . . . before you entered the picture. . . . Now he's gone."

Michelle had been trying so hard not to cry, but now the battle was lost, and the tears rolled down her cheeks. A few grapes slid off the plate in her lap. She patted down her loose-fitting plum dress, one of the few dresses she owned. But no pockets, no tissues.

"He never wanted Ericksen Timber," she whispered.

"The bottom line is that we have one thing left to us," Anthony retorted. "Just one. Our grandchildren. And Nicky is my last chance for an Ericksen heir."

"What do you mean?" Michelle asked.

"This isn't the right time, but there never *will* be a right time," Anthony said stonily. Although he gave no perceptible signal, a black-suited man with gray hair suddenly appeared from behind Anthony and handed Michelle a sheaf of papers. "Mrs. Ericksen, I am serving you with a legal document," the man said in a practiced tone, quickly stepping away from her.

Michelle cautiously placed the papers on the coffee table. The words *Ericksen v. Ericksen,* in larger letters at the top, leapt out at her. But her head was throbbing too hard to try to read anything, let alone legalese.

"We want custody of the children," Anthony said.

a day—30 bucks a month. If you want to become a millionaire faster, then invest more money or find ways to make your money grow at higher rates of return.

You can become a One Minute Millionaire.

- ▲ It only takes a minute to decide it.
- ▲ It only takes a minute to visualize it.
- ▲ It only takes a minute to save it.
- ▲ It only takes a minute to invest it.

A dollar a day—a minute at a time—you can get there. Slowly but surely.

Now, let's talk about the fast way. . . .

A leaf fell onto Michelle's lap.

Autumn. Everything will die.

On Courtney's deck, Michelle sat in a wicker chair, looking out at the yard below, where a few flowers still bloomed. There were marigolds and petunias, although the pink and reddish-purple pansies were no longer vibrant.

She caught the look that Courtney and Summer were exchanging. "I'm all right," she said. "It sure helps being with you guys."

Courtney Dillon and Summer Bindman were two of Michelle's oldest friends—natives, as was she, of Deer Creek, and classmates from high school. Summer was a sweet, naïve soul whose nurturing personality served her excellently in her job at a senior center. Courtney was the practical one of the trio. A few years ago she had opened her own craft store, The Feathered Nest, which sold work by local artists and craftspeople, such as paintings, ceramics, and the quilts that Michelle loved to make.

"We're worried about you," Courtney said.

"Whatever happens, you can't give up," Summer encouraged her.

The two women sat on the opposite side of a table set with tea things. Summer could have passed for a teenager from a distance, with no makeup to cover her abundant freckles. Courtney, as usual, looked as though she had stepped out of the Talbots catalog, in a tweed skirt and twinset.

"Things *are* looking a little grim at the moment," Michelle said. She tried to speak lightly, but what she had to say only depressed her more.

Michelle was insolvent. She and Gideon had taken out a second mortgage to help launch Gideon's Gadgets. He was gifted at designing clever, useful things, though the company hadn't quite taken off the way they'd hoped. He was on his way home from showing the prototype of his latest gadget—a futuristic cell phone holder that no one seemed to want—when he was killed.

CHOOSING YOUR
MILLIONAIRE MOUNTAIN

In the whole wide world of money there are only four major ways of becoming a millionaire. No matter what your background, you can learn to master one of these areas.

1. Investments: Accumulating shares of stock, bonds, CDs
2. Real Estate: Owning properties
3. Business: Marketing products, services, or ideas
4. Internet: Expanding possibilities

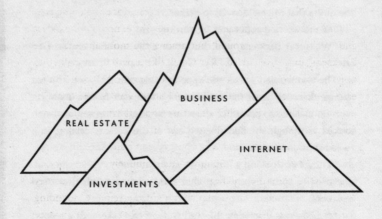

We call this the Mountain Range of Wealth. A lot of routes can be taken to the top of each mountain. We will teach you many different models for creating wealth later on in this book. But for now, realize that you will probably reach your million-dollar goal with a combination of all four. Suppose you make a fortune by launching a home-based business.

As budding entrepreneurs, Michelle and Gideon were good at the creative part, the brainstorming, the *fun* things of running a small business, but less effective when it came to the mundane tasks, like bookkeeping. That's probably how they let Gideon's life insurance lapse.

Michelle was an expert quilter and an organic cook, but if it had once been possible to turn one of these skills into a stream of income, there was no time for that now. Gideon's Gadgets had been a failure, and it seemed unlikely that there would be seed money for another new business in the near future. The house would be gone soon, and a job brewing espresso or bagging groceries simply wasn't going to pay the rent and feed and clothe her children, even in the simple style that they had always embraced.

Meanwhile, the Ericksens were not going to make things any easier. Michelle could not seriously believe that the Ericksens would take her children away from her. But she could not dismiss the possibility, either, simply because of who they were: not just the oldest and wealthiest family around, but among the most powerful. The Ericksens' influence circled Deer Creek like a python strangling its prey. Anthony played chess weekly with the mayor. Ericksen Timber employed hundreds of the residents. Natalie was on the board of every local charity that didn't espouse too left wing a cause; her favorite was one that helped foster children.

"I still don't understand why you just can't sue the driver, and get some money that way," Summer said plaintively.

Michelle started to answer but was relieved when Courtney took over. "Summer," she began with a failed attempt at sounding patient, "have you ever heard the expression 'You can't squeeze blood from a turnip'? The drunk wasn't insured, and he didn't have any money."

"But isn't it a crime to drive without insurance?"

"Yes," Courtney said. "It's also a crime to drive drunk. But even if this upstanding citizen goes to jail, and I hope to God he does,

You'll still need to invest your excess cash in the stock market or other forms of passive investment. Certainly, you will need to buy some real estate along the way—and if you can buy it at wholesale prices instead of retail, it can make a huge difference.

For now, just be aware of the four major mountains. Make an initial "gut" decision to choose one mountain—something that you sense is going to be your primary investment vehicle. Suppose you were enrolled in a University of Money. Which of the four mountains would be your "major"? Which would be your "minor"? Which mountain interests you the most? Which one scares you the most?

Imagine yourself in conversation five years from now. Try these words on for size:

"I made my millions in real estate."
"I made my millions by investing in the stock market."
"I made my millions in business."
"I made my millions on the Internet."

Which one seems right to you?

that's not going to put any money in Michelle's pocket. Michelle, what about *your* auto insurance?"

"We just carried the minimal amount," Michelle said. "It'll just cover the funeral and a month of groceries."

"But—"

"I know what you're going to say," Michelle interrupted. "We waived uninsured motorist coverage."

The three were silent for a few moments. Michelle's gaze drifted out to Courtney's backyard again, as she considered that the savings in their rather minuscule bank account was about to vanish forever. She absently watched as one of the season's last butterflies fluttered above the fading flowers. She wondered where the butterfly would seek shelter in the colder months and if it would live to return in the spring.

"You know, I've just got to get away," Michelle finally said, rather blankly.

"Like where?" Courtney asked.

"There's my Aunt Ginny, up in Cheyenne. The kids adore her, but we don't get to see her very much. Which is too bad, because she's pretty much the only extended family we have."

Summer nodded encouragingly.

Michelle's plan blossomed in front of her, giving her something to think about besides death and being harassed by her in-laws. "We can go today and stay over the weekend."

"Go for it," Courtney agreed. "It'll do you good to get away."

A couple of hours later Michelle headed out to Eleanor Roosevelt Elementary, where Nicky was in second grade and Hannah had just started kindergarten. She had stopped at home and packed for herself and the kids, then filled the Chevy with gas. She and Gideon

THE MILLIONAIRE AHAS

PRINCIPLES

are
simple
yet powerful
models that
help us understand
how the world works.
Principles generate the
same result each and every
time—no matter where, when,
or who uses them. Principles work
when you work them. Gravity is a
principle. When you wake up in the
morning, you don't have to question which
way your foot will go when you get out of bed.
It goes down, never up. Likewise, two times two
always equals four. It never equals five. Principles don't
wear out, rust out, or give out. They last forever. They are
timeless and tireless. Principles cannot be over-used. Life is
the process of discovering principles—of discovering what works.
If you want to make rapid progress, don't fight against principles—
flow with them. Say these words aloud: "I discover the principles that
work and work them. I am forever learning new principles that interaccom-
modate with what I already know, to the betterment of my life and my world.
As principles are revealed to me, I cheerfully record them, use them, and
share them. Principles are, without question, the fastest way to what I want."
We believe that there are at least 24 Principles of Wealth. We call them _Ahas_ . . .

had not even owned the old van outright, and it didn't have much life left. She hoped it would get her to Wyoming that night.

Pulling up to the Cyclone fence around the playground, Michelle spotted Nicky and Hannah waiting at the main gate, as they always did, along with the other children who were waiting for rides home. Michelle bit her lip hard when she saw them. Nicky slumped against the fence while Hannah sat on the pavement, far away from the central group of children. They were both looking down. Hannah's hair, always a challenge to tame, looked ratted and tangled. Nicky's shirt was half tucked in and half drooping out. Michelle wondered, did she comb their hair that morning? Had any of them brushed their teeth in the past 12 days?

They just lost their dad.

For the sake of the children, she knew, she had to get herself together. She was the grown-up. She didn't especially feel like behaving like one, but right now she was going to do the best acting job of her life.

She took her place in the line of cars parked alongside the school, put the van in park, then leaned across the front seat to roll down the window and flash her children a cheery smile. "My Lord and Lady, your carriage awaits," she said playfully.

Nicky and Hannah did not respond for a moment. Then they looked up and slowly registered her presence. Michelle jumped out and went around to slide open the door to the rear seat. She took a deep bow. "Your loyal servant has a surprise for you."

Neither of the kids replied. They seemed to have barely enough energy to hoist themselves up into the van. "Put on your seatbelts," Michelle reminded them.

"Mom, what's going to happen?" Nicky finally asked as they drove away from the school. "I don't want to go live with Grandpa and Grandma. They're really strict."

"Well, *that* I don't think you have to worry about, Nicky, honey." Perspiration made her hands feel slippery on the wheel. She had

THE FIRST AHA:
EVERYONE MANIFESTS

Everyone thinks that the principal thing to the tree is the fruit,
but in point of fact the principal thing to it is the seed.
FRIEDRICH WILHELM NiETZSCHE (1844–1900)

Look around you. Everything you see began as a thought in someone's mind. The chair you sit on. The table you work at. The car you drive. The house you live in. The clothes you wear. The television you watch. First, a thought. Then, a thing—brought forth out of nothing. Voilà! There it is. Everything begins as a thought.

The verb for turning thoughts into things is *to manifest*. It comes from the Middle English word *manifestus* meaning "visible" and the Latin word *manus* meaning "hand." When you manifest something, you metaphorically reach your hand through the invisible curtain separating the tangible world from the world of imagination and pull your desired object into existence.

First, you *think* it, then you *manifest* it. You "materialize" it. You cause it to appear.

Everyone manifests. Some people manifest abundance. Others manifest lack. If you don't have what you want, examine your thoughts. Ask yourself, "How did I manifest this?"

You are the fruit of the thoughts you have planted and nourished. If you want a better harvest, you must plant better thoughts. Just like an apple seed will not produce a peach tree, poor thoughts will not produce prosperity. As surely as the acorn becomes the oak tree, the images in your mind become your reality.

Thoughts *are* things. Every thought has a consequence. No thought lives in your brain rent-free. Each thought is a pebble dropped into the pond of your life—the ripples are real. The more intense the thought, the more

been edgy about driving since Gideon's death. "You might have to go see them sometimes"—she had a feeling they were going to get court-mandated visitation—"but you'd want to go see them sometimes, wouldn't you?" Her voice cracked. She sought out their faces in the rearview mirror, which allowed her to see only the top right corner of Hannah's head and the left half of Nicky's face. Suddenly Hannah dropped out of sight entirely. She had, Michelle knew, collapsed into Mr. Moo-Moo, who was forbidden at school but who had been waiting for her in the backseat.

"This isn't the way home, Mom," Nicky said.

"That's right," Michelle said. Her voice was high-pitched with false good cheer. "I just called your Aunt Ginny. We're going to visit her for the weekend."

Driving northeast, the sun was behind them. Just before it set they stopped at a roadside diner to eat. In the gathering dusk the three of them got back in the van. Just before she pulled out of the parking lot, Michelle felt the first shallow waves of what she knew was a panic attack lapping at her, even though she had never had a panic attack. It was, as nearly as the police had ever pinpointed it for her, within a half hour of the time that Gideon had died. How would she see in the dark? What if the van broke down? When was the last time they had taken this jalopy in for a tune-up?

The kids settled into their seats, full of greasy food and oblivious to her terror. Or so she thought. Because suddenly Nicky asked, "Do you think Daddy's watching us now?"

"Of course he is," Michelle replied, too loud and too eagerly, but feeling the relief flood over her and the panic recede. *Gideon, ask the Lord to protect me. I bet He really thinks you're great. Maybe that's why He couldn't wait to get you there. . . . Tell Him that joke about the skeleton who comes in the bar. Okay, maybe not that one.*

powerful the outcome. An angry thought gets picked up like a radio wave. People can sense it. Animals can smell it. The whole energy system surrounding you is infected. Weed out such thoughts.

Think positive thoughts, intensely. Grow enthusiastic images, boldly. Speak only wonderful words to yourself, constantly. Feel fantastic, NOW! This colors your view of the world. Like a magnet, you attract the resources necessary to manifest the world you desire.

Everything manifested around you made someone a fortune. Everywhere you look, you can see it. The chair you sit on. The table you work at. The car you drive. The house you live in. The clothes you wear. The television you watch. Everywhere you look—every *thing* you see has made or is making someone millions. There are millions of enlightened ways to manifest a million dollars. We want to be your manifestation coaches. We want to support you in changing your economic future. Together we can change the economic future of the world.

THE SECOND AHA: BE-DO-HAVE

To Fly As Fast As Thought
To Be Anywhere There Is
You Must First Begin By Knowing
That You Have Already Arrived
FROM *JONATHAN LIVINGSTON SEAGULL*, BY RICHARD BACH

Properly adding a million dollars to your net worth is a primary objective of this book. Yet to reach this objective—the Enlightened Millionaire way—you must follow three steps in a specific order. They are:

She popped in a Raffi tape that Hannah loved. Nicky complained that it was for babies; he wanted to hear the Backstreet Boys.

"As soon as we get to Wyoming, we switch," she promised.

Forty-five minutes later it was completely dark and she had her high beams on. A little of her nervousness had returned, but once they crossed into Wyoming they'd only be another half hour away, and they'd easily arrive at Aunt Ginny's by nine. She was struck again by the impulsiveness of the trip, but it was like her to make last-minute plans, and she thought the kids had always enjoyed her spontaneity. She knew Gideon had.

"There it is," she said. Her headlights reflected off the small green sign that told them they were entering "The Equality State."

"You know that Wyoming was the first state that gave women the vote," Michelle said. The silence in the back made her realize that her children had fallen asleep. She instinctively pushed the gas pedal a little harder, as if freedom waited on the other side of the sign racing toward her.

The road had been deserted, so she was startled a moment later to see the blinding red, blue, and yellow lights in her rearview mirror. She slowed down so the patrol car could pass her. But it didn't. What was wrong? She pulled over as quickly as she could safely slow the car.

She rolled down the window and looked back. The brutal primary colors on the roof of the state trooper's car kept twirling, and the headlights stayed on, too, casting two large cones of light into which a slim silhouette appeared a moment later. It was a tall, broad-shouldered state trooper, crunching the gravel on the side of the highway as he walked toward the van.

She watched him, frozen, as he placed a hand on the hood and peered in the window, silently. His flashlight did a quick search of the front and backseats. She noticed his Wyoming badge.

BE
DO
HAVE

Of course, to become an Enlightened Millionaire you must DO what you love, add enormous value, and leverage it (more on this later). While these *DOing* steps are critical they are not the first priority. *BEing* comes first! You must first BE an Enlightened Millionaire.

The Enlightened Millionaire knows and acts from the space that

1. abundance comes from making others better off, and
2. the primary reason to get is to have more to give.

For the Enlightened Millionaire, it's all about giving. It is rarely about getting. Giving springs from the wellspring of the abundance that exists. Enlightened Millionaires give because that is who they are—it's the highest manifestation of their true nature. It comes from their BEING.

You must BE an Enlightened Millionaire before you DO anything. From that "BE" space you DO what needs to be done to add as much value to the world as possible. As a result of your Enlightened *Beingness*, your behavior or *Doingness* will be appropriate in each situation.

Granted, it is possible to make millions of dollars by doing and undoing. However, you won't experience the peace, gratitude, and sense of wealth that come from the added-value approach of the Enlightened Millionaire. You will also miss the joy of tapping into the *ocean of abundance*, one of the greatest of earthly pleasures.

When both the *BEing* and *DOing* are correct, you will HAVE your desired outcome. You will have riches beyond your wildest dreams.

"License, registration."

"What—" Her mind went blank for a moment. She fumbled in her glove box. The trooper helped her by training his flashlight on the pile of maps, McDonald's toys, and additional kiddie cassettes that otherwise filled the compartment.

"Here it is, Officer," she said shakily. "I wasn't speeding, was I?"

The young trooper was holding the flashlight on her driver's license. "We had a report of a woman and two children attempting to cross state lines."

"Mommy?" She heard Nicky's groggy voice.

"Yes, sir," Michelle snapped defensively. "I am taking my children to visit a relative. Would you like her name and address?"

"That won't be necessary, ma'am." His tone was matter-of-fact. "Apparently there is a protective order forbidding you from taking them out of state."

Her brief semblance of bravado vanished. She wanted to beg, to plead, to offer him the few dollars in her purse. If he let her go, she would just keep driving. Wyoming was a big empty state. She'd find a town that wasn't even on the map, get a job, start over from scratch, and make all her problems disappear.

"Mommy." Nicky was fully awake, and his single word was full of terror. Since he spoke softly, it must have been that terror that woke Hannah.

"Mommy?" she whimpered.

"It's all right, kids," Michelle said, though her voice was shaking. "Okay, Officer, we'll turn around and go right home. You can even follow us if you want."

The trooper shook his head. "I'm sorry, ma'am, you'll have to get out of the car."

She knew then everything that was going to happen. She stared ahead into the darkness of the state of Wyoming, the blankness of the prairie. *Just drive away. Drive, drive, drive.* As if she could outrun a police car in her old van.

THE THIRD AHA:
LIVE LIFE ABOVE THE LINE

Whenever something doesn't go as expected, most of us tend to "blame" someone else for what went wrong. In doing so, we lose a tremendous learning opportunity.

The world makes progress by learning from mistakes. When we blame someone, it gives that person power over the situation. For example, *"If John had done what he agreed to do, then this would never have happened."* That may be true. However, this statement gives John the power over the situation, and we usually learn very little from the experience.

If we avoid the trap of laying blame, we sometimes tend to *justify* what happened. *"I would have gotten the job done except that I had traveled all night yesterday and I was too tired to focus on the project today."* This is just another form of blame. Instead of blaming a person, we blame the circumstances. Again, no matter how reasonable the justification, we lose an opportunity to optimally learn from the situation.

If we get beyond blaming and justifying, there is another level of suboptimal learning. That is shame—beating yourself up; *"I did the dumbest thing!"* Instead of blaming another person or the circumstance, we blame ourselves. This too reduces the opportunity for learning.

Where, then, is the optimal place to view life experiences? From the point of personal responsibility—from above the line.

↑LEARN

↓BLAME

"Mommy, why is the policeman here?" Hannah was fully awake now, too.

What did they say in the old sci-fi movies? *Resistance is futile.* It was only one of the many crazy things that went through her head as she got out of the van. It seemed to take forever, just the opening of the door, the long step down.

Suddenly there was the cold metal of the car against her hands and bare arms. Her baggy plum dress—the same one she had worn to the funeral—had short sleeves. The trooper had her up against the side of the van, spread-eagled. He was patting her down, his hands as indifferent as a shopper pawing through a sale rack.

Through the closed rear window, in the giant cones of light from the Wyoming state trooper's car, she saw Hannah's face wrench. She could see her crying, even though she couldn't quite hear. She also saw Nicky's big brown eyes fixed on her. Then he pulled his sister close, kissed her head, and hugged her.

"Don't worry about the children, ma'am." A second trooper had taken over, and he guided her more gently than his partner had. "We'll take good care of them. We're taking them just as far as Greeley, and they'll get a ride back to Deer Creek."

Michelle wanted to thank him for the kindness in his voice, but all she could do was sob. When she reached the troopers' car, she was shocked to realize that there was a second car behind the first one. This one had its lights out; she could just discern the outline of two more troopers sitting patiently in the front seat. She thought one might be a woman. She wondered if the woman might be a mother, too.

Two state trooper vehicles patrolling a two-lane highway at least 40 miles from indoor plumbing.

The work of Anthony Ericksen.

❧

Granted, we may not be responsible for everything that happens. However, the more we are willing to view the world from this vantage point, the more the reins to life are in our own hands. By operating "above the line," each of us has optimal control, direction, and command over our existence. From this perspective, "free will" surfaces in each individual action or omission, allowing us to learn as much as possible from each situation.

Life is a succession of choices. The Enlightened Millionaire embraces each outcome from "above the line." As much as possible is learned from each situation. As a result, the next choice is more likely to be wiser.

Choose to look at everything from above the line. The Enlightened Millionaire does.

THE FOURTH AHA: ABUNDANCE IS YOUR NATURAL STATE

Out of abundance He took abundance and
still abundance remained.

THE UPANISHADS

The Universe is fundamentally abundant. There is no shortage, except in our own mind.

Infinite money potentially awaits each of us who apply the principles of acquiring it. You can decide to become wealthy and abundant now, and the Universe will cheerfully provide. Opportunities and blessings come to individuals who embrace an abundant attitude. Others everywhere have created abundance, so can you.

Monday evening, a private dinner in the Fireside Nook at the Mariposa Plaza, Riverdale's only four-star hotel. A cozy, dimly lit room that was set for 12. A flagstone hearth. Fake logs and a gas fire.

Eleven months had passed since Gideon's death; it was early August of the following year.

Michelle felt like a French maid in a Noël Coward play, in her black uniform with its lace-trimmed white apron. She silently removed picked-over salads from the left of the diners. Damp radicchio and butter lettuce lay in the glistening remains of vinaigrette.

She was good at laying the plates up her forearms, overlapping them slightly to maximize the number she could carry at once. Her supervisor, Sarah, said she was a quick learner. But Michelle had forgotten how to take compliments.

Back in the kitchen she unloaded her arms. Sarah, a heavyset Pacific Islander with a blue-black bun, instructed her to arrange the plates for the next course.

"How's it going out there?" Jeremy asked.

"Fine," she snapped. The old Michelle had not snapped; the new one did.

"Chill, girl," Delphine said.

Jeremy and Delphine. Coworkers and, in Michelle's new world order, fellow losers.

Jeremy Cavalieri had high cheekbones and a high-bridged nose, legacies from his Arapahoe mother, and curly black hair, the contribution of his Italian father. Michelle had heard rumors that Jeremy had run a successful computer consulting business but lost everything, even his family, to a gambling addiction.

Delphine Dupre, who was also Michelle's roommate, had a tendency to make a splash at the Mariposa with her Tammy Faye makeup and her big hairdo: brown hair frosted in various shades of blond and red, teased high on her head. She and Michelle lived in a one-bedroom apartment in a dreary complex with washing machines that never worked and a pool chronically filled with slime. Delphine

Once you embrace, experience, and choose to express it, there is only abundance. Who can absorb all the abundance of a magnificent sunset? There is absolute plenty for each of us to drink, absorb, photograph, and share. And it returns again and again—it's endless. In fact, sharing always creates more.

The principle of abundance is exactly the same. The dictionary defines *abundance* as "great supply, plentitude, sufficiency, more than enough." It is a principle that cannot wear out, rust out, get tired, or not deliver the goods. Abundance is. Once you own the principle, the results that follow must be abundant. Abundant thinking multiplies, magnetizes, and magnifies whatever is focused upon.

What is the significance of this? It means there is *more* than enough to attend to the needs of everyone, everywhere and simultaneously create a sustainable ecology and economy.

Real-life models of abundance include such wide-ranging examples as Mother Teresa, Dr. Maya Angelou, Oprah, Paul Newman, Art Linkletter, and Bill and Melinda Gates.

To "out-picture" abundance, we first must successfully and repetitively "in-picture" a mental state of abundance. Why? Because our state of mind creates our state of results. Affirm the following each morning and night for the next 30 days or until it becomes *the truth* for you. Preferably, do this just prior to sleep and just before getting out of bed in the morning. Repeat it with feeling, belief, imagination, and acceptance:

I am abundant in every good way.
Infinite money is mine to earn, save, invest, exponentially multiply, and
  share.
My abundance is making everyone better off.
I embrace abundance and abundance embraces me.

shared the bedroom with her learning disabled daughter, and Michelle had the foldout couch in the living room.

"Which group are we serving tonight?" Jeremy asked.

"A bunch of rich people," Michelle said resentfully.

"A group called EMC^3." Sarah was more specific. "It stands for Enlightened Millionaires Circle. They're a networking and service group of self-made millionaires, and they're excellent customers of the hotel, so be careful how you treat them. Now get out there and see who needs something more to drink."

There was plenty of heat in the kitchen and Michelle would have loved to be anywhere else but here. But she couldn't. It was her life.

What was left of it.

How blessed she had been. She had thought that she'd appreciated what she used to have—her husband, her kids, even her modest home—but she hadn't. Was this God's way of teaching her a lesson? She had not lost her faith in God, not entirely, but if He did exist, He had some explaining to do.

After her arrest, they had released her from jail on her own recognizance. Of course. What would the Ericksens want more than for her to skip town?

Within another two months she had lost her house, her car, and her children, who had been placed in the temporary custody of their grandparents. Back when the Ericksens had first handed her the subpoena, she had foreseen that they would make trouble for her, but she had not really ever believed that she could lose her children. She had underestimated her in-laws.

At the preliminary hearing, Judge Pedroni appeared to be an intelligent man and Michelle could hardly believe that he was fooled by the parade of near-strangers who claimed to have intimate knowledge of how she was an unfit mother. The proprietor of the local hardware store who swore that he had seen her slapping Nicky when he asked her to buy him a tool kit. The landscaper who

THE FIFTH AHA: GIVERS GET

He which soweth sparingly shall reap also sparingly;
and he which soweth bountifully shall reap also bountifully.

2 CORINTHIANS 9:6

The dictionary defines *paradox* as an act or statement that on one level of meaning seem to contradict itself. Yet at a higher level (often called the "meta level") there is a deeper truth or understanding.

Properly adding a million dollars to your net worth is a primary objective of this book. Yet to obtain this you must first *give*. This is one of the Enlightened Millionaire's paradoxes. On one level this makes no logical sense. How can someone *give* before someone *gets*? This is not possible using ordinary logic. Yet on the meta level, that is exactly what happens.

As many of the ancient texts read, *"Give, and it will be given to you."* Reflect for a moment; aren't the people with the most friends the ones who are the most friendly? Aren't the people who receive the most love the most loving? This is the Enlightened Millionaire's principle of "Givers Get." This is the fundamental Enlightened Millionaire's paradox.

Embracing this paradox is a combination of faith and action. It is the process of standing on the edge of a cliff and trusting that there is a fabulous world of abundance in the valley and then leaping. As in a poem by Apollinaire,

> *Come to the edge, he said.*
> *They said, we are afraid.*
> *Come to the edge, he said.*
> *They came,*
> *He pushed them*
> *And they flew.*

worked for a neighbor who said he repeatedly heard screams coming from the house. A doctor friend of the Ericksens who attended the wake and testified about the children's shabby appearance and Nick's bandaged forehead.

"The place was fit for pigs," the Ericksens' housekeeper claimed, raising an upper lip in repulsion. Natalie had so often sweetly insisted that she send Estella over for the day. Once—just once—Michelle had agreed. It was the week before Mother's Day, and Gideon was convinced that Natalie had meant it as a sincere gift.

"There were animal droppings everywhere," Estella testified, greatly exaggerating the number of pets the family kept. "I wanted to throw up."

In the courtroom, her friends did their best, but they were too few, and the legal system was ruled by a system of evidentiary rules so complicated that she couldn't imagine anyone with an IQ under 150 mastering them. Over and over the stories her friends told about her volunteer work, her careful monitoring of her children's progress in school, and the positive example of her loving marriage were struck from the record on technicalities that eluded her—while somehow the Ericksens' psychologist's testimony that Hannah's attachment to Mr. Moo-Moo only confirmed the presence of systematic abuse survived.

At the nadir of the preliminary proceedings, Michelle still did not imagine that she would not get visitation. She did not even believe her attorney when he said that her visitation might be supervised. But Judge Pedroni cited her "kidnapping" attempt as evidence that she could not be trusted. He awarded temporary custody to the grandparents pending a formal trial, which had yet to be scheduled. Michelle couldn't help but wonder if somehow Anthony Ericksen had something to do with the glacial pace of the legal system, though she barely had any fight left in her.

Michelle lived with her friend Summer for a while. She looked for work in Deer Creek and found it strangely—or not so strangely—difficult.

We learn that "givers get" only through the experience. Behaving this way, often a little hesitantly, opens us to the spiritual dimension of wealth building. Give your time, your approval, your smile, your advice, your wisdom, your compliments, your sense of humor, your talent, your attention, your encouragement, your love. All these things will flow back to you in abundance. The spiritual dimension expands, multiplies, and adds value to all that is given.

Giving as you get acknowledges the Universe as truly abundant. Giving taps into the spiritual dimension that multiplies us, our thinking, and our results. The Enlightened Millionaire knows this: There is an ocean of abundance and one can tap into it with a teaspoon, a bucket, or a tractor trailer. The ocean doesn't care.

THE SIXTH AHA:
CHANGING YOUR REALITY IS A SNAP

Do you ever talk to yourself?

Many people have a positive internal voice that encourages them—especially when they've done something good. It's like their own personal cheerleader: *"You can do it." "Go for it." "Good for you!" "You did it!" "Way to go!"*

Do you have a voice like that?

Some people have a voice that is more skeptical: *"Who do you think you are?" "You can't do that." "What an idiot." "Why are you so stupid?" "You can't do anything right." "You're so clumsy."*

Sometimes, without being aware of it, this skeptical voice talks us out

Michelle spied on the children a few times at their new private school, St. James. Hannah's uniform was a white pleated skirt and a midi top. Nicky wore a white polo shirt and navy trousers. Then, worried that she'd get caught and further jeopardize her chances at reclaiming the kids, Michelle cut short her trips to the St. James campus.

She had Christmas dinner at Courtney's house. The food was excellent and Courtney and her husband and young son were solicitous and charming. But she could hardly control her tears all evening, wondering what Nicky and Hannah were doing. She prayed that Natalie hadn't taken it upon herself to tell Hannah the truth about Santa Claus.

After months of living so close but being forced to remain so far from her children, Michelle sank deeper into depression. Christmas was the breaking point. Two weeks later she moved to Riverdale, a town of 300,000 a half hour's drive from Deer Creek. She hoped the move would help her shed the paralyzing grief she still felt and jolt her into action so that she could focus on the upcoming custody battle, but she simply found herself growing angry in addition to feeling sad.

Her bitter acorn of resentment, hurt, and humiliation grew into a mighty oak. She did not make new friends and she cut short her old friends' calls, rarely getting together with Summer and Courtney. In general, men did not pursue her; Jeremy was an exception, but when he asked her out, her reply was rude enough that he did not ask a second time.

Delphine was one of the few people—if not the only person—whom Michelle could tolerate. Perhaps it had to do with Delphine's struggles with her daughter. Mainly, though, Michelle moved in with Delphine to cut costs. Michelle wanted to hire another attorney, but that would take money. Even paying one-third rent, since she slept on the couch, it was still difficult to save. They took so much out of her paycheck. The hotel refused to stop deducting

of our dreams. You have a great idea and immediately this voice fires off in your head, *"Yeah, but . . . "* followed by a string of reasons why it won't work.

We call that voice "Mr. Yabut" (or Ms. Yabut, depending upon your gender), because he or she is always trying to talk you out of something. Frankly, there are some things that you ought to be talked out of. The Yabuts can serve a useful function—trying to protect you, to keep you out of trouble. But more often than not, Mr. and Mrs. Yabut react too quickly to stifle your creativity. Instead of a voice of reason, they try to kill the deal before it has a chance to grow. If you let the Yabuts go unchecked they can cause unnecessary anxiety, muddled thinking, poor health—even ruin your life. If that is the case, you need to learn how to silence them and take control of your thought process.

How?

Notice your positive, cheerleading internal voice right now. Where is it? Is it loud or is it soft? Imagine there is a sound dial that controls the volume of your internal dialogue. Turn up the volume of your positive voice. How does that make you feel? Try finding a volume level that motivates you—that encourages you to be your best.

Notice your negative internal voice. Where is it? Whenever you notice the Yabuts' taking control, just turn the volume down. Notice how that makes you feel.

There is something else you can do to silence the Yabuts for good. You can probably find a thick rubber band in your home or office. When you put this rubber band on your left wrist, it suddenly transforms into a Millionaire Maker. How? Every time you catch yourself thinking a negative or counterproductive thought, you snap the rubber band. Yes, it causes pain. The pain causes a "pattern interrupt." Mentally, and perhaps vocally, you say "OWW!"

Snap yourself every time you find yourself saying . . .

money for her health insurance, though she was willing to risk becoming sick in exchange for the extra cash.

Michelle made the rounds of the EMC^3 table. "More wine, sir?" she asked a man with a blond moustache.

"No, thank you." He covered his glass with his hand.

Michelle picked up snippets of conversation about the Nasdaq, the Nikkei, P/E ratios, and IPOs. *Rich people.* She thought of Anthony Ericksen, and the wine bottle trembled in her hand.

At one end of the table she noticed a striking African-American woman dressed in a flowing African-style robe in blue streaked with gold that made Michelle think of the robes of a wizard. Her outfit was all the more arresting since the rest of the group was so conservatively, if expensively, dressed, in dark suits, although pieces of gold jewelry flashed in the firelight.

Michelle raised her eyebrows, extending her hand toward the woman's plate. The woman nodded absently. Michelle took it, and then hesitated, not wanting to leave her side. She smelled of oranges and sandalwood.

At the kitchen door, Michelle turned backward so that she could push it open with her rear end, since her arms were full. A pale, very thin woman at the end of the table—at the opposite end from where the African-American woman sat—stood up and began to address the group.

"You all know Samantha Munroe. And you're dying to hear her, so I won't waste too much time on an introduction."

Michelle knew immediately that the speaker would be the African-American woman. She was curious to hear her. The woman stood out like a tropical flower blooming in a patch of dry grass. And somehow Michelle knew that her appearance was just the outward expression of what was inside.

As with most people who promise to be brief, the speaker went on at some length. Michelle lingered as long as she dared at the door, even though she feared that someone exiting the kitchen

I can't afford it.

That's out of my league.

I'm not good enough.

I'm not worthy.

I can't do it.

I'm not smart enough.

I don't know where to start.

I'm not well-enough connected.

Replace your internal dialogue with words like these:

I'll find out how to get connected.

I'll start right now with what I have.

I'm smart enough to figure this out.

I can do it.

I AM worthy.

I AM good enough.

That IS in my league.

I CAN afford it if I really want it.

This technique is so simple. Wear the band 24/7 for the next 30 days—that includes to bed and while showering. After a red welt forms on your left wrist you'll start to quickly, safely, and satisfyingly **change your behavior.** No one needs to know you're doing this except you. It works rapidly—within a month. It will amaze and delight you. After you experience these tremendous and fulfilling results, tell three friends about this technique.

Your thoughts have the power to curse or bless. They can lead you to plenty, abundance, surplus, and "have-ness" . . . or to lack, limitation, deprivation, scarcity, and "have-not-ness." The choice is yours. You can control your thinking. Your thinking controls your behavior. Your behavior controls your results.

Put on your Millionaire Maker and snap your way to a vast and ever-improving life and lifestyle. This definitely puts you on the path to becoming an Enlightened Millionaire.

would knock against her and send her plates flying. She learned that Samantha Munroe had just returned from a three-month sojourn in Kenya. She was a founding member of EMC³, a multimillionairess. She was wealthy from real estate, owned several businesses, and was also the author of two books.

Finally Michelle pushed the door open with her derriere.

Delphine quickly took some of Michelle's plates. "We were about to send a search party."

"I—I'm kind of interested in the speaker," Michelle said tentatively.

Jeremy and Delphine looked at each other. "You go ahead, honey," Delphine said. "We can cover for you."

Michelle was embarrassed. She was only a lowly waitress. But at least her black uniform was designed for maximum invisibility. She sat on a chair next to the double doors and tried to project the impression that she was observing for the sole purpose of being available if anyone needed additional food or drink. But even as she was discreetly folding her hands in her lap and crossing her legs at the ankle, Samantha seemed to look directly at her. Michelle raised her chin.

Now that she was standing, backlit by the fire, Samantha presented an even more imposing presence. She was taller than Michelle had anticipated, a stately woman with an ancient and ageless beauty whose long, traditional dress did not hide the curves in her statuesque frame. Her hair was done in a massive weave with what seemed like thousands of delicate, tightly woven braids pouring like a fountain from under a headscarf that matched her robe.

"My friends, I am so blessed to be here with you tonight. Can we join hands?" Her voice was a powerful contralto: commanding yet supple, like a saxophone. Everyone obeyed her request. Even in this circle of self-confident, accomplished millionaires, Samantha

THE SEVENTH AHA:
WORDS TRANSFORM

Use the Millionaire Maker for a few days to "snap" yourself every time you have a negative *thought*. Then focus on the words you *speak*. The spoken word has a tremendous impact on both your external and internal reality. Words have power. Whatever you say eventually comes back to you like a boomerang. Hence, it is critical to use words properly.

Marshall Thurber, a partner in one of the most successful real estate companies in San Francisco, told of a powerful experiment he conducted with his office staff. "There was one discipline that immediately transformed my entire organization. It developed from one of our weekly Monday morning meetings with the entire company. At that meeting I read a page from a book detailing the life of Rolling Thunder, an American Indian medicine man."

These are Rolling Thunder's words:

> "People have to be responsible for their thoughts, so they have to learn to control them. It may not be easy, but it can be done. First of all, if we don't want to think certain things we don't say them. We don't have to eat everything we see, and we don't have to say everything we think. So we begin by watching our words and speaking with good purpose only."

Upon reading this quote, everyone in Thurber's company agreed to only speak with good purpose. That is, *"If it doesn't serve, don't say it."* According to their rules, if anyone was observed not following the policy of speaking with good purpose, he or she agreed to donate $2 to a bowl in the office. At the end of the month the money in the bowl was given to charity.

was the natural leader. When she joined hands with her neighbors, Michelle could see that many of her long fingers were adorned with distinctive rings of hammered gold.

"We are blessed . . . and may we use our many blessings to bless many others," Samantha said simply. She released the hands of the two people on either side of her. All around the table, the chain collapsed, and yet Michelle felt the presence of an energy connecting them.

"I have two orders of business tonight. The first one is to give you all an update on our Millionaire Manifesto.[p. xii] At last month's meeting, Howard and I accepted the assignment of updating our mission statement." Samantha made a nod to a gentleman seated to her right. "We've finished a rough draft and would like to bounce it off you for your input."

As she passed out a single piece of paper to all present, Samantha continued, "For those of you who weren't with us when we formed EMC^3 a few years ago, we wanted to create something unique from all of the other service groups. First, it would consist of only millionaires, but millionaires dedicated to doing good in the world. We wanted to celebrate prosperous people who took the higher road—to distinguish ourselves from the typical millionaire that people read about in the press. To put *our* emphasis on ethics, honesty, and integrity. That's why we called it EMC—the Enlightened Millionaire Circle. Second, we wanted it to be the ultimate masterminding group—to capitalize on the connections among and between us to expand our network exponentially. It's true what they say, it's not what you know, but who you know. And I don't know of a more 'connected' group than those of us in this room. Thus, Exponential Masterminding Connections became another of our goals. And finally, we wanted to not only be Enlightened and Connected but to have Multiple Streams of Income. Thus, our three goals became EMC^3."

The gentleman to the right of Samantha, Howard, spoke up. "I thought of another meaning for EMC: *Everyone Makes Cash*. But Sam vetoed it."

This simple act of putting $2 into a bowl was a transforming experience for this entire office. According to Thurber, nothing he has done before or since had such a powerful impact on a group of people.

We offer this as a challenge: Choose your words carefully. Only speak with good purpose. If it doesn't serve, don't say it. If you catch yourself speaking words that don't serve, put $2 into a bowl. Then watch the results in your own life.

THE EIGHTH AHA: YOU ARE YOUR WEALTH

"Now, here is my secret, a very simple secret.
It is only with the heart that one can see rightly;
what is essential is invisible to the eye."
FROM *THE LITTLE PRINCE*, BY ANTOINE DE SAINT-EXUPÉRY

It all starts from nothing. All of us come into this world naked, helpless, and ignorant. So it is whenever you start a new project—you're like a new baby. The first task is to take stock of your resources. In business, they call this preparing a balance sheet: a summary of your assets and liabilities.

Assets	Liabilities
Cash	Debts
Securities and other liquid investments	Obligations
Real estate	Mortgages
Cars, equipment, and other tangible assets	Bank loans
Furniture, jewelry, and other personal items	Promissory notes

Samantha shot a mischievous scowl toward her counterpart, amid some hearty chuckles from the group. Then she went on, "We decided to call our mission statement a 'manifesto' because it comes from the word *manifest*. Everything in your life is what you choose to manifest.[p. 18] Here is what we want to manifest—abundance for ourselves and for as many people on spaceship earth as possible.

"When I think of abundance, I think of the bumblebee.[p. xiii] He goes from flower to flower, collecting nectar. He's on a mission. To gather nectar to support his hive. So he's already doing well. But in the meantime, he's also pollinating the whole garden. That's what entrepreneurs do: They make money, but in the process they spin off new jobs, and new products and lots of innovation."

Thinking of bumblebees, Michelle remembered Courtney's beautiful garden. When she had left Deer Creek in January it was covered in snow. But now, in August, the lilacs and petunias, the dancing butterflies of late summer . . .

"We're all bumblebees on this bus, Sam," chuckled a gray-haired man in suspenders.

"Exactly, Marshall," Samantha said, nodding to the fellow on her left. "Bees do it by accident. We want to do it on purpose, because, I'm sure you all agree, the ultimate purpose of wealth is to help others."[p. xvi]

Michelle's lips parted. She looked at Samantha. It looked as though the flames from the fireplace were rising from her head. Like a phoenix being reborn. The rest of the room fell away. She thought of the Ericksens—how she had hated them for the way they used their wealth and influence to ruin her life. She had believed that wealth was the same as evil. She and Gideon were proud of not being materialistic, and Gideon wanted to be as different from his father as possible. So they had always lived on the edge. But in the end they had hurt not only themselves but, far worse, they had hurt Nicky and Hannah.

They had demonized Gideon's parents for the wrong reason. Here, in this room, were a group of millionaires who seemed to be

When you subtract your liabilities from your assets, you come up with what is known as "net worth." If you want to be a net millionaire, *what you own minus what you owe must equal more than a million dollars.*

Having such a balance sheet assumes that it is our possessions that make us wealthy. But many essential items are left off the traditional balance sheet. The truth is that these "invisible assets" are the real source for all the wealth we possess.

For instance, what about the original business *idea*? What about the *courage* to implement it? What about the *contacts* and *relationships* that help you accomplish it? What about *creativity, determination, persistence, commitment,* and *knowledge*? None of these attributes appear on the traditional balance sheet, but there can be absolutely no tangible balance sheet without them. The truth is, you don't *have* wealth. You *are* your wealth. So let's prepare your "enlightened" balance sheet. What are some of your invisible assets?

Internal Assets	Internal Liabilities
Creativity, imagination	Anger, small-mindedness
Vision, generosity	Perfectionism, pettiness
Courage, boldness, persistence, integrity	Fear, anxiety, hesitancy
Expert connections and customer databases	Bad reputation
Valuable skills: selling, persuasion, marketing	Laziness
Time management	Poor organization

Literally, as a beginner, there are only three resources you need: a good idea; the commitment to do it; the key contacts who possess all the other resources.

Here is your motto: *Every resource I need (tangible or intangible) is possessed by someone, somewhere at this very moment. How can I find these individuals and persuade them to provide me with these resources?*

different. What if there was a legitimate, kind, nurturing way to make money? What if *she* could make enough to hire the world's best attorney to help her get her kids back? She felt a spark of hope flicker inside her for the first time in almost a year.

She snapped out of her reverie. She'd missed a few words of what Samantha was saying. She wasn't going to let *that* happen again.

"Working with Howard, I got an exciting idea." Samantha paused and, with the subtlest possible movement of her head, seemed to make brief eye contact with everyone at the table. "Ladies and gentlemen, you're the first to hear about the *Enlightened Millionaire Training Manual.*"

Murmurs of curiosity.

"I'm not famous for my modesty, and I'm not going to start now. I have assembled a manual that will teach people to become Enlightened Millionaires.

"I know that most of you have thought about how you became millionaires. For the past several years I've been collecting my own list of principles for financial success. Just recently I've pulled them together into one volume that anyone anywhere can pick up and use as a textbook for their own financial freedom."

I wish I had something like that, Michelle thought.

"My goal is to create a million millionaires from this book."

Michelle leaned forward.

"It's my way of giving back. Mark, here, taught me that one." She glanced over at a tall, blond gentleman in the far corner. "Idea tithing—isn't that what you called it, Mark?"

"That's right," Mark agreed. "It's about taking your best idea and giving it to the world. Like Irving Berlin gave the rights to his best song, 'God Bless America,' to the Boy and Girl Scouts. You know, they've received over $5,000,000 in royalties for that one."

"So," said Sam, "this manual is my gift to the world. All the profits will go to my charitable foundation. The book is the culmination of 20 years of trial and error . . . mostly error. It's the shortcut that I wish someone had shown me when I got started."

THE NINTH AHA: WEALTH IS FREEDOM

Life is a seminar. You were enrolled at birth. You can't get out of it, even by dying. So enjoy it. You came into this seminar with no instruction manual. Allow this book to positively change that.

Financially you may be winning or losing just now. We want you to win. We want you to perpetuate your wins. We want you to catch what we call a "win-fection." With a win-fection, you become an unstoppable magnet that wins, and wins, and wins.

To prepare you for the seminar called "Your Life," we want to teach and inspire you to attract money, and lots of it. This is the incredibly important inaugural freedom—called **money freedom.** You want to have enough money so that all your future days are prepaid. You will work because you want to work, not because you have to work.

You can contribute big-time because you are no longer a wage slave, owned by your job. Because you are free to risk. When this happens, imagine the incredible difference you can make. You can expand your sense of who you really are and become the great server you were meant to be. You can set big goals. You can assemble your Dream Team(s). You can be a fully abundant person, fully functioning. You are a masterpiece in process—becoming ever better, more fulfilled, and totally happy.

Having accomplished your first evolutionary step of money freedom, you now pass "go" and move on to **time freedom.** Time freedom doesn't mean you don't work, it means that your work is your play. Your play becomes your work. You savor it. You own it. Work does not own you. You feel comfortable and calm taking time off. You start by taking off an extra day here and there. You build up to taking off a week per month, or equivalently three months per year, when you can forget about work totally and completely. Yet your income continues to expand, increase,

"Do we get an advance copy?" asked the pale woman who had introduced her.

"Of course—on one condition: that you help me find some . . . well, guinea pigs, for lack of a better term. People to test this material on. Like those family members who are more interested in spending your money than making some of their own . . ."

At this reference, Michelle unconsciously moved to the edge of her seat. She felt a tiny idea pecking at her, like a chick trying to break its way out of an egg.

"Michelle," someone whispered behind her.

Michelle jumped to her feet.

It was Jeremy, peering out through a crack in the double doors. "Chief Sarah is on the warpath."

"Right." How could Cinderella have forgotten her place in the kitchen? She reluctantly ducked back inside.

The last dish was put away, the last counter wiped. But still, out in the dining room, the members of EMC^3 lingered, mostly gathered around Samantha.

Sarah delegated Michelle and Delphine to go into the Fireside Room to strip the tablecloth, a not-so-subtle reminder that the room needed to be cleaned.

Michelle's heart was pounding as she folded the cloth with Delphine. Folding was silly since the cloth was bound for the laundry. But she was stalling.

It was Samantha who took the hint of Michelle's and Delphine's activities. "Let's let these folks get home," she said to the two men and three women who still clustered around her, then motioned with her head toward the door.

"Delphine," Michelle whispered. "I've got a big favor to ask. Could you finish cleaning up without me? I need to do something."

and multiply. When you return to work, you are rejuvenated, refreshed, and ready to have breakthrough ideas that will leverage you forward.

With time and money freedoms, you can pursue **relationship freedom.** You and your loved ones will have one of life's most precious gifts— love and time to explore it. You can go deep into your primary relationship and make it sing, whistle, hum, and dance. You have what others only dream about—the freedom to make your commitment to each other deep, poignant, meaningful, intimate, and lastingly cherishable.

You can now investigate your spiritual beingness. You can work toward achieving **spiritual freedom.** You can discover who you are in God and who God is in you.

Let's not forget **physical freedom.** Health is the ultimate wealth. With time to exercise and money to buy the finest nutrition, nutritional supplements, and health care, you can maintain your health for as long as humanly possible.

These five great freedoms give you **Ultimate Freedom**—the ability to pursue your real genius. According to groundbreaking research by Dr. Howard Gardner at Harvard University, each of us has genius in us. With Ultimate Freedom you have a choice to discover your true genius and how you can uniquely apply it. (See the Thirteenth Aha.)

"Sure."

Trying not to think about how furious Sarah would be with her, Michelle rushed back to the employee lockers, removed her apron, grabbed her purse, and went searching for Samantha Munroe. Out the door, down a hallway, into the lobby. *Had Samantha gone already?*

No. Thank God. She was sitting on a circular banquette, flanked by the pale woman who had introduced her and the man in suspenders whom Michelle recognized from EMC[3].

Michelle stopped about 10 feet away. Her heart was pounding. *It's for Nicky and Hannah.* She forced herself to take the final steps. The three on the banquette looked up.

"Ms. Munroe," Michelle blurted out. "I think I can help you."

Samantha gazed steadily at Michelle. "You're the waitress from the dinner, aren't you?" she observed leisurely, but kindly.

"Yes." Michelle squirmed. "But don't hold it against me."

"Why would I do that, miss?"

"I don't know, I . . . Ms. Munroe, I was listening to your speech. I—I think you have a really incredible idea."

"Me, too."

What calm, what confidence radiated from Samantha Munroe! "You were talking about . . . guinea pigs," Michelle reminded her. "For your training manual."

Samantha gave her that mysterious one-corner-up smile that Michelle remembered from her talk in the Fireside Room. She felt the stirrings of hope.

"What's your name, young lady?"

"Michelle Ericksen."

"Tell you what, Michelle Ericksen. When the book is printed, I'll send you one of the first copies off the press. Why don't you give me your business card."

"I don't have a card," Michelle said, a bit shortly.

"Well, then, here's my card. Call my office and give your address to my assistant and I'll make sure to send you a copy."

THE TENTH AHA:
IT ALL STARTS WITH A DREAM

Where will you be five years from today? Are you still living in the same house? Driving the same car? Working at the same job? Does five years pass and make you older, grayer, fatter, deeper in debt?

Or do you see a brighter future? Let's go there.

Ask yourself, "How good could life be five years from today?" Pretend that all of your dragons have been slain, all your demons have been banished. The way is clear before you. Just you and anything you want in five years or less.

Lift yourself above the burden of your current life and ride on wings of imagination into the future. Imagine your dream home. Walk up to the front door and step inside. What's the first thing you see? Smell the smells in that house; hear the sounds. How does this resonate with you?

Who lives in that house with you? How exquisite are your relationships? How does it feel to love and be loved?

What do you look like in five years? Are you healthier? More fit? Let the "ideal you" emerge.

Are you in tune with your Higher Power? Are you living the Divine life? Do you enjoy peace of mind, expanded awareness, even bliss?

Give yourself permission to dream a big dream. See yourself living a life of balance: financially, spiritually, socially, physically. You've got it all—and it's good!

Tonight, as you drift off to sleep, imagine this bright future in vivid detail. Tomorrow, when you wake, awaken inside your dream world. See it, taste it, hear it, smell it, feel it. Do this every day for the next 90 days and notice the amazing things that will start spontaneously happening in your life.

Michelle took the card. It was simple yet elegant—a black card with gold-embossed lettering and the logo of a phoenix. *A phoenix!*

Samantha nodded her head as if to say "we're done now" and returned to her previous conversation with her companions. Michelle stood there, awkwardly, and tucked the card in her blouse pocket. She didn't know what she had expected, but she felt dismissed. Still, she couldn't bring herself to leave.

After a moment Samantha rose gracefully from the banquette and turned to leave. Michelle heard her say good-bye to the others, who headed in different directions.

Michelle watched her go, until she disappeared through the sliding glass doors of the Mariposa Plaza.

"Wait!" Michelle called. When Michelle caught up with her, Samantha was waiting under the porte cochere, presumably for the valet to bring her car. She turned calmly toward Michelle. "I see you've handled the first rejection."

Michelle wrinkled her brow.

"The first rejection," Sam repeated. "Most people can't handle the first rejection. That's why they never get rich."

Michelle nodded, beginning to understand.

Sam continued, leaning forward as if to share a secret, "It's after the third rejection where the big money is made." By this time the attendant had brought the keys to Sam's car, a deep-green Mercedes with sparkling chrome wheels. Sam turned to walk toward her car.

"But . . . ," Michelle called after her.

Samantha glanced back over her shoulder. "It will all be explained in the book I'll send you." Samantha tossed her briefcase into the backseat and just before she slipped into the leather frontseat, Sam looked back and held up her two fingers toward Michelle. *A peace sign?*

Michelle stood there helpless. It was all happening so fast. Somehow she knew that this woman was the key . . . the missing number of the combination to the vault . . . the way to get her life back on track. All she could think of were her two children being raised by

What's important to you about transforming this dream into reality? Write it down. When you do this, you are becoming an Enlightened Millionaire.

_____

_____

_____

_____

THE ELEVENTH AHA: CLARITY IS POWER

Every book on success talks about the importance of goals. But almost none of them talks about *how to think about* your goals. Decades ago, a success philosopher named Neville gave us the secret. He said,

Don't think *of* your goals, think *from* your goals.

In other words, rather than thinking *of* your future dream home, think *from* your dream home. Imagine yourself actually living in that dream home—as if you were already there. Imagine walking in the front door of your dream home. What do you see? What do you smell? What do you hear? What can you taste? How does it feel to have acquired this home? What are you saying to yourself? Actually experience living there. That's the difference between simply thinking *of* your dream home and thinking *from* it.

How important is it to do this? In his book, *Golf My Way*, Jack Nicklaus revealed how he used this technique to become one of the greatest

those stuffy, conniving Ericksens, and something bubbled out of her. A renewed strength she hadn't felt in months.

"WAIT!" she called out.

The car stopped and the driver's-side window rolled down. Samantha looked out.

"I'm it," Michelle blurted out. "I'm your guinea pig. I don't need to read your book. I'm ready now. I need it NOW." She spoke with a sense of focus and power that surprised even herself.

"I'm sorry, Ms. Ericksen, I just don't have the time." Samantha stayed there, slightly smiling, her car not moving, the window still rolled down—almost as if she were waiting for Michelle to speak. Now Sam held up three fingers.

And then, Michelle understood the game that Sam was playing with her. "That's the third rejection, isn't it?"

Samantha smiled. She gestured slightly with her head toward the passenger-side door.

Michelle ran around the front of the Mercedes and jumped onto the buttery leather seat next to Samantha. The smell of new car washed over her. She looked over at Sam. Sam returned her gaze, with another slight nod, as if tipping her hat in respect.

"You learn fast, missy."

Sam put the car in gear, and off they drove into the cool Colorado night.

When Michelle awoke she didn't immediately remember where she was. Then the branches of the crab apple tree outside the window came into focus. *Samantha Munroe's house.*

Michelle had been surprised when Sam had driven up to the nondescript two-bedroom bungalow on the outskirts of Riverdale. "This was my first investment property," Sam had explained. "I figure this will be an excellent place to begin our training."

golfers of all time. Before each shot, he created a mental movie of the entire golf shot in his head.

> I never hit a shot, even in practice, without having a very sharp, in-focus picture of it in my head. It's like a color movie. First I "see" the ball where I want it to finish, nice and white and sitting up high on the bright green grass. Then the scene quickly changes and I "see" the ball going there: its path, trajectory, and shape, even its behavior on landing. Then there's a sort of fade-out, and the next scene shows me making the kind of swing that will turn the previous images into reality.

Here's another great example. The world held its collective breath during the 1984 Olympics as American gymnast Mary Lou Retton stood at the end of the mat preparing for her final vault. The stakes couldn't be higher. She had to get a perfect score, a 10, or lose it all—lose the dream, the gold, the team pride, everything. She closed her eyes for a few seconds, then got into position, ran like a demon on fire, and nailed a perfect 10 off the pommel horse to clinch the gold medal for herself and Team USA. When asked by reporters afterward what she was thinking when she closed her eyes before her run to victory, she told them she saw herself doing every motion precisely, flawlessly, and achieving a perfect score.

There are times in life when everything IS on the line. It's either 100% or nothing. Trying and striving doesn't get you brownie points, only achieving does. That's why it's so critical to visualize your goals clearly. As you practice this new method of vivid visualizing, you will find that your self-image begins to conform to these new images in your mind. You will literally begin to grow into the new millionaire you.

The guest room that Michelle now occupied was small, painted white, and looked suited for a young girl. Photos of Sam's own extended family and some nieces and nephews of her late husband adorned the dresser. Michelle wondered, would she ever have a place to put pictures of her own up again? No matter where she lived, it wouldn't be a home without Nicky and Hannah. For a while she hadn't even let herself think about them. She had cut off her feelings the way she used to prune back her plants. But now she almost dared to hope again. In the early morning quiet she began reflecting on the affirmations—Sam called them Manifestations[pp. 96, 120, 152, 188, 208, 224, 266]—that Sam had already instructed Michelle to do first thing each day. *I am rich. I am successful. I am standing under the spout where all good things pour out.*

She felt a little silly even repeating them silently in her mind. *Samantha must know what she's talking about.*

"It'll happen," came a voice.

Michelle sat up, startled. Samantha was in the doorway, dressed in dark green jogging pants and a matching sweatshirt. A dime-store bandanna replaced her usual headscarf.

"How did you . . . ?"

Samantha laughed. "Intuition. Come on, Private, it's time for your morning drills. If you're going to live here, it's not gonna be to laze in bed till all hours."

"All hours? It's 6 A.M.!"

"What do you bet that daddy-in-law of yours is eating some venture capitalist for breakfast by now?"

Michelle jumped out of bed. Five minutes later she had brushed her teeth and put on the old sweats and running shoes that she had retrieved from her apartment the night before. Samantha was outside, at rest in her porch swing.

"Samantha . . ."

"You can call me Sam." And Sam was on her feet, the porch swing rocking behind her. Without looking back she skipped one of

THE TWELFTH AHA:
MORE CLARITY IS MORE POWERFUL

Goals are critical to your success. We recommend you start a special note-book for your goals. Whenever you think of something you would like to accomplish in your life, write it down in your goal book. Then, on a daily basis, write your six major goals. Do this each morning as you start your day. Don't just read your goals aloud, but physically write them down again on paper. We learned this idea from Brian Tracy, the famous public speaker. He writes his major goals down *every day*. It magnetizes his mind to what he really wants to accomplish that day.

To keep yourself balanced, record your top six goals, in each of the six major areas or resources of your life:

Body: Your physical goals
Brain: Your intellectual goals—the books you read, the amount of
    daily study
Being: Your spiritual goals—the time you spend meditating or
    praying, etc.
Time: Your organizational goals
People: Your people goals—concerning the most important people in
    your life
Money: Your financial goals

In addition, affirm each of these six goals daily, *as if you'd already achieved your success,* in writing on a 3 × 5 card. For instance, if your money goal is to earn $100,000 this year and take plenty of time off, you would write the following on the card: "I am so happy and grateful that I am earning $400 per day, working only 250 days this year."

the three steps down to the sidewalk, took a left, and hit the ground running. Michelle felt a surge of adrenaline. She and Gideon used to run together; she hadn't been out since then. She was out of shape, but surely . . .

"We'll be running every morning," Sam called back over her shoulder.

The sun wasn't yet strong enough to burn through the early morning mist. Sam led the way down the quiet suburban street. By the time they took a right 10 minutes later, the gap between Michelle and Sam was nearly a half a block long—and Michelle suspected that Sam wasn't going at full speed. "You'd better put the pedal to it," Sam shouted, this time without looking back.

"I'm trying," she puffed.

This new street ended in a park. Sam ran straight across the grass toward a narrow paved path. Michelle, feeling the oxygen leeching from her muscles, willed herself to follow. They passed picnic tables and a large play structure, but there were no children out yet—only a few joggers on the path that she now joined behind Sam.

"Keep it up."

Michelle looked up at the wooded hill ahead of them with a feeling of dread. But Sam didn't slow, and as the path began to climb, Sam did, too. Soon they were entering a stand of pine trees that became denser as they went on. Michelle kept her eyes on her prize in the green sweats.

Then, suddenly, Samantha disappeared. She had left the path. Michelle was afraid she had lost her. But after a moment she caught sight of her darting among the trees, heading in a direction that she seemed to have memorized.

Michelle continued her pursuit, wheezing harder than before as she kept pushing uphill. Then, just as she felt her second wind giving out, she saw light breaking through the trees beyond. A few moments later she followed Sam into the open. It was if she had stepped out into another world.

Note that you start your goal affirmation with "happy," because most people don't know if they are happy or sad. Choose to be happy. It doesn't cost any more. It's an *attitude* that will give you *altitude* in business and life. It's a state of mind that will attract many good things.

Then write what service, product, or information you plan to render and in what quantity and quality: "I am providing excellent value by selling x number of products to x number of satisfied customers each day." (If you miss a sale on Monday, you must make two on Tuesday, and so on.)

Keep this 3 × 5 card with you as you go throughout your day. On this single card affirm all six of your major goals. Read these goals aloud four times a day, at breakfast, lunch, dinner, and just before you go to sleep. This last step is most important, because your mind never sleeps.

Sign and date this card and get one other person to whom you are committed to do the same. Follow up with this person weekly to prove you are on track. Change and upgrade your card at least monthly.

Think only of what you want, never what you don't want. Visualize yourself earning the kind of money needed to reach your goals.

Write it. Read it. Say it. See it. Notice how your goals magically materialize into your life.

THE THIRTEENTH AHA: TAP INTO YOUR GENIUS

Are you a "genius"? Expressing your genius is knowing what you want to do with your life and doing it because it expresses who you really are. Tiger Woods, Oprah, Warren Buffett, Bill Gates. They're expressing their genius. They're living the life they were born to live. It's hard to imagine them doing anything else. No wonder they're so successful!

Sam was standing on a flat outcropping of rock—a promontory that extended beyond the thick line of trees. Her arms were stretched wide toward the sky. A valley dipped below her: It was deep and narrow, drenched in early morning sunshine and alive with yellow dots that Michelle guessed were black-eyed Susans. A bright creek coursed through the bottom. The forest was awakening with the sounds of bluejays and skittering squirrels, and in the distance, the Rocky Mountains rose in all their blue majesty.

"This place is blessed, this day is blessed, and we are blessed," Sam shouted out over the valley.

"I don't remember a Samantha Munroe winning an Olympic gold medal in track." Michelle, holding on to her side, finally had enough breath to speak.

"Before your time, Butterfly," Samantha chuckled. She continued to gaze over the valley. "Come out here on the point with me."

Michelle chose her footing carefully among the rocks until she reached a flat spot near the edge. She leaned over; the drop looked to be about 100 feet. She quickly took a few steps back, feeling dizzy.

"Now stand up straight," Sam coached, looking straight at her, down from her extra six inches, with kindness and love. "I want you to take a slow, deep breath . . . the deepest breath of your life."

Michelle closed her eyes and concentrated on pulling in a massive quantity of the pure mountain oxygen. She held it for a long time. And then slowly exhaled every last molecule.

"Perfect. Do that again. But even slower this time. Breathe in all the good things and breathe out all the things you fear."

Michelle allowed herself to be coached through seven all-purifying breaths. When she completed the last and longest breath, her face was flushed and her skin was zinging. She opened her eyes, almost tipsy with excess energy.

"Wow." She scanned the horizon with renewed appreciation.

"Come over here and sit down by me," Sam coaxed.

Here are four characteristics of people who are expressing their genius.

1. **Passion:** They love what they do. If they weren't getting paid, they'd do it for free.
2. **Talent:** They're good at what they do. Call it talent, ability, or genius—they've got it.
3. **Values:** Doing what they do is extremely important to them.
4. **Destiny:** They have a sense that they are doing what they were born to do—making their own unique contribution. It's almost a spiritual thing. It's their destiny.

Is genius only found among the great? Absolutely not! We believe every person has unique genius—including you. You have unique talents, abilities, interests, and values that only you can bring into greatness. You have a destiny that only you can fulfill.

How do you begin to tap into your genius? Please complete the exercise on the next page to compile your own four-part Genius List.

The purpose of this exercise is to help you become aware of more aspects of your unique personality. The more you access these parts of yourself . . .

- ▲ the more *energy* you will feel in your daily activities
- ▲ the more *fulfillment* you will experience
- ▲ the more *success* you will have
- ▲ the *faster* you will become a millionaire

Michelle saw that Sam was pointing to a huge stone, almost as smooth as a table, to their left. Sam slid easily onto the edge, then scooted over to make room for Michelle and patted the space beside her. After another uneasy glance down, Michelle joined her. She swung her legs over the side. "I've always been a little scared of heights," she admitted.

"Time to get over it" was Sam's response.

"Gideon was the one who took Nicky on all the amusement park rides," Michelle remembered. "Hannah was more like me that way."

Sam leaned over and picked up a shiny, yellow-brown pinecone from among several that were scattered around them. "A lot of getting over fear is just doing what you're afraid of."

And as the crisp breeze ruffled her hair and she watched the stream below glimmer in the ascending sun, Michelle did feel her fear recede.

Sam lobbed the pinecone into the valley. "There'll be a lot of new scary things to try . . . if you really want to be a millionaire."

"Well, I do," Michelle said firmly.

"What would you do with all that money?"

"First, I'd fight to get my kids back."

"And then?"

"Then I'd make *them* pay for what they did."

"Them?"

"Yeah, the people who ruined my life. Like that drunk driver," she nearly spat.

"Hmm."

Michelle caught something odd in Sam's tone, but she barreled on. "And the Ericksens. I'd like *them* to know what it's like to sleep on someone's couch for six months."

"So you want revenge."

"Works for me," Michelle agreed.

"Because they *ruined your life*."

MY GENIUS LIST

Passion:
What Do I Love to Do?

What activities give me satisfaction?

What excites me about life?

What is my secret ambition?

What are my hobbies?

1. _____

2. _____

3. _____

4. _____

Talent:
What Am I Good At?

What do I get complimented on?

Where have I excelled in the past?

Where have I been successful?

What are some of my strengths?

1. _____

2. _____

3. _____

4. _____

Values:
What Is Important to Me?

What would I do if I were wealthy?

What do I stand for?

What won't I stand for?

What would I risk my life for?

1. _____

2. _____

3. _____

4. _____

Destiny:
What Was I Born to Do?

What is my unique mission in life?

What does God want me to do?

What are my unique opportunities?

Where can I make a difference?

1. _____

2. _____

3. _____

4. _____

Michelle squirmed. "Well, they *did* ruin my life," she said sulkily.

"There is only one person who can *ruin* your life. And that's you."

This made Michelle angry. She glared back, stabbing a finger toward the other woman. "My husband was killed by a drunk driver. *That's a fact.* His parents stole my children. *That's a fact.* I lost my house. *That's a fact.*"

"I don't dispute your facts, Counselor," Sam said, as if she were a judge in a courtroom scene. "But *you* get to decide whether these facts make you a victim or a victor. And right now, you're acting like a victim."

"But, I AM a victim!"

"Missy, every one of us is a victim of *something,* but some people don't *act* like victims. I have a friend who's a quadriplegic. Do you know what he does for a living? He draws cartoons with a pen he holds between his teeth."

Michelle looked down at the valley. It suddenly seemed even deeper. "And you're telling me this *because . . . ?*"

"Because my friend is *not* a victim, he's a victor. A victim blames. A victor *learns.*"[p. 24]

Michelle looked down at her knees. "What is there to learn from losing everything?" she asked.

"You tell me."

Michelle blinked back tears. "I learned that I don't like rich people."

"Hey," Sam teased. "*I'm* rich."

Michelle retreated hastily, "I learned that I don't like *some* rich people."

"What else did you learn?" Sam tossed another pinecone over the edge.

Michelle was silent. She didn't like this game.

Sam prodded her. "Did you learn that you could survive?"

Michelle nodded, grudgingly.

THE FOURTEENTH AHA: LOVERAGE

It is much easier to ride a horse in the direction it's going.

ABRAHAM LINCOLN

To become rich one minute at a time requires that you do what you love doing and you are passionate about it. Our friend Mike Litman has coined a word to describe the power that flows from a person who is living the charmed life: *loverage.* The success of the Enlightened Millionaire is derived from loverage.

Remember, the force that propels human action is emotion. Feelings—not cold cognitions—drive Enlightened Millionaires to turn good ideas into great value. If you love what you are doing, it is much easier. Go back to the Thirteenth Aha. Which items on your Genius List make your emotions sing? List of all of them below.

MY POTENTIAL PATH TO RICHES LIST

1._____

2._____

3._____

4._____

BrightHouse is an "ideation company," and a perfect example of loverage at work. They charge clients like Coca-Cola, Georgia Pacific, and Hardee's between $500,000 to $1,000,000 for a single idea. Says Joey Reiman of BrightHouse, "We do heartstorming, not brainstorming; creativity is much more about what people feel than what they think."

"Did you learn that you loved your family more than your own life?"

Michelle blinked again, but this time the tears came anyway. But if Sam noticed them, they didn't slow her down. "You take it from here."

Michelle whispered, "I learned that I'd do almost anything to get them back."

"And . . . ," Sam prompted.

Michelle thought for what seemed like a long time. It hurt to get the words out. "I learned that I need to take care of business. If I hadn't let the insurance lapse . . ."

"That was a hard lesson," Sam said gently.

Michelle pondered for a moment. "Here's something else I learned. That I'm not very good with money."

Sam spoke in a mocking tone, "Poor me. I didn't get the 'money genes' so I guess I'll always be poor."

"Well . . . I'm *not* good with money."

"Let's suppose that you're right. Do you want to be *right* or do you want to be rich?"

Michelle reflected on this.

"Anybody can learn to be good with money,"pp. 238, 240, 242 Samantha said. "I believe that even you can do it—if you choose.

"Ultimately, the victors are the ones who figure out what went wrong and rearrange their life so that it never happens again. Otherwise life just keeps throwing the very same lesson at you until you 'get it.' My daddy always used to say, 'The third time you get bitten by a dog, you can know one thing for sure: it ain't the fault of the dog.'"

Michelle smiled.

Sam picked up another pinecone; this one she chucked to Michelle. "Do you know anything about these?"

Michelle tossed the cone once in the air. "Hannah would say that's where baby pine trees come from."

Becoming an Enlightened One Minute Millionaire is as easy as one, two, three:

1. Do what you love.
2. Add enormous value.
3. Loverage it.

This is the path. Millions follow when you walk it.

THE FIFTEENTH AHA: IMAGINATION TRUMPS WILL

Almost 100 years ago, a French doctor named Emile Coué said something profound,

> "When the will comes in conflict with the imagination, the imagination invariably carries the day."

In other words, when your will—your rational, logical self—comes in conflict with your imagination—your creative, right-brained self—your imagination always wins.

Put simply, your imagination is the key. Case in point: A child is told there are no monsters under the bed—but when the lights go off, the childlike imagination runs wild. If you want to calm the child, you'll have more success by appealing to imagination than to logic. (*Don't worry, dear. The monsters in our house aren't the kind that hurt kids. We only let in the kind that protect kids.*)

"She's right. That pinecone comes from the lodgepole pine." Sam pointed out a stand of tall, straight trees ringing the edge of the valley. "The kind your father-in-law lusts to turn into two-by-fours."

Michelle's face darkened.

"Inside that pinecone are thousands of seeds. Do you know what finally releases them?"

"When the male pinecone pays for dinner?"

"No," Sam laughed. "The seeds are only released by a wildfire."

"Really?"

"Wildfires are part of nature's renewal process." Sam reached over to touch the pinecone, without taking it from Michelle's hand. "Every hundred years or so, a wildfire roars through these woods, and the heat is so intense that these cones explode, and that releases the seeds for a brand-new forest."

After a pause, Sam went on, "Sometimes *people* have wildfires. It takes a while . . . but things grow back."

Michelle wrapped her hands around the shiny cone.

"Let's get up and walk."

A little reluctantly, Michelle pulled herself to her feet. "Yes, this is a special place," Samantha said. By now Michelle was used to having Samantha read her thoughts. "I call it 'the Rock.' I take it with me everywhere I go, metaphorically speaking," she added with a chuckle. "I recommend you do, too."

Michelle followed as Sam climbed back over the stony ground to the more welcoming earth of the forest. Michelle's muscles were ready to move her again, and she enjoyed the more leisurely pace, with time to admire the silvery leaves of the blooming wild sage and to spot butterflies. The sight of one prompted Michelle to ask, "Sam, why did you call me 'Butterfly'?"

"Because you are a butterfly," Sam replied. "Once you get out of that cocoon."

Sam fell quiet again and Michelle sensed that she was giving her time to absorb some of the matters they had discussed. After a

We adults are no different—and the monsters we imagine are no less threatening. Have you ever held back for fear of rejection? Sure, we all have. We are all soft and fuzzy inside. We seek acceptance by our peers. We want to be loved. We crave it. And we hate to look like fools.

Often we end up imagining the worst. We see "them" turning us down—hanging up on us or refusing to do business with us. We end up "mind-reading"—projecting thoughts into other people's minds. *"I'll bet she doesn't like me." "He can probably tell that I'm not as successful as I appear."*

Why don't you imagine the best? Picture yourself succeeding. See them accepting you, liking you—your ideas, your projects—saying Yes! Imagine how good it could be. Insert positive thoughts into their minds. *"They probably need what I'm selling." "This just might be the answer they've been looking for."*

Here's the point: Imagining the best doesn't always work. Sometimes the worst *does* happen. But imagining the best works *more often.*

Why?

Because people *actually do* read your mind. What you "think" is projected through the airwaves to the person you're meeting with. They pick it up subliminally. So if they're going to be reading your mind anyway, make sure that what they read is worth reading.

Imagine the best-case scenario. Project the best possible outcome. That's what Enlightened Millionaires do.

while Sam began to ask casual questions about Michelle; soon she responded in kind by telling Michelle some of her own life history.

Sam had had her own wildfires. She had always wanted to have children, and she and her husband had tried for years through many miscarriages. Then her 42-year-old husband succumbed to a brain tumor. After caring for him through his illness, Sam was as broke as Michelle. But she had managed to buy the small house in Riverdale. From that start she had built a miniempire with properties and businesses in five western states. Sam focused the energy she had hoped to lavish on her own children to fostering at least one deep mentoring relationship every year. This helped Michelle understand why a successful businessperson like Sam, already so extended in her commitments, had agreed to take her on.

Finally Sam led Michelle back to the promontory. Michelle was happy to see the breathtaking vista again. The sun was a little higher. Once again they picked their way to the edge. Sam stood on the flat rock and motioned for Michelle to join her. The height still made Michelle's heart beat a little faster, but this time there was more thrill than fear. They stood on the point together, Sam's arm on Michelle's shoulder.

"So, Michelle Ericksen, let me ask you again—after you get your kids back, what will you do with a million dollars?"

Michelle's voice was low and hard. "I'd get my finances so strong that no one would ever be able to hurt me—or my family—again."

"Good," said Sam. "What else do you want? *Dream.*"[p. 48] she added in a whisper.

Michelle looked over the horizon as she described what she began to see in her mind. "I'd buy a farm. Not a working farm. I don't want to churn butter or grow corn. But I want a big, big place with lots of rooms and lots of land so we can have all the pets we want and the biggest garden in the world."

"What else?"

"Isn't that enough?"

THE SIXTEENTH AHA:
THE SIZE OF THE QUESTION
DETERMINES THE SIZE OF THE RESULT

If you ask yourself "How do I earn or create a million dollars?" your mind goes to work to discover the answer. Your mind is compelled to work ceaselessly until a satisfactory answer is found.

Note that most individuals ask themselves questions like these: "How do I get a job, salary, or work?" or "Can I earn $50,000 doing this?" The wrong question will generate the wrong result or a less than outstanding outcome.

Questions predetermine the answer. The size of your question determines the size of your answer. Few people ever ask million-dollar earning, inventing, innovating, generating, and creating questions. They are yours to ask.

Ben Feldman, known to many as the world's greatest insurance salesman, once taught Mark that the difference between earning $100,000 per year and a million dollars per year was effectively one zero. To earn $100,000 per year, a commissionable salesperson must work 250 days @ $400 a day. To earn a million a year, the $400 must be increased to $4,000 per day. The difference is one zero. The mandate to make it happen was: "If your loved ones' lives depended on it, could you do it?" The answer was almost always resoundingly "YES!"

What that means is that individuals who ask the wrong question are living below their true potential. They have more ability and talent than they are utilizing. This is true for almost everyone. We are encouraging you to rethink what you could do and do it now!

When we decided to create this book, we asked: "How do we write a totally original book that stimulates the creation of one million millionaires

"Does it have to be? Why can't you have everything you want? Is it hurting someone if you do?"

"No . . ."

"So, keep going. Tell me—just how good could your life be? It's not just about money, now."

Michelle shook her head. "I don't want to do this."

"You don't want to get your hopes up."

"No."

Sam leaned closer. "Look," she said in a stage whisper, "there's nobody here but us chickadees. Take a chance. Let yourself dream. *How good could it be?*"

Michelle hesitated.

"Go for it," Sam pushed.

"Okay . . ." Michelle began slowly. "We have that farm. And the kids are back with their old friends, and they have new ones. Hannah isn't so shy anymore. They love school and they get all A's." She paused for breath.

"Keep going."

"They have all the clothes and toys and books they want, but they're learning to give back, too." The little hopes were sprouting up in her like the black-eyed Susans in the valley. "We travel. All the places we've all wanted to go. And Hannah has the lead in the school play and Nicky is the best shortstop that Deer Creek ever saw."

"And who's responsible to make that happen?"

"I am."

Sam nodded. "Now, that's how a *victor* talks. I can work with that."

"Great." Michelle let out a happy sigh.

"Oh, you're not done yet, Butterfly." Sam winked. "One more thing. Now you need to shout it."

"I beg your pardon?"

"Tell the Universe! Out loud!"

Suddenly Michelle understood. She looked across the valley

and four hundred billionaires in this decade?" Bob had perfectly named the book: *The One Minute Millionaire*. It was a leading-edge title with a big mission to serve greatly. Why? *To change the economic future of the world we need to create jobs.* Entrepreneurship is the best, lasting, and most fulfilling way to do it.

Statistics prove that each millionaire creates 10 *new* jobs and each billionaire creates 10,000 *new* jobs. Therefore, this book, with its requisite seminars, teleconferences, and trainings (visit our website, www.oneminute millionaire.com, for more information on these services) will achieve our objective. All of this happened because we kept asking others and ourselves strong and important questions. Each question had big goals and dreams attached to it.

As you ask yourself and others better questions, your results will vastly improve, the world will be better off, your quantity and quality of service will expand, the difference you make will experience quantum change, and you will leave a profound legacy in the footprints of time.

THE SEVENTEENTH AHA:
YOU ALREADY KNOW THE ANSWER

Touch your finger to your forehead and say, "This is the most powerful computer on the planet." The computer that is your brain records everything that happens to you—for millions of different inputs simultaneously—heat, light, moisture, sound. It keeps your body functioning, your heart beating, your lungs working—all of this beneath your conscious awareness.

Everything you have ever learned in your life is indelibly recorded. Everything you have ever heard, said, read, seen, and experienced. This is

spreading out before them, at the mighty Rocky Mountains. She stretched out her arms. "I want . . ."

"No! Say it as if it's happening *now*."

Michelle filled her lungs to bursting. Then she called across the valley, "I'm with my children!"

She was startled to hear it come back to her with almost the same intensity.

Children . . . Children . . .

The echo.

"Go on."

"We live on a great big farm . . ."

Big farm . . .

" . . . with lots of pets . . ."

Pets . . .

" . . . and we are as happy and successful as we could ever imagine!"

She kept her arms stretched out wide, alone with Sam on the very top of the world, listening to the final words of the echo:

Imagine . . .

Imagine . . .

Imagine . . . p. 50

🦋

Over the next week, Michelle and Samantha followed the same routine: Up at six, they jogged out to the Rock. Each day Michelle found the trek a little bit easier, until, on the seventh day, she raced ahead of Sam and beat her to the promontory by a good 60 seconds. When she heard Sam break through the woods behind her, Michelle was at the end of the point, shouting out her goals, her hands up in the air like Rocky at the top of the Philadelphia courthouse stairs.

"Great job, missy!" Samantha called her approval. Michelle suspected that her new friend had cut her a little slack, but it still felt good.

the database you are carrying around with you. Some even have suggested that your DNA carries with it the wisdom of previous generations or a previous lifetime. In short, your unconscious data bank is enormous. People don't have bad memories. They have *perfect* memories. They just have a bad system for accessing what is already there.

Now, how does your intuition work? Suppose you're "stewing" on a decision. Your intuition scans through your enormous data bank of information, evaluating and processing, until it comes to a conclusion. It now tries to signal you.

Here's the hard part. Your intuition is like a deaf mute . . . with perfect vision. It can see clearly what to do, but it only has "subtle" ways to "signal" you. Each person has a unique pathway to intuition. For some, the signal is a peaceful feeling. For others, it is a quiet, reassuring internal voice. For others, it is a flash of insight. It may be a combination of all three. How does your intuition signal you?

Remember a time when you had a "hunch"—when you knew something was right. Go back to that time in your mind. Rewind the memory till just before the "moment of hunch" and then advance the memory, frame by frame, and notice any internal signals inside your body associated with the hunch. What do you notice? An image? A voice? A feeling? How do you "know" it is signaling the truth? You just "know."

Where do you know it? Notice where the feeling of certainty is centered in your body. Is it warm or is it cool? Is it clear or is it confusing? Does it ring true or is it muffled?

You already possess an amazing ability to "know" which direction to go. You simply need to learn how to interpret your own signals.

Take time to cultivate your intuition. Before you make a decision, check with your "inner knower." Go with your "gut." It is almost never wrong.

After enjoying the view silently for a few moments, and catching their breath, Samantha motioned with her head toward the flat rock. She proceeded to lie down, folded her hands behind her head, and crossed her legs at the ankle. Then she let out a contented sigh. "Dr. Freud was on to something, having people lie down to get themselves analyzed." She looked over at Michelle. "C'mon, Butterfly, join me."

The sun shone on Michelle with comforting warmth. And the sunbathed Rock also sent its heat flowing back upward into her body. But it was so much more than physical warmth. She felt at peace for the first time—not just since Gideon's death, but in a way that she had rarely felt in her life before.

A calming presence encircled her. She associated it with Sam— she knew it was brought to her by Sam—but it was so much more than Sam, too.

"Where do we start today?" Michelle asked, after a few moments of silence.

"Midterm."

"Oh, boy." Michelle rolled her eyes.

"Don't worry, it's an oral test. Tell me about the *ahas* you've had this week."

Michelle immediately knew what Sam was talking about— they'd spent many hours talking about the *ahas* of the Enlightened Millionaire.[pp. 16–94] Sam had taught her that it was one thing to learn a lesson intellectually, but quite another to "get it" emotionally. Without that flash of insight—the *aha* experience—the lesson wasn't complete. Sam called it "transformational learning"[p. 148] as opposed to "informational learning." Heart learning versus head learning. It meant using metaphors and games and various exercises until the lights came on. Sam had told her that it wasn't enough to get an *aha*. It was just as important to share the *aha* with someone else as soon as possible. In this way the lesson was learned at a deeper level.

THE EIGHTEENTH AHA: BE CONGRUENT

Sunlight focused through a magnifying glass can start a fire. But the conditions must be "just right." If the magnifying glass is held too high above the paper, the rays are diffused and don't generate enough heat to make fire.

When you heat water to 212° Fahrenheit, it begins to boil. If the temperature only reaches 211°, the water won't boil.

An airplane has to attain a certain ground speed before it lifts off into the sky. Any speed less than this will not produce flight—only a spectacular crash at the end of the runway.

A satellite must reach "escape velocity" to break free of earth's gravitational pull. Then it falls into an effortless orbit where the breath of a baby is enough to propel it. But if the spacecraft doesn't reach escape velocity, it tumbles back down to earth.

Some people expend enormous amounts of energy trying to become financially successful. They seem to do almost everything right—set goals, read books, go to seminars. They go through all the right motions. Still, success seems to somehow elude them. Yet others appear to go through the same motions and are literally awash in abundance. What is the difference? To manifest abundance, you need to achieve *congruence*—the condition where all parts of you are in alignment. You need to align three key parts.

The first is desire: You've got to want it. The second is belief: You've got to believe you can make money—lots of it. The third is self-acceptance: You've got to believe that you deserve to be wealthy—to your very core. If one of these is out of alignment, your energy is diffused, ineffective. For example, you may want to become wealthy and even feel you deserve it, but after several unsuccessful attempts, you form the belief that you're just not cut out for it. Two out of three isn't enough. You're not congruent.

Michelle scanned back over the week, reviewing her favorite *ahas*. "Givers get,"[p. 30] she said. "That was a new concept for me. I always thought of rich people as stingy, penny-pinching, money-grubbing. But you showed me how I could 'give my way' to wealth. I like that."

"Give me another *aha*," Sam prodded.

"Writing down my goals every day,"[p. 54] Michelle replied immediately. "The first few times I did it, I heard that voice in my head. . . ."

"Do you mean Ms. Yabut[p. 34]?" Samantha smiled.

Michelle nodded. "I'd start writing a goal, like getting Nicky and Hannah back"—she flinched, but found she could go on—"and I'd hear that voice saying, '*Yeah, but* it's too late. *Yeah, but* you're not smart enough. *Yeah, but* you'll never get the money.'"

"Whoa. You're good at yabuts."

"*Yeah, but* I had a good teacher," Michelle laughed, "who gave me one of these." Michelle held up her slender, freckled forearm, now tanned from her week outside. From it dangled a purple rubber band.[p. 34] "This is my second one. I snapped the other one so many times, it broke."

"Ouch." Samantha winced. She took Michelle's wrist and silently regarded the faint red mark above her watch.

"I'm still snappin'. But not nearly as much."

Samantha let go of Michelle's wrist. "That'll be gone by next week. Along with Ms. Yabut."

For the next 15 minutes Sam reviewed Michelle's goals with her—coaching her to visualize each of her goals in full sensory detail as if she were experiencing them in present time. Although Michelle was beginning to feel more confident about the future, something was nagging at her—an underlying worry she was having trouble putting into words. Finally she asked Sam about it.

"Learning these *ahas* has been great, but I was wondering . . ." Michelle struggled to avoid offending her mentor ". . . when are we going to get to the millionaire stuff?"

You're only firing on two engines, and it takes three to reach escape velocity. You fall back to earth. Sound familiar?

To produce enough heat—to reach the boiling point—to attain the right ground speed—to achieve escape velocity, you need to be congruent. EVERY part of you must "buy in"—your heart, your mind, and your spirit. *All systems GO.* The Enlightened Millionaire is congruent.

THE NINETEENTH AHA:
YOU ARE A MONEY MAGNET

You—a money magnet? Absolutely! Magnetism is one of the prime moving forces in the universe. It is the power that binds the galaxies together. It is the force that moves the tiniest subatomic particles in your own body. The earth itself is a huge magnet. In everyday life, you find magnets in telephones, televisions, radios, computers, stereos, video cameras, and in all electric-powered home appliances—refrigerators, microwaves, and so on.

Around every magnet, there is an invisible "magnetic field" of attraction. When a nail comes in contact with this magnetic field, it is drawn to the magnet—as if by magic. The nail has no choice. It never says to itself, "I think I'll ignore the magnetic field today."

Did you know that when a nail comes in contact with a permanent magnet, the nail becomes a temporary magnet itself—acquiring powers of attraction that it did not previously possess? As long as the nail remains near the magnet, it retains these new magnetic powers. If the magnet is taken away, the nail returns to its original state. Why is this?

When you examine the atoms of the nail under a microscope, you discover that they possess magnetic attributes—but they are disorganized.

Sam must have heard the question but didn't immediately respond. She continued to stare at the clouds. It appeared to Michelle that she was pondering how to answer.

Sam finally spoke, her voice low and deep. "This *is* the millionaire stuff." The way she said it, Michelle got the impression that Sam was a bit disturbed by the question.

"Yeah, but . . ." And then Michelle caught herself and snapped her rubber band.

Sam picked up on it. "What was the thought you just snapped?"

"I just keep telling myself that this is going too slow. I don't have time for *ahas*. I need to get to the making-money stuff . . . you know, how to buy real estate, how to launch a business, how to make a million dollars."

"Have you ever noticed how quickly skyscrapers seem to go up?" Sam asked. "What you don't see are years of advance planning with the architect and the general contractor. Then they spend months excavating the soft soil and then driving steel columns or piles sometimes hundreds of feet deep until they reach bedrock. The taller the building, the deeper the piles. As for your 'building,' I'd say we're still in the excavation phase."

Michelle was silent for several minutes. "How do you know so much about buildings?"

"Well, my office building isn't a skyscraper . . . just ten stories, but the principles are the same."

Michelle leaned up on her elbow, impressed. "You *own* a ten-story office building?"

"Yup. Me and the bank," she chuckled. Then, after a short silence, Sam spoke softly. "Just trust me, Missy. The money'll come. Faster than you can imagine. But first, the foundation."

"Okay," said Michelle, feeling like a child who has just been told that there'll be no dessert unless she finishes her vegetables.

Sam launched ahead. "When was the last time you just *knew* something was right?"

The atoms of the nail point in all different directions and, thus, cancel out one another's electromagnetic charge. By contrast, the atoms of a magnet are in perfect alignment—their north and south poles face in the same direction. When a magnet attracts a nail, the atoms in the nail begin to line up to match the atoms in the magnet—becoming "like" the magnet. The more aligned these atoms become, the more the ordinary nail behaves like a magnet. (Can you smell the analogy coming?)

Your own body is a field of electromagnetic activity. Each of your trillions of atoms is a tiny machine that generates magnetic energy. You are a walking factory of magnetic power.

- ▲ You, too, possess magnetic properties—dormant powers of attraction.
- ▲ Since "like" attracts "like," you attract the things you like or want.
- ▲ The more aligned you are with the things you want, the more powerfully you attract them.
- ▲ The things you *congruently* want have *no choice* but to be attracted to you.
- ▲ People who are aligned or congruent are attractive, magnetic—even charismatic.
- ▲ When you are with another congruent being, his or her magnetic power "rubs off on you."
- ▲ The more congruent you are, the wider the "magnetic field" around you.
- ▲ When you are "fully congruent," you are irresistible!

As Napoleon Hill writes in *Think and Grow Rich,*

"Our brains become magnetized with the dominating thoughts which we hold in our minds, and, by means with which no man is familiar, these "magnets" attract to us the forces, the people, the circumstances of life which harmonize with the nature of our dominating thoughts."

In other words, you become a literal magnet for the things you want. If you *really* want money, money literally can't say no.

"That's easy. When I met you."

"No extra credit for buttering up the teacher."

"Seriously."

"But *how* did you know?" Samantha twisted one of the hammered gold rings she wore on her fingers. "What did it feel like when you met me? Not just in your head—in your body."

Michelle closed her eyes and took herself back to the Mariposa Plaza. That night she felt so desperate and alone. She remembered how *that* felt well enough—from morning until night. The heaviness in her body. The dimness of the world—as if she were wearing sunglasses all the time.

"I'm not sure. . . ."

"Go back to that experience. Relive it. Notice the subtle things that were going on."

Michelle kept her eyes closed. She saw again the flames of the fire lapping behind Samantha. She remembered details she hadn't been consciously aware of before, because there had been so many other things going on in her mind at the time.

"Take yourself forward frame by frame," Sam coached.

As Michelle followed Samantha's instructions, reliving that night, she felt as though she were seeing a movie for the second time and picking out elements she had missed on the first viewing. And then she noticed something. She spoke as if she had been thinking aloud. "There is this tiny voice in my head whispering, *'This is it. Go for it.'*"

"Ms. Yabuts?" Sam asked.

Michelle shook her head, "No. Not that voice. Another one."

"How did this new voice make you feel?"

"Hmm . . . peaceful . . . all over my body . . . and lighter . . ."

Michelle continued to reenact the scene up to the moment when she got into Samantha's Mercedes.

"Where is the feeling now?"

"Right here." Michelle opened her eyes wide, then squinted in the sunlight. She tapped her chest. "In my heart."

THE TWENTIETH AHA:
KNOCK AND IT SHALL BE OPENED

Study this quote:

> "Until one is committed there is hesitancy, the chance to draw back, always ineffectiveness. Concerning all acts of initiative (and creation) there is one elementary truth, the ignorance of which kills countless ideas and splendid plans: that the moment one definitely commits oneself, then Providence moves too. All sorts of things occur to help one that would never otherwise have occurred. A whole stream of events issues from the decision, raising in one's favour all manner of unforeseen incidents and meetings and material assistance, which no man could have dreamt would have come his way. I have learned a deep respect for one of Goethe's couplets: 'Whatever you can do, or dream you can, begin it. Boldness has genius, power and magic in it.'" W. H. Murray, *The Scottish Himalayan Expedition* (J. M. Dent & Sons Ltd., 1951)

Commitment is the spark that ignites the fire. Commitment is the key that starts the engine. When one lays down a line in the sand and declares, "I am committed to do this—whatever it takes, for however long it takes," then an invisible signal goes forth, like a radio beacon, resonating with whatever resources are necessary to complete the task.

These resources begin to "materialize" as if by magic. Ideas begin to flow. Time slows down or speeds up to accommodate. People suddenly arrive as if summoned.

How does this happen?

Have you ever played with a tuning fork? When you tap the fork, it begins to vibrate and hum, sending out sound vibrations of specific pitch

Samantha propped herself up on one elbow. "Some people call it *intuition*.[p. 70] I call it your *true self*. Now you know what it sounds like . . . and how it makes you feel."

Michelle nodded. "Where did you learn this?"

"From my grandfather." Sam smiled, remembering. "He was a very successful businessman. One day—I was about 14—I observed him in a business meeting in his living room. I noticed that whenever he was asked to make an important decision, he paused, pursed his lips, put his hand on his heart, and tapped three times. Then he rendered his decision. Afterward, I asked him about it. He said he always checked with his 'true self' before he made up his mind about anything important."

"Hmm . . ."

"So what does your intuition tell you is the next step?" Sam asked.

Michelle hesitated. Then she closed her eyes once again and put her hand over her heart. "I don't like it." She squirmed on the Rock. "It's telling me that it's time to go see Ericksen . . . but . . ."

"Yeah, but . . ."

"This is different," Michelle shot back. "I'm just so . . . so afraid of him."

"You always talk about him like he's as big as King Kong and twice as mean. But you know, that's your perception."

"Mine and a whole lot of other people's."

"Still your perception," Samantha insisted. "You can change that."[p. 64]

Michelle waited.

"Picture him," Sam instructed. "Picture him in as much detail as you can."

Michelle closed her eyes.

"What's he wearing? What does he smell like? How far away is he standing? How tall is he? What's surrounding him?"

Michelle cringed as the image of Anthony took shape in her

through the air around it. If you place another tuning fork nearby, calibrated to the same note, the second fork picks up on this vibration and slowly begins to hum and vibrate in harmony with the first fork. If the second tuning fork is not pitched to the same note, it does not vibrate.

In a similar way, you send out silent and invisible signals. Most of the time, these signals are weak and unfocused. However, when you reach a certain level of commitment, the intensity of your vibrations increases. Your spirit, your soul, your life force—or whatever you want to call it—begins to oscillate at a higher frequency. These vibrations, like invisible radio signals, are picked up unconsciously by everyone you meet. The message is subtle but clear—*I am committed.*

When you are committed, the cells in your body are energized by the passion of your purpose. Enlightened Millionaires are committed.

Please go back and read the quote again. Are you committed? Have you memorialized your commitment by going to www.oneminute millionaire.com and making your commitment public? When you make your commitment public, you get the support of thousands.

THE TWENTY-FIRST AHA: SHARING IS HAVING MORE

The Enlightened Millionaire knows that giving is the highest form of manifestation of one's true nature. It is a combination of faith and action. What is the specific act we mean? Tithing. Enlightened Millionaires donate the first 10% of all of their incomes to the charities and/or churches in their communities. This giving multiplies prosperity a thousandfold.

mind. She'd latched on to her memory of the first time she met him. He was red-faced with rage—an expression she often saw again over the years. She'd been one of the picketers in front of the Ericksen Timber building, protesting against his company's reforestation policies, or lack of them. She met Gideon the same day, when he'd come out to try to negotiate with the picketers. Maybe she was guilty of some revisionist history, but she also believed that she had fallen in love with Gideon the first moment she saw him.

"You're drifting. Get back to Mr. E."

She went back to Anthony, this time imagining steam coming out of his ears when she and Gideon announced their engagement. He had been outwardly polite, but his feelings were no secret.

"Looks like you've got it," she heard Samantha say. "Now make him smaller. That's right. See all that stuff around him? It's getting bigger. Not just the fancy paintings and furniture, but his clothes, too. He only has those clothes because he bought them, you know, and he's just a naked man without them."

Michelle stifled a giggle. She'd never seen Anthony without a $3,000 suit on. She had never stopped to think what was underneath. He was nearing 70.

"Is he getting smaller? Good. Keep going. Smaller and smaller until he can fit in the palm of your hand. He's still naked, by the by."

Michelle put out her hand.

"See him there."

Tentatively, she opened her eyes. "I do."

Sam went on, "He's getting smaller. He's starting to not look human. He's featureless, like a worm. Now he's even smaller. He's—"

"—a speck of dust."

"Now blow him away. Just like blowing out a birthday candle."

Michelle blew on her palm and as the speck of dust that had once been her red-faced father-in-law floated away, she made a wish.

It worked for John D. Rockefeller, who was a meticulous tither. It also worked for Carnegie. Recently it worked for Oprah, who has donated at least 10% of her annual income to charity, most of it anonymously, throughout her adult life. One of the world's greatest investors, Sir John Marks Templeton, founder of the successful Templeton Fund, said, "Tithing always gives the greatest return on your investment." Go behind the scenes of most great fortunes, you'll find a common pattern—the more they gave, the more they got.

Why is this? Because giving expands money. How? Just as water exists in three forms—ice, liquid, and vapor—we find it useful to think that money exists in three dimensions: the frozen state (material), the liquid state (mental), and the ethereal or spiritual state. When you give money from an attitude of gratitude and abundance, it thrusts you from the material state into the ethereal or spiritual dimension.

Just like water expands when it's heated, money expands when it is given away. Giving literally magnifies, multiplies, and exponentializes money. Conversely, the tighter you squeeze your money, the more compact it becomes. Dickens's mythical figure Scrooge vividly demonstrates the consequence of being tightfisted, stingy, hard, and parsimonious with one's money.

Many people in poverty consciousness think that money shrinks when you give it away (100% − 10% = 90%). The Enlightened Millionaire knows that giving money actually expands in the spiritual dimension (100% × 10% = 1,000%). This is spiritual math. **Tithing is a money multiplier, not a money subtracter.** It expands, multiplies, and adds value to all that you do. When you begin to live this law, you'll lay claim to a multiplied harvest of 30-fold, 60-fold, or 100-fold.

When you pick one apple off a tree, Mother Nature makes sure that next year there are two apples where that single apple was picked. One apple seed can create an apple tree, an apple crop, an apple forest, and enough apples, over time, to feed apples to everyone—forever.

The Enlightened Millionaire knows that giving is a seed that multiplies infinitely. Tithing is the tool. One of the richest men in Australia, industrialist Peter J. Daniels, said: "You cannot be greedy if you tithe."

Michelle had not been back to Deer Creek since January. Now it was September; a full year since Gideon had died.

Michelle experienced a confusing range of emotions as she recognized landmarks on the two-lane highway that meant they were drawing closer: the hand-lettered "Fresh Cherries" sign on the edge of the Parsons' farm, and a few miles later, the pile of used tires that had been there all her life. Those same old sights she'd taken for granted now seemed so precious. It was early morning, and the air was still delicate with the last of summer, black-eyed Susans still crowding the side of the road.

"We'll get to the junction in about 10 minutes," she alerted Jeremy. If someone had told her 10 days before that she would be driving to Deer Creek with Jeremy Cavalieri, she would have pointed her index finger at her temple and made a few circles. But as Sam had said with a wink when Michelle left, "Any road round the mountain is going to have lots of curves."

Michelle had stayed in touch with Delphine and Jeremy, who had offered to drive her to what felt like the most important meeting of her life. She hadn't felt like this since Gideon drove her to the hospital when her contractions were five minutes apart. "You sure you don't want me to go in with you?"

"I've got to do it by myself," Michelle replied. "But thanks."

Funny how good a friend Jeremy was turning out to be. "Funny what you find out when you stop pushing people away," Sam had said.

"Well, I'll be hanging outside. You can call me on my cell phone if you need help."

"That's really nice, Jer."

"You know, this is my last week at the Mariposa, too."

She jumped. "Turn here!"

❧

The Enlightened Millionaire donates the first 10% of all of his or her income. This giving multiplies your prosperity a thousandfold. Committing to this will transform your life and make you richer than you ever dreamed possible.

Are you willing to commit?

THE TWENTY-SECOND AHA:
GOD KNOWS WHERE THE GOLD IS

The Gallup Poll estimates that 95%
of North Americans believe in God.

If our spiritual life is so important to most of us, why don't we tap into the spiritual realms more often to reach our monetary goals? People don't usually associate money with spiritual matters. It's as if we want to maintain the "separation of church and state" in our personal affairs as well as in our politics.

Is it that money doesn't mix well with God? Frankly, we think it's quite ridiculous to learn to master money without involving the Author of all Wealth. As someone said, "God knows where the gold is." If you think about it, He probably also knows which stocks are going to go up tomorrow, which real estate is bound to triple in value next year, and which business ideas are destined to make some deserving person a millionaire.

Before you start thinking that the Bible teaches that poverty is a virtue, remember that Abraham, revered as "Father" by three great religions—Judaism, Islam, and Christianity—was also one of the wealthiest men in the world at the time. A billionaire by today's standards. (*And*

Michelle would also not have believed it was possible to learn so much in so short a time—it had been less than four weeks since she'd met Sam. One thing that Sam had taught her in their time at the Rock was the importance of personal presentation. "I like to pay homage to my ancestry," she said. "But another reason I wear the ethnic clothes is—well, if you were in a meeting with me and 10 other people, who would you remember afterward? Me or the six dudes in double-breasted suits?"

"It helps to be six feet tall and gorgeous."

"Five ten. But who counts?"

The day before, Samantha had taken Michelle to her personal stylist. Michelle had let her hair grow long and uneven, but the stylist had cut it to a casual, fashionable shoulder length. Sam had also taken her shopping. Today Michelle was wearing some of their purchases: a teal blazer over a crisp white blouse and perfectly creased charcoal slacks.

As Michelle stood at the intercom in front of the Ericksens' automatic gate, at the bottom of their drive, she did the warm-up exercises[p. 64] that Samantha had taught her.

Breathing. She took seven deep breaths, careful to exhale every molecule.

Visualization. She mentally surrounded herself with a light, intense purple, the color that gave her the most energy.

Aural. She called up a song that always stirred her, a rousing Reba McEntire tune.

She pressed the intercom button.

"Yes?" It was Estella, the Ericksens' housekeeper of 25 years and the woman who had claimed Michelle's house was unfit for the children.

"It's Michelle, Estella."

"Are they expecting you?" came the voice from the intercom.

"Yes. My appointment is at 9:00." She was exactly on time.

The gate rolled open.

Abram was very rich in cattle, in silver, and in gold [Genesis 13:2].) These material blessings were not a curse, but a *reward* for his faithfulness.

Almost every spiritual path has sacred writings that teach about the abundant universe and the importance of sharing our abundance. Here are two of our favorite passages:

> *Trust in the Lord with all thine heart; and lean not unto thine own understanding. In all thy ways acknowledge him, and he shall direct thy paths. . . . Honour the Lord with thy substance, and with the firstfruits of all thine increase: So shall thy barns be filled with plenty, and thy presses shall burst out with new wine.* (Proverbs 3: 5–6, 9–10)

> *Bring ye all the tithes into the storehouse, that there may be meat in mine house, and prove me now herewith, saith the Lord of Hosts, if I will not open you the windows of heaven, and pour you out a blessing, that there shall not be room enough to receive it. And I will rebuke the devourer for your sakes, and he shall not destroy the fruits of your ground; neither shall your vine cast her fruit before the time in the field, saith the Lord of Hosts.* (Malachi 3: 10–11)

In our study, we find no other promise made so clearly. God challenges us to prove Him—to put Him to the test.

We have put this principle to the test. It works. The Enlightened Millionaire acknowledges that God knows where the gold is. Allow God to show you.

Heading up the steep drive, Michelle thought longingly of Nicky and Hannah. When she had called Anthony to arrange this meeting, he had made it a nonnegotiable demand that she not see the children. It had been painful to agree, but she knew that by doing so she would shorten the time necessary to arrange the meeting.

She used another visualization to toss the distracting image of her children from her mind. Sam had taught her how to isolate a negative thought, to mentally package it, and then to dispose of it. Every time Michelle did this exercise it became a little more natural, and she could foresee a time in the not-too-distant future when she was truly mistress of her thoughts.

It was a challenge, though, as she looked up at the house. It was a tribute to ostentation, a re-creation of an English lord's manor, with elaborate stonework and gables. In the center of the circular drive, planted in a perfect round of green grass, a tall pole flew the American and the Colorado flags.

Estella met her at the front door. She wore a robin's egg blue uniform, with a broad white apron and cap that made her look like a nurse from World War I. She wore heavy foundation to cover a poor complexion and turquoise eye shadow and heavy liner.

"Hi, Estella," Michelle said, trying to sound neutral. For some reason, Gideon had adored her, so she must have another side to her cold personality. Somewhere.

"Yes," Estella said coolly. "Mr. Ericksen says to wait in the library."

The library. That was the two-story room crammed with books with the ladder on wheels. It wasn't all for show: Anthony was an avid reader, with a special interest in history. Natalie was a lover of romance novels, but her husband made her keep them in a separate room.

Michelle followed Estella. Her uniform made a rustling sound, but her crepe-soled shoes were as silent as a snake crawling underfoot.

THE TWENTY-THIRD AHA:
DESTRUCTION IS CREATION

After you have made the decision to become an Enlightened Millionaire, you may, like many people, run up against the phenomenon of "hysteresis" (pronounced hiss-ter-EE-sis.) Technically, the term describes the tendency of materials to snap back to their original shape once the pressure being applied is removed. For example, when a piece of steel is heated, it expands. Stop applying the heat and the steel returns to its original condition as it cools. Hysteresis has taken place.

Something similar takes place with human beings. Often an individual returns to her or his original state when a new force is no longer being applied. It "remembers" where it was before the new force arrived and it returns to that familiar place.

To create permanent change within a material or a human being, a force must be applied that is strong enough to exceed the "elastic limits" of the object or old conditioning of the individual. How do you transcend your old habits and move to a new level in your life?

First start focusing on your future vision. The vision must be so strong that it dominates your thoughts, your choices, and your activities. What *one* attitude or habit can you eliminate right now that is hurting your ability to manifest a million dollars? Maybe it's blaming others when something doesn't go right. Whatever it is, commit to making that behavior "off limits." Start with just one off-limits behavior and commit to keep it off limits.

At the same time identify one pattern that you are certain you must have to reach Enlightened Millionaire status—maybe it's getting proper nutrition so you have more energy to do the things necessary to be a millionaire. Whatever it is, commit to making that behavior a "must" instead of a "maybe." Then commit to stay "on target" until it becomes part of your new habit pattern.

Estella left her alone in the library. Michelle sensed they would make her wait, partly to demonstrate who was in control and partly to let her anxiety level build. There were two new portraits of Nicky and Hannah prominently displayed above Anthony's desk, the one wall not lined with books. Hannah was outfitted for tennis, and Nicky for lacrosse. Michelle rose to study the portraits, examining the new and subtly more mature lines of their faces. It hit her hard that she had not seen them since before the previous Christmas. She had missed a birthday each. She closed her eyes, reassuring herself that Anthony wouldn't leave her too long in a place she might snoop. Samantha's thought-mastering exercises were getting more difficult by the moment.

After 10 minutes, Anthony entered with Natalie behind him. Natalie was in a crimson silk lounging suit. Her hair was pulled back into a tight bun. Fleetingly, Michelle wondered if it was possible that Anthony was faithful to her.

"You have five minutes," Anthony announced, sitting behind his mighty desk. "My bridge club is meeting in the second-floor lounge."

"And I have the Junior League." Natalie remained standing like a sentry next to her husband.

"I have a meeting, too," Michelle said casually. "I don't need more than five minutes." She gazed straight at her former father-in-law, calling up the image of the harmless speck of dust in her palm, ready to be blown away into nothingness.

"You said you had a proposal for me." Anthony reached for a gold-plated ballpoint and a leather-bound appointment book, making a show of not paying too close attention to her.

"Anthony, Natalie . . . I came to talk to you, parent to parent, as it were," Michelle began. She remembered an insight that Samantha had shared earlier in the week: There was nothing to be gained by demonizing the Ericksens—by labeling them as jerks, let alone stronger curse words. They were on their own path, reaping what

Now write both commitments and put them where they can be seen each morning and each night. When you fail to keep your commitment (most people will), just acknowledge the failure and recommit. Remember what Henry Ford said, "Failure is the opportunity to begin again more intelligently." When you have gone seven sequential days both staying "on target" with the behavior you desire and "off limits" with the behavior you want to eliminate, then celebrate! Hysteresis has lost the majority (if not all) of its power. You have moved to the next level!

When that objective is reached, it's not an end, it's the beginning of the next phase. Focus again on your vision and add the next off-limits task and on-target behavior to the same paper and repeat the process.

Each cycle moves you closer to being an Enlightened Millionaire.

THE TWENTY-FOURTH AHA: PUTTING IT ALL TOGETHER

Have you ever sabotaged yourself? Was there a part of you running around inside your mind setting booby traps to slow you down? Leaving land mines, setting ambushes, blowing up your own bridges, flattening your own tires, emptying your own bank accounts, spreading lies and rumors about you? Better catch that little saboteur before he does any more damage—better catch him and convert him to your side. It's worth the effort to get congruent.

they sowed. Looking at them now, this was a slippery insight to keep hold of, but Michelle swallowed and vowed to do her best. "I want to see my children. Surely you'd agree that would be in their best interest."

"Michelle." Anthony's voice was unctuous. "Let's leave the visitation issue for the courts to decide. I only agreed to see you because my lawyers suggested it would be to our benefit. You won't be able to say to the judge that I stonewalled your every request. But I certainly cannot allow you to see them now."

"You tried to run away with them," Natalie snapped.

"I did not," Michelle insisted. "We were going to visit—"

"As if we'd trust you again—"

"Dear." Anthony put his hand out, but stopped short of touching his wife. "We'll stay civil."

Michelle looked from Nicky's to Hannah's picture. They were so close . . . maybe even in the house . . . yet so far away. . . . "You can stay in the room with me, I don't care, I just want to talk to them, to hug them once. . . ." *Don't lose control.* "You can't really believe that would hurt them."

"Yes, it would, though." Anthony threw down his gold pen, put his hands on his desk, and tilted his chair back. "Be logical. They're young and pliable. They're forgetting you and forming new attachments. Gideon was on the right track until he got mixed up with you. Fortunately, Nicholas has inherited my intelligence and head for business. Unlike his poor late father, he is excellent with numbers. I arranged with the principal at St. James to start a Young Entrepreneurs Club, and Nicholas will be the first president."

Natalie leaned over Anthony's desk. "It's time to put this behind you, dear. You're young, some men would find you attractive, you can have more children. We really mean what's best for the children. Nicholas and Hannah are *Ericksens*. We were the first settlers."

"Not counting the Native Americans," Michelle murmured, even as she was blinking back tears.

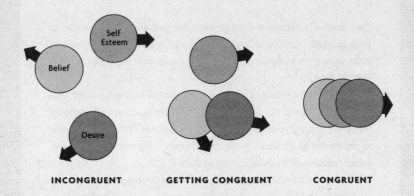

INCONGRUENT   **GETTING CONGRUENT**   **CONGRUENT**

Desire. Belief. Self-esteem. When you have these in alignment, you are a power to behold. But this process of alignment doesn't happen all at once. Sometimes it takes years. Other times it takes a near-death experience or some other "close call" to suddenly force you to wake up and get your act together. When you don't have any other choice—when it's a matter of survival—you usually figure things out. Whether slowly or suddenly, you wake up one morning and realize that "your someday is now." You want it. You believe it. The seed you planted so long ago is now ripe and ready to bear fruit.

It may seem like we're spending a lot of time on the inside stuff—but this is the hardest part. If you can get congruent, all the rest is child's play. Anyone can learn *what to do*. It's *getting yourself to do it* that's hard.

Stephen Covey likes to quote Lincoln, who said, "If I had eight hours to chop down a tree, I'd spend seven sharpening my axe." Getting congruent is having a sharp axe.

Most people get lost hacking their way through the jungle in pursuit of their goals. When you're congruent, you fly confidently over the jungle and land next to your objective to claim what you have so clearly envisioned.

Getting your act together is the final key to manifesting what you want in your life.

"They're thriving here," Natalie went on, as if Michelle hadn't spoken. "They eat the best food. Hannah has lost five pounds of baby fat. I gave her such a lovely birthday party. We had a professional magician and pony rides and three kinds of cake, all nonfat."

"I'm their *mother*," Michelle said helplessly. Why wasn't this working? Then she remembered her session with Sam at the Rock from just a couple of days before. Her intuition.[p. 56] In her growing desperation, she had lost touch with that. She closed her eyes, took the deepest breath of her life, and tapped her heart three times.

When she opened her eyes both Anthony and Natalie were looking at her as if they feared she might finally have proved their longtime suspicion that she was crazy. But Michelle let a smile spread slowly across her face. While accessing her intuition she had remembered a key insight that Samantha had illustrated early on. *The size of the question determines the size of the answer.*[p. 54]

"I just have one question for you. . . ." Michelle paused. "On what conditions would you allow me to get my children back?"

Anthony Ericksen responded immediately, "I can't imagine any scenario where we would allow that."

Natalie shook her head in agreement.

The first rejection.

"Come, now," Michelle replied. Although there was no rational reason, she began to feel calmer than she had felt since the moment she had stepped inside. "There must be some way. . . ."

"If you get them back, dear," Natalie said in a tone that might have passed as concerned, "how are you going to feed them? I can't imagine that food stamps cover everything."

"What my wife is pointing out is that since you're still as insolvent as you have been all your life, it doesn't seem likely that you'll ever have the financial resources to take care of a family, let alone *my* grandchildren."

The second rejection.

THE FIRST MANIFESTATION

"I am enough."

Today, I am enough.

I am smart enough.

Wise enough.

Clever enough.

Resourceful enough.

Able enough.

Confident enough.

I am connected to enough people to accomplish my heart's desire.

I have enough ideas to pull off magic and miracles.

Enough is all I need.

Enough is what I have.

I have more than enough.

As I do all that I can do, I'm able to do more and more.
I am excited to be alive. I rejoice and re-choice every day to make my life better.
I am happy, healthy, prosperous, successful, rich, loving, loved, and beloved.
I am comfortable with myself, so I am comfortable with all others.
I confidently greet each day with a smile on my face and love in my heart.
Everyone who meets me is warmed by the radiance of my attitude.
I work on my attitude continuously. I read positive, inspiring, and uplifting books.
I listen to audiotapes and CDs during my driving and exercise times.
I associate with friendly, caring, nurturing people who are involved doing important things.
The people with whom I associate want more for me than I want for myself.
The projects with which I am involved WOW my soul.
I am passionately on-purpose to do good, be good, and help others do the same.
I am enough. I have enough. I do enough.

Michelle asked boldly, "Just what kind of financial resources would I need?"

This question seemed to catch both of the Ericksens off guard. Was this a slight crack in her opponent's resolve? She pressed on. "How much? A hundred thousand? Two hundred? A million?"

"You? A millionaire?" Anthony laughed heartily. Michelle didn't think she had ever heard him laugh before, and it was a frightening sound. "Michelle, thank you. Mayor Quarls always starts our weekly bridge games with the best joke, but I think I'll have him beat this time."

Natalie looked less amused. Perhaps she was anticipating what Michelle said next.

"I'm serious."

"The answer is no." Anthony sounded impatient now. "And I don't have any more time to waste." He picked up his phone with the intention, Michelle guessed, of calling his private security to escort her out.

The third rejection.

So she spoke quickly. "I never thought I'd see you back down from a wager."

"Wager?" he echoed. He held the handset of the phone in midair. "What kind of wager did you have in mind?"

Natalie shot her husband an angry look.

"Don't worry, dear," he said. "Michelle?"

The idea had taken shape in her mind in just the past few moments. Now she let the words come out in a rush, trusting them to take her to the right place. "Let's say . . . I make a million dollars . . . in the next 12 months. If I do, you drop your suit for permanent custody . . . and I get my kids back."

"And if you don't?"

"I'll leave the state and you'll never see me again."

"Oh, for God's sake," Natalie blurted out.

"Be quiet, Natalie," Anthony said sharply, but in his irritation

ACRES OF DIAMONDS

In 1870, 27-year-old Russell H. Conwell was serving as an international correspondent for the *American Traveler*, a weekly journal published in Boston. On assignment, he was riding in a camel caravan along the valley between the Tigris and Euphrates Rivers in Mesopotamia when he heard his Arab guide weave tales to entertain his American tourists.

The young Conwell was deeply impressed by a legend about a prosperous Persian farmer, Ali Hafed. Lured by the stories of a Buddhist priest, Ali Hafed deserted his own fruitful farm to search for immense wealth in mythical diamond fields.

Far and wide Ali Hafed roamed, footsore and weary. Youth and wealth disappeared, and he died far from home, an old and disillusioned pauper. Not long afterward, the guide related, acres of fabulous diamonds were found on Ali Hafed's own land.

To the other tourists, this was just another alluring story, but in Conwell's mind a great truth had been sown. To him it said: "Your diamonds are not in faraway mountains or in distant seas; they are in your own backyard if you will but dig for them."

Throughout his life Conwell applied this valuable lesson numerous times. Although he authored 40 books, he is most remembered for his famous lecture, "Acres of Diamonds." In the early 1900s he became America's foremost platform orator. By the end of his life, in 1925, he had delivered the lecture more than 6,000 times in town after town across America. It was heard by millions from pulpits and public platforms, and by radio, and today others are still reading his practical, optimistic essay* and hearing it on cassettes. The money from his speeches

---

*For the full text of Conwell's speech "Acres of Diamonds," go to www.temple.edu/about/temples_founder/acres_text.html.

Michelle felt a sudden lifting in her heart: The gambler in him was tempted. Better yet, there was no financial risk involved for him, and once this nonsense was over she'd be out of their lives for good.

"There are limits," he said, tapping his pen against the appointment book. "You have to earn it. You can't borrow it, receive it as a gift, or win it in a contest. And it must be cash. I'll need proof. In fact, I'll need to see your million dollars with my own two eyes."

"Agreed." She returned his gaze without flinching.

"And," he paused, "you'll have to bring it to me in 90 days."

"90 days to make a million dollars? You can't be serious!"

"That's the bet. Take it or leave it."

Michelle was in a panic. He'd outmaneuvered her! Samantha had taught her how to find her center at times of stress, and she groped for each step now: picturing herself at the Rock, its warm strength flowing into her, sitting next to Samantha, her hand in the older woman's hand. *Take the Rock with you wherever you go.*

Two voices inside her head were arguing.

Don't do it.

You can do it.

Are you crazy?

You'll figure it out.

She listened first to one, and then the other. And then she spoke.

"Have your attorney draw up the papers."

"Turns out my lawyer is upstairs right now. About to play bridge. Natalie, will you go get Martin for me?"

Michelle shifted in her chair as she watched Natalie leave. It was going to happen. Now the panic began to return in even bigger waves.

"Once Martin gets here we'll wrap this up quickly," Anthony said. Pause. "Well, as quickly as we can. You know, I don't want to leave any loopholes."

THE ENLIGHTENED WAY TO WEALTH   99

was used to fund scholarships for Conwell's other great love—Temple University in Philadelphia. How this came about is a great story by itself.

One evening in 1884, a young man approached Conwell and expressed a desire to prepare for the Christian ministry. Conwell offered to teach the youth one night a week, but on the agreed-upon evening seven earnest young men appeared. Conwell's class grew in numbers, the services of other teachers were enlisted, and it was necessary to rent a room, then a building, then two. Within a few years the studious group had grown from seven to several hundred students, and a charter for "The Temple College" was issued in 1888. Of course, Conwell already had been elected its president, a position he held for the next 38 years. A charter for Temple University was issued in 1907.

Today, Temple University boasts 29,000 students. It is the 39th largest university in the United States and the largest provider of professional education (law, dentistry, medicine, pharmacy, and podiatric medicine) in the country. No doubt you've heard of Temple's most famous trustee and alumnus—comedian Bill Cosby. Temple's founder, Dr. Russell Herman Conwell, lies at rest in the Founder's Garden, surrounded by splendid buildings of the attractive main campus of Temple University. Temple University itself is an enduring monument to his vision—truly his own "Acres of Diamonds."

This material is adapted from an article on Conwell at the Temple University website: www.temple.edu.

Michelle stood up to see if she could regain control of her emotions. She tried to act calm. "You don't mind if I look at your books while we wait, do you?" She gestured to one of the crammed walls.

"By all means." Anthony smiled. "I'm particularly proud of my Napoleon shelf. And I have an early edition of Machiavelli's *The Prince*. If you've never read it, now might be a good time."

She turned to glance back at him. He had folded his well-cared-for hands over his flat stomach.

"Michelle, my dear, you couldn't make a million dollars in a million years."

90 Days and Counting . . .

What have I done? Michelle asked herself over and over.

She barely spoke to Jeremy on the ride back. He seemed to sense her need for silence; in any event, he was supportively quiet.

When he returned her to Sam's cottage in Riverdale, Michelle raced through the empty rooms until she found her friend in the backyard. Sam was kneeling in the earth next to her tomato plants. She was wearing a broad-brimmed straw hat and quilted gloves.

"Sam." Michelle sunk to her knees next to her, grinding her slacks in the dirt. "Sam, I'm in trouble." Her words ended in a sob.

"Whoa, slow down, Butterfly," Sam said calmly. "Will you hand me that little trowel over there? With the red handle?"

"Sam!" *Doesn't she see this is serious?*

"Why don't you start from the beginning."

Michelle wiped a teal sleeve across her teary eyes. Then she told Sam what had happened—how nervous she had been, how Natalie had taunted her, how she had used her intuition—and finally, how she ended up making what she thought was the most foolish decision of her life.

"Anthony's right," Michelle said quietly, feeling another painful lump in her throat. "I can't make that kind of money. . . ."

ONE MINUTE REVIEW OF MILLIONAIRE AHAS

1. **Everyone manifests.** If you don't have what you want, ask yourself, "How did I manifest this?"
2. **Be. Do. Have.** First, be. Then, do. Then you can have all the prosperity you want.
3. **Live life above the line.** If you are willing to *learn* instead of to *blame*, life will go more smoothly.
4. **Abundance is your natural state.** Opportunities and blessings flow to individuals who embrace an abundant attitude.
5. **Givers get.** Give, and it will be given to you.
6. **Changing your reality is a snap.** Control your thinking and you control your results.
7. **Words transform.** Speak only with good purpose. If it doesn't serve, don't say it.
8. **You are your wealth.** All you need is a good idea and the commitment to do it. All the rest can be borrowed.
9. **Wealth is freedom.** The six great freedoms are money freedom, time freedom, relationship freedom, spiritual freedom, physical freedom, and the freedom to pursue your genius.
10. **It all starts with a dream.** Give yourself permission to dream a big dream. You can have it all.
11. **Clarity is power.** Don't think *of* your goals, think *from* your goals.
12. **More clarity is more powerful.** Write your six major goals down every day.
13. **Tap into your genius.** You have unique talents, abilities, interests, and values that only you can bring into greatness.
14. **Loverage.** Do what you love and the money will follow.
15. **Imagination trumps will.** When the will comes in conflict with the imagination, the imagination always wins.
16. **The size of the question determines the size of the result.** As you ask yourself better questions, your results will vastly improve.
17. **You already know the answer.** Take time to cultivate your intuition. Go with your "gut." It is almost never wrong.

"Of course you can't."

Michelle looked up, startled by the answer—expecting something more positive from her mentor.

"*You alone* couldn't make that kind of money. But you and I and the right *team* of sharp people might stand a chance."[p. 162]

"But . . ."

Sam rolled her eyes. "Besides, it was *you* who proposed the arrangement to Mr. Ericksen. Now, where did that come from?"

"I don't know . . . it just sort of . . . bubbled out of me . . ." Michelle stammered, but the tears had now stopped. "It felt so right at the time but . . . but as soon as I got out of there I said to myself, *What have I done? I've lost them forever!*"

Sam used the clippers in her hand to snip off a couple of wilted leaves. "You're listening to Ms. Yabuts again," said Sam. "I thought we talked about that. Feed your dreams, starve your doubts."

"But, Sam. A million dollars in 90 days! That's impossible."

"Impossible, huh?" Sam rolled back on her haunches. She was in one of the warm-up suits she wore when they jogged out to the Rock. "Do you think anyone has ever created an *impossibly* large amount of money in an *impossibly* short period of time? Of course," she said, answering her own question.

"But how?"

Sam closed her eyes and slowly shook her head. "Wrong question. The more important question is, *why?* When your 'why' is big enough, the 'how' takes care of itself."

"You're not making sense," argued Michelle.

"Precisely!" replied Sam cheerfully. "Doing the impossible never makes sense. You've heard the story about the woman whose child gets trapped under a car. She grabs the bumper and lifts the car off the child. How did she do it? It seemed impossible. But she had a big enough *why*. She just did it."

Michelle fingered a tomato plant. She saw that her hands were trembling. She clasped them together to make them stop. "I'm scared."

18. **Be congruent.** You've got to want it. You've got to believe you can make money—lots of it. You've got to believe that you deserve to be wealthy—to your very core.
19. **You are a money magnet.** You are a literal magnet for the things you want. If you *really* want money, money literally can't say no.
20. **Knock and it shall be opened.** *"Whatever you can do, or dream you can, begin it; boldness has genius, power, and magic in it."* (Goëthe)
21. **Sharing is having more.** Tithing is a money multiplier, not a money subtracter.
22. **God knows where the gold is.** Become a partner with the Author of all Wealth.
23. **Destruction is creation.** Hysteresis is the enemy. Break through to a new level of results.
24. **Putting it all together.** Getting your act together is the final key to manifesting what you want.

"Michelle, I'll be honest with you. This will be the most high-pressured goal I've ever been a part of. By the way, when does the 90 days start?"

"It started about an hour ago, as soon as I signed the agreement."

"Hmm . . ." Sam paused to think. "Well, I have faith in your intuition, even if you don't. You needed to do something extreme to nail Ericksen. He could play around with you for years, torture you with the custody suit, while your kids get halfway to college. This way you're going to get the situation resolved quickly. The sooner you make the million, the sooner you're tucking them in at night."

At this image Michelle couldn't hold back her tears. "Forgive me, Sam, but I just don't see how that can happen."

"Do you think you can handle one more analogy?" Sam grinned.

Michelle shrugged.

"See that boulder next to the fence?"

Michelle nodded. It was a good three feet across and half sunk in the ground.

"Could you move it over here for me?"

"If I were a human-sized ant, maybe."

Michelle immediately regretted her sarcasm, but Sam ignored it. "How *could* you do it, if you *had* to?"

"I don't know." Now she sounded sullen.

"A man named Archimedes once said, 'Give me a lever long enough and a place to stand and I could move the whole world.'"

Michelle had a brief flashback to her eighth-grade science class, when she had learned about levers and pulleys.

"You want your kids badly enough, so you'll find the leverage."[p. 116]

Michelle's first step was to put together her Dream Team.[p. 164]

"No one succeeds alone," Sam had reminded her.

LEVERAGE

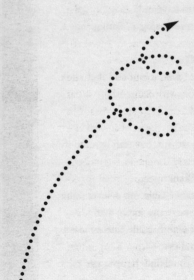

"You're one person." Sam held up the index finger of her right hand. "And I'm one person." She held up the index finger of her left hand. Then she brought the two fingers side by side. "Together we're the power of 11."[p. 162] She paused. "And when we add more people to our team, we're exponential."

Michelle did understand Samantha's lesson: that her greatest leverage lay in her ability to attract a powerful team. The members did not have to be rich, famous, or pretty—only as committed as she.

Michelle knew immediately who those people would be: her old friends from Deer Creek and her new friends from Riverdale.

Although Michelle regretted dragging her Deer Creek friends out on the half-hour schlep to Riverdale, both discretion and speed were of the essence. On the Riverdale end, Michelle had invited Delphine to participate, but because of her special needs daughter, Delphine couldn't commit the time necessary. Michelle vowed to help her old friend once all of this was behind her.

By contrast, when Jeremy had asked to be included, Michelle had only agreed after a quick consultation with Samantha. "What does your intuition tell you?" Sam had asked, as she often did. Michelle concluded that he was *supposed* to be there, although she wasn't quite sure why.

It didn't hurt that Jeremy had completely dropped his romantic pestering. On their drive to their Deer Creek meeting with Ericksen, he had revealed more of his past to Michelle. He and Jennie had married young. His early years were not only happy but prosperous, as he ran a highly successful computer consulting business. But a weakness for gambling—he'd started just with a little online trading—had become a runaway obsession. "Jennie tried to get me help. When I look back, I can only respect her for bailing out. I think it was forging her signature on the second mortgage papers that was the real deal-killer."

Somewhere along the line, when things were falling apart, an unplanned son had come along. Jeremy Jr. was four when Jennie

LEVERAGE = SPEED

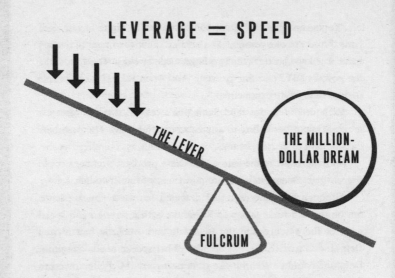

Leverage equals speed. If you want to create wealth, you need leverage. Lots of it. There are three parts to leverage. The first part is the objective (the Dream) that you intend to bring into reality. The Enlightened Millionaire focuses on a dream that advances humanity; it adds value. In this way, every dollar earned is an "enlightened" one. In addition, the precessional events are always positive, and, as the dollars mount to millions, a sense of gratitude permeates the Enlightened Millionaire's being.

The second part is the fulcrum. That is you. You are the object upon which the lever pivots. Without you there is no height to the lever and the objective will never move, no matter how long the lever or how much force is applied to the lever.

The third part is the lever itself. When the objective and the fulcrum are in place, success depends on the length and strength of the lever. Assuming the lever is strong, it is all about the length of the lever. The longer the lever, the *less* force that is needed to move the object. A long lever works easier and faster than a short one.

Enlightened Millionaires know speed is the new currency of business. Hence, Enlightened Millionaires create very long and strong levers.

left. "It got me in recovery." He concluded sadly, "Up till a year ago, I was thinking I was going to get them back, but then she met some-one else. Now *they're* a family, and Jennie's having another kid, and she says it's just better for everyone if I stay away."

For now, Jeremy begged for a chance to make some kind of con-tribution to the team with his computer expertise. He'd quit his job at the Mariposa and had enough money socked away to last him several months. He was ready.

The final team consisted of Michelle's two best friends, Court-ney and Summer, plus Jeremy and Michelle's teacher-friend, Renee (who now, ironically, worked as a substitute teacher at the same private school that Nicky and Hannah attended).

They had told her, one by one, when she phoned them, how glad they would be to help her. "Why have you been so distant?" Sum-mer had fairly wailed. "Didn't you think we cared?"

"I was so humiliated and angry," Michelle had explained, "and there wasn't anything for you to do anyway."

But now there was. As Michelle stood at the head of the table in Sam's conference room, the sight of those beloved faces threatened to make her weep. But this was not the time or place to weep.

So she made an attempt at humor. "Fasten your seatbelts, ladies and gentleman." Michelle smiled. "We're ready for takeoff."

"Wherever we're going," Courtney said, in her practical tone, "you've made it clear that we don't have any time to waste."

The conference room table was a heavy oak, surrounded by high-backed chairs. The room was not small, but the table was so large that there wasn't a lot of room at the periphery. Fresh flow-ers—a dramatic bouquet of gladiolas and irises—graced the center of the table, mirroring the edgeless pastels of the Monet reproduc-tions on the pale peach walls. On the far wall, lit from the ceiling, in raised gold letters, was the name of the company, "SAM, Inc.," and then below in elegant script, *"Samantha Ann Munroe, Incorporated."*

THE LONGER THE LEVER,
THE GREATER THE IMPACT

*Give me a lever long enough and a place to stand
and I will move the entire earth.*

ARCHIMEDES (C. 287–212 B.C.)

A movie star makes a movie once. The leverage comes when thousands of prints are made and the movie is shown all over the world. The money comes when millions of people pay to view it.

A baseball player plays baseball. The leverage comes when he is watched by tens of thousands of fans at the stadium and viewed nationally on television. The large salary a ballplayer makes comes from the revenues of this leverage.

Teachers, on the other hand, usually have 25 to 40 students per class. They have very little leverage and thus their salary is relatively low. Both the baseball player and the teacher add value (with the teacher generally seen as adding more value), yet the baseball player has the greater leverage and thus is able to demand and receive more money for his services than a teacher.

All large sums of money embrace the generalized principle of leverage. For example, the first volume of *Chicken Soup for the Soul* added lots of value. It was a book that was written once, yet it was purchased by millions. Once the book became a hit, the authors were able to leverage the "Chicken Soup" brand into many other books (e.g., *Chicken Soup for the Teenage Soul*) as well as other products, like the Chicken Soup calendars. Tens of millions of these products have been and are continuing to be sold. This leverage creates continuous income streams not only to the authors but also to the publishers, distributors, bookstores, and many others.

Sitting to Michelle's right was Sam, as usual the most striking presence in the room, with her regal calm and her bountiful weave flowing from her sepia-toned headscarf. Earlier that morning, to Michelle's great pleasure, Sam had complimented her on the progress she had made—she was becoming much more assertive and direct. "More like me," Samantha said unself-consciously.

In the little kitchen next to the conference room, everyone had helped themselves to coffee or herbal tea. Their cups rested on coasters with Samantha's company logo, the phoenix.

"Well, let's get on with it, then," Renee said. She wrapped her hands around her red raspberry tea. She had a reserved demeanor, but Michelle knew her as a devoted teacher and reliable friend.

Michelle looked instinctively at Samantha, who gave her a faint smile of encouragement. In her phone calls to her friends, Michelle had outlined her million-dollar wager with Anthony in broad strokes. Now she prepared to fill in some blanks. She took a deep breath. "You know I want my kids back. That overrides everything else. So. The first million dollars is legally and officially mine, free and clear. To fulfill the bet with Ericksen. But once I have my kids back, I plan to pay you all for your time, and then plow as much as necessary back into the business to keep it going. Then, after that, we share profits.

"Samantha has agreed to lend us her in-house counsel to draw up articles of incorporation. We'll be a closely held corporation. Everyone here will receive a percentage of the stock based on the time she or he can commit." She winked at Jeremy, the only "he" in the room. "Eventually we'll hire staff as necessary at regular salary, but for now, we can't afford to do that."

"This sounds pretty well thought out," Renee said with a light laugh. "Only thing is, we still don't know what this company is going to do."

"Yes, well, there is *that* little matter." Michelle grinned. "For this, I'd like to turn things over to my vice president, Samantha

The book *Nothing Down* explains the power of leverage in real estate. For example, if you put 10% down on a $200,000 home that goes up in value by 5% in one year, then the property is worth $210,000. You get the leverage not only on your $20,000 but also on the remaining $180,000 that you have borrowed. Your $20,000 investment has earned you $10,000, a 50% return on your money.

When you are able to buy real estate for no money down and it goes up in value, you have created a return on someone else's money. Of course, some time and effort are involved. However, computing a financial return on no money invested shows an infinite return. That is infinite leverage.

THE AWESOME POWER OF LEVERAGE

Leverage is the power to control a lot with just a little. Big doors swing on little hinges. In the business world, there are five kinds of leverage.

- ▲ **OPM—Other People's Money.** In real estate investing we buy residential real estate with 10% down and yet we control 100% of the property. The classic investment book *Nothing Down* teaches how to achieve ultimate leverage: how to buy property with little or no money down. Thousands of people have become millionaires using this system.
- ▲ **OPE—Other People's Experience.** It takes too long to learn it yourself, so borrow or learn from others. The easiest way to become rich is to apprentice personally with someone who is rich. Learn all they know, meet all their contacts, and do what they do—do it even better. If this isn't possible, read their books, listen to their tapes, watch their videos, interview them if possible, and attend their seminars. One

Munroe." Samantha rose, making, as Michelle anticipated, the striking impression that Michelle remembered from the first night at the hotel.

Sam scanned the little group with the subtle gesture of her head that Michelle also remembered from that first night. "A company thrives with a strong mission, and I don't think I've ever helped to launch a venture with a stronger one. But it won't be easy. A million dollars in 90 days."

"Sounds like we need a miracle," Jeremy said.

"We do." Sam paused—for effect, if Michelle knew her mentor. "The miracle of leverage. And even then, it's probably going to come down to the very last minute."

"What do you mean by *leverage*?" Summer asked.

"Glad you asked," Sam said. "Open your folders."

Each person flipped open the green folder in front of them, to find a single illustration.

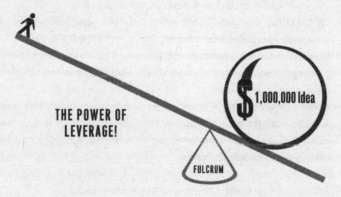

THE POWER OF LEVERAGE!

$1,000,000 Idea

FULCRUM

Sam motioned to the picture in front of them. "Your mission is to move that million-dollar stone . . ." she looked at her watch ". . . in only 89 days, 2 hours, and 45 minutes."

Michelle glanced at her friends. The look in their eyes was a mixture of fear and excitement.

idea you learn can save you 10 years of work effort. Leverage is about maximizing your results in a minimum amount of time. Therefore, absorb lifetime bodies of information and insight—compressed into instant usability just for you—in the forms of books, tapes, CDs, films, videos, and seminars. This is the cheapest and quickest way to gain OPE.

▲ **OPI—Other People's Ideas.** When Mark wanted to become a professional speaker, he attended the National Speakers Association meeting in 1974. Cavett Robert, the "dean of speakers" and cofounder of this association, talked about how to create multiauthored books. Within a month, Mark had adopted the idea and created a book with Keith DeGreen called *Stand Up, Speak Out and Win.* They enrolled 14 co-contributors who each invested $2,000 to obtain 1,000 books each. It was Mark's first zero-cash investment. He capitalized on someone else's idea to personally earn $200,000 in that year (selling 20,000 copies at $10 each). Your objective is to associate with people who can share with you their powerful moneymaking ideas.

▲ **OPT—Other People's Time.** Individuals will sometimes volunteer their time in certain circumstances, but most will sell you their time, talent, connections, resources, and know-how relatively inexpensively. Leverage yourself with professionals who are excellent and unique at employing their abilities.

▲ **OPW—Other People's Work.** Most people want a job. They want security, rather than opportunity. Hire and delegate to them everything that you don't want to or can't do as well. Leverage yourself through other people and grow.

Millionaires are masters at using all five kinds of leverage.

Sam continued, "To pull this off, we need to find a million-dollar idea and then leverage it. Leverage is not only about moving large objects with minimal effort. It's also about speed."

"And what is the fulcrum?" Courtney asked.

"The fulcrum is *us*," Sam said, "and our commitment. Like the lever, everything hinges on that."

Sam picked up a thick green marker from the tray on a flip chart at the head of the room and drew the same leverage diagram that was in front of them. Then, she drew six arrows along the length of the lever and added the following words:

- ▲ Mentor
- ▲ Team
- ▲ Network
- ▲ Infinite Network
- ▲ Skills & Tools
- ▲ Systems

THE POWER OF LEVERAGE!

SYSTEMS · SKILLS & TOOLS · INFINITE NETWORK · NETWORK · TEAM · MENTOR

FULCRUM

"We're going to apply six kinds of force to our lever.pp. 106–124 Each one individually might not be strong enough. But taken together . . ." Sam trailed off, and Michelle knew that this time she was encouraging them to use their imaginations.

APPLYING MAXIMUM LEVERAGE

Alone, you are without leverage. You have to rely on your own knowledge, your own experience, your own money, your own resources. This is the long, slow way to wealth. Eventually, your resources run out. You become discouraged. You quit.

Your first form of leverage is to acquire a mentor. Your mentor has tackled this mountain before you. Your mentor knows the terrain, the challenges, the pitfalls. Your mentor knows what to do. More important, your mentor knows what NOT to do. This is the first shortcut—avoiding lost time and money in trying to correct rookie mistakes. Your mentor also knows the shortcuts, the time-savers, the little tricks. You need a mentor.

Your second form of leverage is to acquire a team. Together, you all achieve more, faster, easier. You can spot one another's blind spots. You can encourage discouraged team members. They can encourage you when you're down. They fill in the gaps in your skill sets. They can be strong where you're weak. As a team, you all run faster. A 4-by-4 relay team runs the mile about two seconds faster than the individual runner. If you want speed, you need a team.

Your third form of leverage is a network. Each team member knows at least 100 valuable contacts. A team of 6 therefore knows 600 people. If each of these people knows 100 valuable contacts, then you have access to 60,000 valuable contacts. But these numbers are deceiving. It has been calculated that the value of a network is the *square* of the number of people in it. If your immediate network consists of 600 people, then your ultimate reach is 600 times 600, or 360,000 valuable contacts. Obviously, a one-person team is not enough. You need the power of a network. In that network, there are several *key contacts*—people who control huge networks of people. A key contact has "make it happen" power. One word

After a moment, Sam went on. "The first form of leverage is to find a *mentor*[pp. 126–150]—someone who has actually done it. In our case, *that's me*. I'm good," she said, "but I'm not *that* good. So we add a *team* of committed individuals. That's where you come in." Sam gestured to the group in front of her. "But together, we still may not be strong enough. But when you combine the *skills, tools,* and *systems* of all these forces plus that of their interlocking *networks,* you tap into enormous power."

Michelle thought of Sam's two fingers making the number 11, but she noticed that the others had furrowed their brows.

"Okay," Sam continued. "Suppose our million-dollar idea is to sell a widget. Our profit is a dollar a widget. So we'd need to sell a million of them in 90 days. Who do we know who can buy a million widgets?"

They all looked at one another, shaking their heads.

"That's the point—the six of us at this table don't know *anyone* who could buy a million widgets. But each of us easily knows 100 people.[p. 204] And those 100 people know at least 100 other people. By this very modest calculation, that's 60,000 people in our network. Maybe even the president of this here U. S. of A."

"Six degrees of separation,"[p. 198] Renee acknowledged softly.

"That's right. What are the odds that one of those 60,000 people knows *the key contact*—someone who knows someone who is looking for a million widgets?"

"You mean, like the guy who started Wal-Mart—Sam Walton," Jeremy said.

"Or his successor," Renee said.

"Jeremy's right," Sam said. "When he was alive, if you had walked into Mr. Walton's office and showed him the world's greatest widget, and he loved it, he could have snapped his fingers and had 10 million of them in stores across the country within a few days."

Michelle found herself nodding with all the rest and, for what must have been the hundredth time that day, thanking the Power

from this key contact and things happen. The value of a large network is the increased probability of finding the key contact. Remember, all it takes is ONE key contact.

Your fourth form of leverage is the Infinite Network. There is a spiritual connection that links us all up. This is the realm of coincidence, serendipity, chance, a twist of fate. Tapping into the Infinite Network is the ultimate form of leverage.

Your fifth form of leverage is the use of tools and skills. Millionaires use the tools of wealth—computers, the Internet, e-mail—for fast communications, fast calculations, fast decisions. If you want a speedy result, you need instant information.

Your sixth form of leverage is systems. Every millionaire has systematized, streamlined, and organized the processes of wealth. The most efficient form of information transfer is to learn your mentor's system and follow it—whether you've chosen real estate, the stock market, business, or the Internet. Learn the system.

When the combined force of mentors, teams, networks, Infinite Networks, tools, and systems is applied to a strong, long lever, miracles can happen in minutes.

that had led her into Sam's life. "This is what Samantha calls 'the *key contact*.'[p. 116] The key contact has Make-It-Happen power." Michelle was eager to show Sam that she had been paying close attention during all their lessons.

Encouraged by a "good-for-you" look from Sam, Michelle went on, though now more tentatively. "There's a principle called Occam's razor." Although she and Sam had discussed it twice, she was still struggling a little with the concept. "Occam's razor was named after a fourteenth-century English scientist, William of Occam, who put forth the theory that 'the *best* solution to a problem is almost always the *simplest* solution.' In our case, rather than selling one widget to a million people, we might find one person to buy a million widgets." Michelle leaned back, feeling satisfied. Sam was right; by sharing lessons with others, one learned it at a deeper level.

After another hour, Michelle felt much the same as she did after her first few jogs to the Rock with Sam: a mix of exhaustion and exhilaration.

It was clear from the hands massaging eyes and the pens now lying untouched on the table that the rest of the group felt similarly; after all, this was their introduction to Sam, which was a little like taking a drink from a fire hydrant.

When Sam announced lunchtime, everyone straightened up a little and a few words went around the table about nearby Chinese and Mexican restaurants. Michelle smiled to herself, knowing what was coming.

"In your dreams, my friends," Sam announced as these plans began to be verbalized. "We'll have lunch, all right—Chez Samantha."

Chez Samantha, it was soon revealed, was a small roof garden on top of the building where Samantha's headquarters were located.

THE SECOND MANIFESTATION

"I am a money magnet."

I am a money magnet.

I like money and money likes me.

I attract money.

I attract money 24 hours a day.

I earn bountiful amounts of money.

I wisely know how to create money.

I know that I will always have more money in my future than I do now.

The money that I create keeps multiplying, duplicating, and replenishing itself.

I am forever enjoying more and more money.

I have infinite money—more than enough for my every want and need.

I cheerfully save money.

I faithfully save 10% of all the money I earn.

I wisely invest my money.

I see my money re-creating itself effortlessly.

I cheerfully give money to good and worthy causes and philanthropies that make a lasting and ongoing difference.

My estate is in perfect, updated order and will be a lasting legacy that makes an important and memorable difference.

Money rushes to me in every form and fashion.

I have lots and lots of money.

I have money in my mind, in my future, in my pocket, in my wallet, in my safe, in my bank accounts, in my businesses, in my investments, and wherever it keeps growing.

I enjoy money and money enjoys me.

Money and all its equivalents are attracted to me.

Money is forever making me infinitely better off.

All that I do creates surplus, abundance, and plenty for myself and everyone else.

One of Sam's assistants had sent out for box lunches—turkey and vegetarian sandwiches from a nearby gourmet deli.

Sam let small talk go on just about as long as it took for everyone to get settled on the white wrought-iron chairs. She took a turkey sandwich out of the cardboard box on her lap and held it in two hands, close to her mouth. "I could just about eat this in one bite," she said. "So, since Michelle was doing such a good job, I'm going to let her keep talking for a while." She hardly had the last word out before the Kaiser roll went into her mouth.

"Well . . ." Michelle wriggled, thinking that she'd like to be digging into her own sandwich. "I guess the leverage concept we haven't discussed is *Infinite Networks*."pp. 214–222

"Oh, boy," Jeremy sighed. "Here comes the 'woo-woo.'"

"If you want to call it that," Michelle said defensively. "I mean, most of us believe in a Higher Power, don't we?"

"I do," Summer said eagerly, and though a couple of others looked uncomfortable at the personal question, most of them nodded.

"It doesn't matter what you call it," Michelle went on, paraphrasing Sam and having forgotten her lunch entirely. "The Universe, God, Higher Power—"

"Did you know that there are 627 different names for God?" Sam *mm'phed* through her food.

Michelle forged ahead. "The point is, the Infinite Network is made up of the Higher Power plus all of the invisible forces, or spirits, or angels, or guides,pp. 218–220 or whatever you want to call them. All around us, right now. Ready to help us."

The look on Jeremy's face said that he still wasn't convinced.

"But what if there was such a network, Jeremy?" Michelle pressed. "What if there was a way to tap into it? I'm not asking you to believe it will work. Just open your mind to the possibility."

"It's just too fuzzy for me." Jeremy swirled what was left of his Snapple in the bottom of his bottle. "I'm a computer guy. I want zeros and ones."

THE REAL ROCKY STORY

In 1974 Sylvester Stallone was a broke, discouraged actor and screenwriter. While attending a boxing match he became inspired by a "nobody" boxer who "went the distance" with the great Mohammed Ali.

He rushed home and in a three-day burst of creative output produced the first draft of the screenplay entitled *Rocky*.

Down to his last $106, Stallone submitted his screenplay to his agent. A studio offered $20,000 with either Ryan O'Neal or Burt Reynolds playing the lead character. Stallone was excited by the offer but wanted to play the lead himself. He offered to act for free. He was told, "That's not the way it works in Hollywood." Stallone turned down the offer though he desperately needed the money.

Then they offered him $80,000 on the condition that he wouldn't play the lead. He turned them down again.

They told him that Robert Redford was interested, in which case they'd pay him $200,000. He turned them down once more.

They upped their offer to $300,000 for his script. He told them that he didn't want to go through his whole life wondering "what if?"

They offered him $330,000. He told them that he'd rather not see the movie made if he couldn't play the lead.

They finally agreed to let him play the lead. He was paid $20,000 for the script plus $340 per week minimum actor's scale. After expenses, agent fees, and taxes, he netted about $6,000 instead of $330,000.

In 1976 Stallone was nominated for an Academy Award as Best Actor. The movie *Rocky* won three Oscars: Best Picture, Best Director, and Best Film Editing. The *Rocky* series has since grossed almost $1 billion, making Sylvester Stallone an international movie star!

Follow your gut. Stick to your guns.

Sam put down her half-eaten sandwich, obviously ready to take over again. "I can respect that, Jeremy. To use computer terminology, I believe that there is *Spiritual* Internet that links us all up. All of us are logged on to it 24 hours a day. When we want something intensely, it's like we broadcast bulk e-mails out over this Net. And we get responses back . . . hunches . . . like e-mails in our intuition inbox. If we act on these hunches, things usually turn out for the better."

"Mmm," Jeremy said. "I can buy that."

Sam now spoke to the entire group. "So, my friends, do you think the Higher Power already knows which stocks are going to go up tomorrow? Or which real estate corners will increase in value in the next five years? Or which businesses are bound to succeed or fail?"

"If there's a God," Courtney said, "and I do believe there is, then it only makes *sense* that He knows." Her eyes were wide; she'd clearly never thought this way before.

"Then," Sam continued, "the Higher Power already knows what our million-dollar idea is."[p. 86]

Summer picked up the thread. She spoke in a whisper, as if a huge *aha* was dawning in her head. "And *already knows* the names of all of the key contacts . . ."

"Exactly," Sam said. "We are one great idea and one key contact away from our million dollars."

They brought their trash down off the roof to throw away. "Get psyched up for an intense afternoon," Sam warned them cheerfully as she opened the door that led to the stairs.

The woman is like the Energizer Bunny, Michelle thought.

As they filed back into the conference room, Summer made a short announcement. "By the way, I brought a special clock for the occasion." She held up a small rectangular box with an LCD display. "It counts down the days, hours, and minutes left to reach a

ONE MINUTE REVIEW OF LEVERAGE

1. **Leverage equals speed.** To make a million dollars in a minute, you must master the principle of leverage. The more leverage you have in your added-value activity, the easier and faster you make money.

2. **The longer the lever, the greater the impact.** Enlightened Millionaires know that ease and speed are the new currencies of business. Hence, Enlightened Millionaires create very long and strong levers.

3. **Millionaires are masters at using all five kinds of leverage in the business world:**
   - ▲ **OPM**—Other People's Money
   - ▲ **OPE**—Other People's Experience
   - ▲ **OPI**—Other People's Ideas
   - ▲ **OPT**—Other People's Time
   - ▲ **OPW**—Other People's Work

4. **Millionaires are constantly looking for leverage.** Enlightened Millionaires constantly ask: How can I leverage this situation, this opportunity, this idea? To become an Enlightened One Minute Millionaire, your mantra must be, "Where's the leverage? Where's the leverage?"

5. **There are six key forms of leverage that give you maximum leverage.**
   1. Mentors
   2. Teams
   3. Networks
   4. Infinite Networks
   5. Tools and skills
   6. Systems

   Apply all of these forms of leverage to a pure, enlightened goal, and you are unstoppable.

deadline." She took the small box and placed it on top of the television/VCR stack in the corner of the conference room. It read:

88 Days, 22 Hours, and 51 Minutes

Michelle shuddered, not sure whether she should thank her friend or shake her. When this clock blinked down to the last minute, Michelle would either be the happiest woman alive or a woman who would live the rest of her life in regret.

The next three hours were spent in a feverish brainstorming session that started with the question: What is our million-dollar idea? They began with an exercise called "Unique or Weak" that helped them discover which of their own unique talents, skills, and interests they could turn into million-dollar ideas. Then they looked at their own weaknesses with the goal of creating products or services to solve some of their own problems. No idea was rejected.

"Remember the Acres of Diamonds story,"[p. 98] Sam had coached them. "We're looking for *any* idea you might already have, or that someone you know might be sitting on. A recipe. A special tool. A game. An idea for a book."

By 4 P.M., they had filled up dozens of flip chart pages and plastered them on all of the walls of the conference room.

After a 15-minute break, Sam explained that the purpose for a Dream Team was not only to come up with ideas but to make sure those ideas were sound. Some people on a team are naturally good at seeing opportunities. Others are good at seeing obstacles. Neither is wrong. Both are necessary to implementing an excellent idea. So Sam split the group into two groups: the Hares and the Turtles.[p. 176] The Hares, consisting of Sam, Michelle, and Summer stayed in the conference room. The Turtles—Jeremy, Courtney, and Renee—went into Sam's corner office to get a head start on writing down their list of 100 contacts.[p. 206]

MENTORS

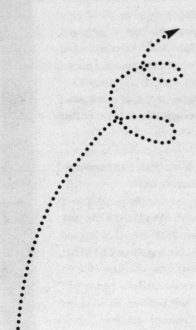

While the Turtles were out of the room, Sam directed the Hares to narrow the many lists of million-dollar ideas into a short list of only 10 "high-probability" candidates. A half hour later, the Turtles were invited back in the room with one purpose in mind—to play devil's advocate. As they heard each idea presented, the task of the Turtle group was to foresee the problems that might arise. Through this process, they were able to narrow their list down to the three ideas with the fewest obstacles. Then both teams helped to come up with contingency plans for every potential problem—if Plan A didn't work, they would be ready with Plan B.

Finally, Sam split the group into three pairs. Each pair took one idea and became responsible for implementing it.

The first pair, with Sam and Renee, zeroed in on real estate. This was, after all, Sam's expertise. Renee had been a Realtor® and still had a real estate license, so it was natural for her and Sam to work together—with assistance from Michelle.

Jeremy and Summer were partnered together in the second pair. Their objective was to use Jeremy's Internet experience to find a product or service to market online.

Michelle and Courtney paired off to try to capitalize on Courtney's merchandising know-how. They had narrowed their choices for a product to sell to five or six possibilities . . . but nothing felt quite right.

"Why don't we focus on the best idea and throw all of our resources at it to make it happen?" asked Summer.

"Multiple Streams of Income,"p. 262 was Sam's answer. "We don't know which of these ideas might work. So we launch all three. Maybe none of them makes a million by itself—say we make $200,000 in real estate, another $500,000 online, and $300,000 by selling a product. All together, we've got our million. Then again, none of these ideas might pan out. The 'Mother of all Million-Dollar Ideas' might still be floating around out there. So don't stop

THE POWERFUL LEVERAGE IN
A MENTORING RELATIONSHIP

*A single conversation across the table with a wise man
is worth a month's study of books.*

CHINESE PROVERB

The dictionary defines the word *mentor* as "a wise and trusted counselor or teacher." Another common definition is "a coach." Very few people achieve great success without personal mentors. Here is why we need mentors.

First, a mentor can give us perspective. Often, we are too close to see things objectively. We are caught up in the emotions of the situation—the fear, the excitement, the wonder, the anxiety, the confusion, the overwhelm. A mentor is detached and can see things from a distance. Experience plus time equals wisdom. A mentor can give us the wisdom of a lifetime of experience.

Second, a mentor can give us proficiency. A mentor fills in the gaps of our ignorance. In mastering any new task, an experienced mentor can simplify the process, guide us through the complicated parts, help us avoid the pitfalls, and warn us about the dangers. In short, a mentor helps us avoid the school of hard knocks—the most expensive kind of education in terms of time, money, and emotional pain. A mentor gives us a shortcut.

Third, a mentor gives us patience. In learning any new skill, there is a learning curve. A mentor can teach us patience as we struggle through failure to achieve mastery. Do you know any successful person who doesn't have a mentor? Look, for instance, at the story of Warren Buffett.

Buffett is the richest investor in the world—a billionaire many times over. When Buffett was a senior in college he read a book by Benjamin

looking. As you go through each day, turn your awareness into a Geiger counter . . . constantly sweeping the area around you for million-dollar ideas."

Renee looked puzzled, as if she didn't quite agree with what Sam was saying.

Sam continued, "Renee, have you ever driven off the car lot in a new car and almost immediately you began to notice other people driving your same car, same color, everything? Why does that happen?" Sam asked. "One day you hardly see any cars like yours. The next day it seems like there are hundreds of them." She let this question hang in the air. "It has to do with awareness. Once your mind is magnetized[p. 76]—emotionally charged—you start to notice things—things that were always there, but which remained below your awareness. I'll tell you this: Million-dollar ideas are floating around us every day. Even right now."

Sam reached up her hands and began to pluck imaginary thoughts out of the air around her head. "What million-dollar idea is floating around your head this very moment that you simply need to become aware of? The minute you become aware of it, you're a One Minute Millionaire—all the rest is just execution."[p. xi]

When they finally adjourned for the evening, Sam gave them the assignment of completing their 100-name lists and then, using intuition, prioritizing the names into two separate lists, A and B— the A list being made up of the top 10 people with the greatest probability of eventually leading to the *key contact*. The B list was made up of everyone else.

"Remember," Sam said, as she ushered them out of the conference room, "Occam's razor. Tell me what that is again?"

Michelle led the not-quite-in-unison response. "The best solution to a problem is almost always the simplest solution."

Graham called *The Intelligent Investor* (still considered to be one of the great stock-market classics). For Buffett, this was an epiphany. When Buffett learned that Graham was teaching at Columbia University he enrolled, studied under Graham, and received a master's degree in economics.

After graduation, Buffett attempted to work at Benjamin Graham's investment firm (even offering to work for free). Graham finally agreed, after repeated rejections of Buffett, to hire him three years later. Buffett spent the next two years being mentored by the famous author.

At age 25 Buffett returned home to Omaha, Nebraska, and launched, with seven investors, Buffett Associates. Buffett's original stake was $100. Within five years Buffett was a millionaire and on his way to becoming the most famous stock investor in history.

Remember, there is no synergy on your own. It takes at least two. Almost all Enlightened Millionaires have mentors. They recognize the need to have a mentor. It is part of their leverage. You are only as powerful as your mentors.

THE MENTORING MODEL

A feeble man can see the farms that are fenced and tilled, the houses that are built. The strong man sees the possible houses and farms. His eye makes estates as fast as the sun breeds clouds.

RALPH WALDO EMERSON

Study anyone who's great, and you'll find that they apprenticed to a master or several masters. Therefore, if you want to achieve greatness, renown, and superlative success, you must apprentice to a master. Usually, the apprenticeship is two years or longer. You will want to absorb their

86 Days . . .

Sam was lecturing her students, who'd nicknamed themselves the Millionaire Eagles, at the Rock.

"An eagle's eyes," Sam had told them, "are the sharpest in the animal kingdom. They can spot their prey from hundreds of feet in the air. They ferociously guard their nests and their young. They're noble, dignified birds who've survived because they're strong."

This trip to the Rock was the first time any of them other than Michelle had ever been introduced to Sam's private training sanctuary. It was just after 8 A.M. and the warm sun was bathing everything. In front of Sam, most of the group was seated cross-legged, except for Jeremy, who was actually lying on his back on the flat stone with his eyes closed, feigning a deep concentration, but from time to time Summer had to nudge him as he began a soft snore. He wasn't used to being up before 10 A.M.

"Yesterday," Sam continued, "I told you about the Butterfly Effect[p. ix]—the fact that tiny adjustments you make in your life today can cause enormous results later on. Let's brainstorm: What are some small changes—one minute habits, one minute activities, one minute thought patterns—that could transform your life?"

Summer piped up, "Like the way you taught us to visualize our goals with vivid vision?"[p. 50]

"Exactly," said Sam. "In one minute, you can scan through your dreams in vivid detail, magnetizing yourself to the person you want to become."

"How about writing down your goals?" offered Renee. "Writing down our top six goals each day takes about a minute but imprints them deep in our mind and heart."[p. 54]

"Very good. Anyone else?"

Michelle was ready with her answer. "Exercise—like this morning. It takes longer than a minute, but the small amount of time it takes really makes a huge difference."

entire body of information, learn all their sources and secrets, meet all their contacts, and study all that they studied, are studying, and will study. Learn their cognitive style. Learn to *think like they think* to obtain the results that they are obtaining.

All masters take on assistants to do their "grunt work"—to help them leverage their time. Accept it. Do it better, faster, and with a more upbeat attitude than anyone else. Offer constantly to go the extra mile. Anticipate the master's needs, wants, and desires.

Mark was a mentee and research assistant to Dr. R. Buckminster Fuller. From Fuller, Mark learned to think comprehensively and globally, to make the world work for 100% of humanity. Mark worked around the clock to fulfill "Bucky's" requests. This included driving Bucky's wife, Anne, on errands.

Bob was a mentee in graduate school to the business philosopher-genius Dr. Stephen R. Covey, co-owner of the billion-dollar Franklin-Covey Enterprises. From Covey, Bob learned the power of goals. One of Bob's original goals was to write a book. Six years later Bob's book became a number one *New York Times* bestseller. Impressed with Bob's results, Covey asked him to provide input into the original draft of Covey's *Seven Habits of Highly Successful People,* a book that is now an international bestseller. Bob, the mentee, had become the mentor!

Decide on the disciplines that you want to master. Decide to take ownership of that awareness. Become a mentee to a great and inspiring mentor. You must want to become a mentee, as much as you want your next breath of air. When you do, you will discover a way.

In business, you are either leading edge, cutting edge, dull edge, or trailing edge. You need to be at the leading edge. To be there you must master a discipline. The quickest, safest, and easiest way to do this is to apprentice with someone who leads in that field. Absorb everything you can from the master and then blaze forth with your own Dream, find your Team, and build your Theme.

When you do, riches will follow.

In the continuing discussion they came up with dozens of answers: prayer, meditation, deep breathing, snapping a rubber band for negative thinking, yoga, noticing a hunch.

"In a business context," continued Sam, "the way you hand someone your business card can cause a butterfly effect. In the Far East when someone hands you a business card, it's a 'big deal.' They use both hands. It is considered bad manners to use just one hand. And on the back of their business cards they list their lifetime goals."

"What a great idea!" Jeremy offered, who had begun to listen.

Sam nodded. "Even the habit of shaking hands can leave a lasting impression. When you shake someone's hand, don't let go until you can determine the color of their eyes. This simple habit lets them know that you're real—that you're interested. As you get to know people better, you can graduate from a firm handshake to a handshake/arm touch. Then to a two-fisted handshake. Me, I like hugs. It only takes a few seconds but makes a more profound connection. And," Sam added, "don't forget their name."

"Ohhh," groaned Summer. "I'm terrible with names."

"Keep telling yourself that," Sam shot back, "and you'll never be good. Say instead, 'I'm getting better at remembering names,' and soon you will be. Remembering a person's name is one of the most valuable but least expensive gifts you can give—it's a gift to the person you're greeting, and to yourself, too. If I gave you a thousand dollars to remember a name, could you do it?"

"I'd figure out a way," Jeremy said as he sat up.

"Exactly," Sam said. "Each contact you have with somebody needs to be improved—tweaked, made more important. Those little things pay big dividends." She paused. "Speaking of money. Every time you spend money, take an extra minute to spend it right—the millionaire way.^{p. 238} Buy right. Avoid getting into debt. Plan your purchases. The further in advance you plan, the cheaper your life becomes. Expect a discount. Check your receipt. Balance your checkbook. Figure out a way to turn an ordinary expenditure into a business

SERENDIPITOUS MENTOR

Goliath was the best thing that ever happened to David.

DOUG WEED

As the saying goes, "When the student is ready, the teacher appears."

Why is this true? Because when the student is finally committed, he or she suddenly becomes aware of the teachers and mentors that exist all around them. Mentors are everywhere!

There are three kinds of mentors: (1) serendipitous mentors, (2) hands-on mentors, and (3) hero/shero mentors.

The most common form of mentorship is serendipitous. *Serendipity* means "to make desirable discoveries by accident." If you are open and teachable, each person you meet can "accidentally" teach you something to advance your cause. Since "there are no accidents," you need to practice this discipline: Every encounter, no matter how trivial, has the potential for serendipitous mentorship.

Do your best to make it a two-way exchange. You may be the serendipitous mentor for someone else—carrying just the right message or *aha* to lift that person to a new plane of understanding. In your conversations, keep in mind the question "Who is the mentor here?"

A serendipitous mentor doesn't always need to be a person. It can literally be anything that causes you to change course in life, like . . .

A life-threatening disease
Or losing a job
Or reading a powerful book
Or an encounter with another life form

expense. Investing that extra minute to spend money wisely can make you a millionaire. People with money problems won't do these things—no wonder they are always a day late and a dollar short."

Sam continued, "When you think about it, to change your life you don't have to make a massive shift. Just a few little things every day—a few flutters of a butterfly's wings—can transform you into the person you want to be."

As they finished their lesson at the Rock, Sam had them all stand on the edge in a line, repeating aloud lines from a Manifestation about Team,P. 188 the second form of leverage.

As they spoke the Manifestation, the valley echoed their words.
"With the right dream . . ."
Dream. Dream. Dream.
"And the right Team . . ."
Team. Team. Team.
"We can achieve . . ."
Achieve. Achieve. Achieve.
"Miracles!"
Miracles. Miracles. Miracles.

85 Days . . .

Michelle's molars were banging together so hard that she felt as though she could chew through wood.

Courtney was driving her to Golden House, the Deer Creek senior residence facility, where Michelle would finally see her children, although Nicky and Hannah would not be able to see her. She would be watching them from the wings—or such wings as there were—as they performed for the residents, as part of the St. James children's chorus.

Michelle was terrified that something bad would happen. Maybe she'd get caught by the Ericksens. Maybe the chartered bus that always took the St. James kids on field trips would crash. Michelle

The world's greatest marine artist, Wyland, has said, "Once you've looked a whale in the eye, your life is nevermore the same."

Each day notice the serendipitous mentors that "accidentally" flow through your life. Remember, your problems are good. They are power in disguise.

What are they trying to teach you?

THE HANDS-ON MENTOR

If people knew how hard I worked to get my mastery,
it wouldn't seem so wonderful after all.
MICHELANGELO

The second kind of mentor is called a hands-on mentor.

Take a few moments to scan back over your life and you'll probably find you've had numerous one-on-one, hands-on mentors—from an athletic coach to a favorite aunt or friend. Robert Allen counted up 42 mentors whom he had worked with. Some of these relationships lasted years, others lasted just minutes . . . but each one came at an important "turning point" in his life. Many of these mentors just "showed up." Others, he sought out, asking for their advice and help.

On the journey between where you are now and your future millionaire goal there will be dozens of points along the way where you will need to be mentored. You'll find yourself lacking in an attitude, an awareness, a skill, a habit, a technique, or a strategy. Often, this requires a hands-on, nitty-gritty, in-the-trenches, day-to-day kind of mentor.

If the day-to-day kind of mentor doesn't spontaneously "appear," you must seek him or her out. How is this done?

had not been an overanxious mother until Gideon's death had demonstrated that she and her loved ones lived under no special protection.

Golden House was a large modern building on spacious grounds on the edge of town. Courtney pulled into the adjacent parking lot, and they went in together.

"What's in there?" Courtney asked, pointing to the white shopping bag that Michelle was clutching as they waited for Summer in the lobby. Summer was the social activities director at Golden House.

"Just a gift for the kids." She was trembling with anticipation.

"Won't that get you into trouble?" Courtney frowned, ever practical.

"I'm getting it to them one way or another," Michelle replied stubbornly.

She had dreamt of Nicky and Hannah almost nightly for the last year. Often her dreams were nightmares, of watching them drift out to sea, or being trapped on the second floor of a burning house. Sometimes the dreams were happy, dreams of such sweet relief, when they were all together again, sometimes even with Gideon— but then, when she woke up, she had to lose them all over again.

Now, as she watched them through a porthole in the kitchen door, she couldn't decide if it was like the good dreams or the nightmares. Michelle could see them but not touch or talk to them. *Maybe this is how it feels to be dead,* she thought. They were both in their white and navy St. James uniforms. It struck her that when she dreamt of them, they were almost always in those uniforms, too.

Nicky's hair was shorter than it had been in the picture on Ericksen's wall. Hannah's once-long auburn curls now barely touched her shoulders.

Before the choir performance was finished, she slipped away.

1. **Make a List of Missing Resources.** Writing down the resources that you feel you lack to help you reach your goal.
2. **Network Within Your Own Circle of Contacts.** You probably already know someone—who knows someone—who has the answers to your questions. Call them up and ask: Do you have the answer or solution? Or do you know someone who might know the answer? Make a list and call. Use the name of the person who provided the name as a referral. Repeat the preceding questions.
3. **Widen Your Search.** Once you know what you are lacking, you can usually find the names of potential mentors in the Yellow Pages or on the Internet—for a price.

Remember, you're seeking more than simple answers; you want a mentoring relationship—someone who can coach you to success. These types of relationships aren't cheap, but they are much less expensive than the school of hard knocks.

Also remember that potential mentors will usually be extremely busy pursuing their own goals. A request for mentorship will fall at the bottom of their to-do list. The only way to move to the top of their to-do list is to find out what your mentors want, attach yourself to one of their top priorities, and help them accomplish it. In doing so, your mentor will recognize your value, and through the law of reciprocity (you scratch my back, I'll scratch yours) your mentor will naturally want to help you achieve your goals.

In other words, give first and then you shall receive.

Summer had planned a short reception for after the performance and it gave Michelle the opportunity to check in quickly with Renee and get an update about the children. They met in an empty residents' lounge, a comfortable room with few sofas and chairs, a card table, some well-stocked bookcases, and a big-screen television.

"I don't have long," Renee said apologetically. "The chorus director and the chaperones will wonder where I am." She looked over her shoulder.

Though Renee was on the St. James campus a few times a week as a substitute teacher, she rarely saw Nicky and Hannah and up until now had not been able to give Michelle any new information on the kids. But last week she'd been assigned to work in the music department and had spent a couple of afternoons with Michelle's children at chorus rehearsals.

"Go on," Michelle said. "I can take it."

Renee sighed. "Mickey, I've spoken with both their teachers. There have been some problems, especially with Hannah."

"Like what?" Michelle felt hysteria beating against her chest, like the wings of a trapped bird.

"Well . . ." Renee folded her arms across her chest. "Hannah's been having some bathroom accidents."

"And what set that off?" Michelle snapped. "Hannah never even wet her bed, not once—but I suppose there's some reason why that's my fault, too."

Renee looked down. "Obviously, what's happened has been hard on the kids, first Gideon, then the new school...."

"Go on."

"Apparently, your mother-in-law got rid of Hannah's blankie." Renee winced.

Michelle couldn't speak for a moment. Then she thrust the white shopping bag into Renee's hands. "Can you get this to them for me?"

WHO IS YOUR HERO/SHERO MENTOR?

*If you can tell me who your heroes are, I can tell you
how you're going to turn out in life.*

WARREN BUFFETT

The third type of mentor is the hero/shero mentor. These are your heroes
and sheroes who are bigger than life—your champions, your role models,
your inspiration.

In the corporate world, they are (or have been) leaders like Lee Iacocca
of Chrysler, Jack Welch of General Electric, or Katharine Graham of the
Washington Post. In the investment world, they are the Warren Buffetts or
Peter Lynches. In the spiritual world you have Jesus, Moses, Buddha,
Confucius, Mohammed, Mary Baker Eddy, and Joseph Smith. Each indus-
try has its icons, alive and dead:

Donald Trump
   Julia Roberts
      Rush Limbaugh
         Cleopatra
            Buckminster Fuller
               Margaret Thatcher
                  Sir Winston Churchill
                     Diane Sawyer
                        John F. Kennedy
                           Princess Diana
                             Abraham Lincoln

Usually these leaders are inaccessible to the general public. Only on
rare occasions can you break through to their inner circles. But that doesn't
mean that you can't have access to their courage, wisdom, and insight.

"Do you mind if I ask . . . ?"

Michelle collapsed on the sofa, covering her face with her hands. "When Gideon started the new business, he was on the road a lot. Trade shows and stuff. He hated it. But he always left a tape for the kids to listen to when he was gone. Sometimes he read a story, or he sang a song, or he said a prayer."

"So?" Renee peered into the bag.

"He was so good at tinkering with things. That's how we got the idea for Gideon's Gadgets. Before he died, he had just figured out a way to put a tiny tape player inside a pillow. When the kids would put their heads down on it, it would trigger the tape."

"That's so sweet," Renee said softly.

Michelle gathered her strength. "I was helping him with it. So I knew enough to put a couple together with my own tapes. I used small pillows so that it'll be easy for the kids to get them home from school and into the house. I've got one for each of them with a story recorded on it. Just in case the Ericksens do find it, I didn't want to record a more personal message. This could just be—"

"That might just work." A voice seemed to come from nowhere.

Michelle jumped. She was afraid to turn around—expecting police or the looming figure of Anthony Ericksen. But it was an elderly woman in a wheelchair, her gnarled fingers poised above the buttons that moved the contraption back and forth.

"I didn't see you there," Michelle said, as soon as she could breathe again.

"Not as a pillow, of course," the old woman continued, talking absentmindedly to herself.

Michelle glanced at Renee, who looked uncomfortable. Michelle guessed that Renee was thinking the same thing that she was—that this unfortunate, confused old soul was living in another world.

"Pillows belong in housewares. They'd never take it as a pillow." And then she began to chuckle to herself as if she were remembering something.

We encourage you to become an avid student of the lives and teachings of successful people.

1. Read the biographies and autobiographies of people you admire.
2. Watch the Biography Channel as well as other television programs that chronicle the lives of great or famous people. You will learn that their lives have been full of challenges and setbacks that they were able to overcome through persistence, commitment, and stamina.
3. Read magazine and newspaper articles containing information and interviews about them.
4. Study books, tapes, and videos by them or about them.
5. When convenient, visit their birthplaces and/or locations they made famous.
6. When possible, have your photo taken with them, and display these photos on your wall.

And finally, we encourage you to assemble a Dream Team of your favorite heroes and sheroes, present and past. Form an imaginary Council of Light consisting of your selected leaders. Imagine being able to counsel with them as if they were communicating with you in person. Imagine what they might say to you. What special counsel might they give you? During your daily meditations, imagine that you are able to draw inspiration and wisdom from your own personal Council of Light.

MY COUNCIL OF LIGHT

_____   _____

_____   _____

_____   _____

_____   _____

_____   _____

Michelle and Renee exchanged another glance, this time with their eyebrows raised.

"If it's a toy it has to *look* like a toy," the old woman babbled on. "That's the way we did it, when I was president."

This last comment confirmed Michelle's suspicions. The woman was tiny in her wheelchair, her hair sparse, frizzy, and dead white. Still, she spoke in a confident voice.

Renee bit her lip. "I've really got to get back to the chorus," she said.

Michelle sagged. *Nicky. Hannah.* But there was no help for it. "Don't forget the pillows."

"You know I won't." Renee gave her a reassuring hug.

"Nicky will know how to sneak them in," Michelle went on. She rose from the sofa and grabbed at Renee's hand, as if somehow that would keep her children close a little longer. "I don't like to teach them to be dishonest, but . . ."

Renee gently pulled her hand away. "Mickey, we all know what you're about." She glanced toward the woman in the wheelchair. "I have to go now." She spoke loudly, apparently assuming the woman was hard of hearing.

"My name's Tilly, by the way," the woman replied in kind, in a louder than normal voice. "Tilly Walczak. I'd shake your hand, but I just got a manicure from one of those little girls who come round once a week and do our nails."

"Nice to meet you," Renee murmured. Michelle kept her eyes on the white shopping bag as Renee beat a hasty retreat.

"I'm serious about that pillow—what did you say your name was?"

Michelle roused herself. "Michelle Ericksen." She started to put her hand out but then remembered the manicure. She wanted to be nice to Tilly. Probably many people brushed her off. What would Sam do? She would be compassionate and tithe some of her time. She would also tell Michelle that doing something nice for someone else would make her feel better.

THE LESSONS OF THE CLIFF

There is a cliff in the Canadian Rockies reached by a short hike up a rugged mountain trail. Nestled in the basin above the cliff are three pristine alpine lakes—the Lineham Lakes—teeming with schools of huge, hungry rainbow trout. Unfortunately, the only way to reach the lakes is to traverse the steep cliff along a dangerous, narrow ledge.

You decide to do it.

Your guide coaches you across the cliff (you wouldn't want to tackle this alone!). Your fingers cling to the sheer rock face as your feet dangle over a 300-foot drop. Heart pounding, you force yourself to not look down. You come to a hidden ravine and clamber up using trees and roots as leverage.

When you emerge into the upper basin, you discover three deep-blue lakes ringed with majestic pines. The fishing is fantastic! You catch one with nearly every cast—dozens of fish fighting for your bait, their silver bodies flashing in the sunlight.

At the end of the day, you beg your guide to return with a helicopter—anything to avoid that cliff! Not possible, he explains. Somehow you make your way back, bringing with you memories of the harrowing adventure.

Later, you ponder the lessons of the cliff.

▲ **Lesson One: The fishing is best where only the brave dare go.** The easy lakes get fished out fast. The shores are lined with anglers. The fish are small and hard to catch. Conversely, the hard lakes are full of fish—big ones. But you have to dare to climb the cliffs to get them. The risks may be great, but the rewards are greater. If you want to prosper, look for the cliffs.

▲ **Lesson Two: Always take a guide.** To you, a beginner, the cliff is frightening. To your guide, it is a routine experience. No matter what

Just then, Summer came rushing through the swinging doors.

"Michelle, I've been looking for you," she said. Then she noticed the woman in the wheelchair. "Oh, I see you've met Tilly."

"Yes, we were just—"

"Tilly's a firecracker," Summer kept on as if Tilly wasn't in the room. "But you've got to watch out for her. She can talk your ear off."

"Don't patronize me, young lady," the older woman grumbled.

"C'mon, Tils, you can take a little ribbing." Summer patted Tilly affectionately on the shoulder, adding to Michelle, "She can tell you stories about the things she's done that will knock your socks off. But not right now. Courtney's been nagging me to find you. She says we need to get back to work." A bit louder, "Tilly, I've got to take Michelle away from you."

"Don't worry about *me*," Tilly replied cantankerously. "*I* came in here to watch one of my dramas." She maneuvered her wheelchair around Michelle, picked the remote up from a coffee table, and pointed it at the TV.

Summer grabbed Michelle by the elbow and pushed her out into the foyer. Out the window they could see the St. James school bus pulling out of the parking lot, its exhaust fumes spewing into the air.

"Thanks for rescuing me," Michelle said.

"If we didn't have to get back to Sam's office, I think you'd enjoy getting to know Tilly. She's amazing. Her body might look old but she's got every last one of her brain cells."

"I just figured she was drifting into her own world—she said something about being president, about toys. . . ."

"Toys?" Summer shot back. "She's the *queen* of toys. Didn't she tell you?"

"Not really."

"She had her own toy company until she sold it to Hasbro about 10 years ago. They're still selling her toys, even today. Haven't you ever heard of Doggie Surprise?"

the "cliff" in your life—a speech to a group, a sale to an important client, the launch of a new business—find a mentor who has conquered the cliff and have him or her take you.

▲ **Lesson Three: Face your fear.** As in all fairy tales, if you want to marry the princess, you have to slay the dragon. The greatest dragon you'll ever face is your own fear. If you can learn to live with the fear, the world is yours. Face your fear today.

TAKE A MILLIONAIRE TO LUNCH

The shortest and best way to make your fortune is to let people see clearly that it is in their interest to promote yours.

JEAN DE LA BRUYÈRE

Search out a millionaire a month. Request an audience, either in person, by phone, or by e-mail. Pick the millionaire's brains. Here is a list of questions. Something magical will happen as you ask these questions. Write down the millionaire's answers.

1. How did you make your first million?
2. How long did it take you?
3. How long would it take you today?
4. What is the system that you used to make it?
5. Is this system transferable?
6. How long would it take you today to mentor somebody to your same level of success?
7. What would you recommend that I do to become a millionaire?
8. What's the most important lesson you ever learned?

"Sure—Hannah had one when she was younger."

"That *one* toy made her $11,000,000. That's not just according to her, either."

"Then, what's she doing living here?"

"Her son lives in Riverdale. She wanted to live *near* but not *with* him. So her best choice was Golden House. It's the nicest senior assisted-living center in the area."

"I sure was mistaken about her," Michelle said.

"I made the same mistake the first time I met her," Summer confessed. "But then my boss let me in on a secret. Tilly anonymously pays for about 10 of the residents of Golden House who can't afford to live here on their own."

And out of nowhere, Michelle had a major *aha*. "Summer, did you have Tilly on your list of 100 contacts?"

"No, why?"

Michelle looked at Summer. Then together, the two women said, "Occam's razor."

84 Days . . .

Courtney rushed in and joined the rest of the team members seated at the conference table. She looked as if she hadn't slept. Sam glanced at the clock. It was 8:10 A.M. "Good morning, little flock," Sam began. "We made a lot of progress yesterday. We only have till noon today. I've got meetings in Denver, and Michelle has a lunch appointment. So I'd like to get a progress report from each team-pair. Michelle and I had a teleconference with Renee earlier this morning before she had to leave for school. I'll give you a report on our real estate project in a minute. First, were there any *ahas* from yesterday's session?"

Courtney couldn't wait to talk, the words spilling out of her, "I just couldn't get to sleep last night. Finally, about two A.M., I drifted off. And this memory hits me. I sat bolt upright and said, 'That's

9. How do you integrate spiritual values into your life?
10. What is the legacy you want to leave?
11. What's your most important habit?
12. What opportunities do you see that you don't have time to take advantage of?

After the interview, become quiet and reflect on what you just experienced. Ask yourself these questions:

1. What most resonated with me about this millionaire encounter?
2. What insights (or *ahas*) did I have?
3. What specific actions am I going to take as a result of this interview?
4. What trait or quality about this person can I emulate?

TRANSFORMATIONAL LEARNING

Each one, reach one. Each one, teach one. Until all are taught.

MARK VICTOR HANSEN

Change expert Don Wolfe teaches that there are two kinds of learning: informational learning and transformational learning—or head learning and heart learning.

Informational learning is predominant in our educational system. Teachers talk; students listen, take notes, take tests, get grades, and so on. It's all about memorization and regurgitation.

Transformational learning is about empowering students to discover the answers for themselves. It's a slower process, but much more profound. That's why it's transformational.

it!' Last year, at the Chicago gift show, I was walking the aisles scanning for new merchandise for my store. There was this woman handing out a paperback book to people passing by her booth. They glanced at the title, opened it up, and immediately broke out laughing. I was curious, so I walked over and she handed me a copy. *Everything Men Know About Women*, by Dr. Alan Francis.[p. 344] There is no Dr. Francis. The real author is the woman who handed me the book, Cindy Cashman. I opened it up. The book was completely blank. One hundred and twenty-eight blank pages and not a single word."

At this, all the women at the table burst out laughing.

"And your point is . . . ?" Jeremy responded.

This brought another bout of laughter from the women around the table.

"I mean," said Jeremy realizing his mistake, "what does this have to do with *us*, with *our* project?"

"I'm getting to that," said Courtney, holding up one finger. "So I asked the author, 'How's business?' 'Booming!' she said. Women's clothing stores buy it by the caseload as an impulse item. She prints them for about 50 cents each, sells them to the store for $1.50, and the store sells them for $2.95. Guess how many she has sold?" Courtney paused. "*One million copies*. This woman became a millionaire selling a book with *no words* in it."

"Now, that's my style," said Summer.

Jeremy, who had recovered from his female ribbing, now injected himself into the conversation. "While we're talking about unusual ways to make a million dollars, this 'blank book' story reminds me of the guy who sold the Brooklyn Bridge."

"You can't sell the Brooklyn Bridge," said the ever-practical Courtney.

"I know," Jeremy agreed, "but this guy named Paul Hartunian figured out how to make a fortune from selling *pieces* of the bridge. This is a true story. Hartunian was working as a paramedic, looking for his lucky break. One day he was watching a newscast of some work crews

Informational Learning	Transformational Learning
Left brain	Right brain
Intellectual	Emotional
Head	Heart
Structured	Creative
Serious	Curious
Rigid	Spontaneous
Told the answer	Discover the answer
Repetition	Intuition
Passive involvement	Active involvement
Hold back	Let go
Fear	Trust
Being *the* best	Being *your* best
Knowledge	Understanding
Uh-oh!	Aha!
Oh, no	Oh, yes

We live in the age of too much information and not enough transformation. When people get stuck, it's rarely because they don't know enough. It's because they lack the ability to act on what they already know. Transformational learning is not about taking notes in a notebook. It is about writing the lessons on your heart and in every cell of your body—so that your behavior flows effortlessly, without compulsion, from the wellspring of your natural desire to live the life you were born to live.

God designed life to be a transformational experience. Similarly, we can't "inform" you into a millionaire. We can only "transform" you into a millionaire.

The main goal of transformational learning is to cause you to experience "*ahas.*" An *aha* is when your awareness expands—when you "get it." The lights go on and you say to yourself, "*Aha!*"

What did you *aha* today?

repairing parts of the Brooklyn Bridge—taking down old wooden beams and carting them away. And this idea popped into his head. He immediately called down to the construction site and asked the project manager if he could buy the old wood. Of course, the manager thought the wood was worthless so he was happy to get rid of it.

"Hartunian took the old beams of lumber and had them sliced into one-inch-square and ⅛-inch-thick pieces of wood and glued them onto an official certificate saying that the holder of the certificate had purchased the Brooklyn Bridge, or a piece thereof. Then he did something quite remarkable. He sent a press release to hundreds of media outlets that said, 'New Jersey Man Sells the Brooklyn Bridge for $14.95!' His phone rang off the hook! Literally hundreds of media outlets called him on the phone and wanted to learn more. He ended up selling thousands of these pieces for $14.95, *plus* a couple bucks for shipping and handling. He turned those old, worthless beams into SEVEN MILLION DOLLARS. No lie."

"That's a great story, Jeremy," Sam commented. "It's exactly what I've been trying to teach you. Your million-dollar idea can come from the most unusual places, *if* you're open and aware."

Courtney raised her hand to command the floor. "Let me finish my *aha* about the blank-book idea, because I think this is a perfect million-dollar idea for our group. Just think, if this single woman can sell a million copies of a blank book all by herself, shouldn't we, with all of our interconnecting networks, be able to sell a million copies of some simple book that we create?"

"A million books . . . that's a lot of people," Summer said.

Michelle joined in, "But if we sold to companies, and each company bought a hundred books . . ."

Jeremy did a quick calculation in his head. "You'd need 10,000 companies."

"That's a lot of companies," Summer added.

Sam sat watching this brainstorm, amused. Then she spoke. "Why not sell a million books to one single customer? Occam's razor."

THE THIRD MANIFESTATION

"I attract millionaire mentors."

I attract successful mentors.

When I am ready, they suddenly appear.

My mentors offer to mentor me and guide me to the success I desire.

My mentors enjoy sharing with me their most important success secrets.

I feel confident in asking my mentors for advice.

My mentors intuitively know how to help me make the most important breakthroughs.

I am able to glean from the relationship with my mentors exactly what I need to launch me toward the goals that I seek.

My mentors enjoy the relationship with me.

It's exciting to be with individuals who possess the truth that I am seeking.

My mentors willingly share, encourage, and coach me to experience and express my full genius, abilities, talents, and resources.

They see more in me than I see in myself.

Their gentle, sequential guidance makes all the difference to my accomplishments.

My mentors know how to bring out the best in me.

I study them up close and personal—if possible.

I cheerfully apprentice and pay my dues to my "masters," as they did with their "masters."

I read, study, and apply all that they have written and that they recommend.

I meet all my mentor's friends, colleagues, and loved ones and make them part of my ever-growing million-dollar Rolodex.

My life is made infinitely more meaningful with a mentor-teacher who wants to be in service to my greater growth and development.

I catch my mentor's passion for life and living fully and richly.

I realize no one has ever achieved greatness who did not have mentors.

I am willing to have great and inspiring mentors throughout my life.

I am learning from my mentors how to be a mentor myself.

I am prepared to mentor others when the opportunity presents itself.

This seemed to pour cold water on the group. It was too big an idea.

"Why would *any* company buy a million copies of one book?" asked the ever-practical Courtney, who had brought the original idea that morning.

This question lingered in the air. Michelle thought, *The bigger the question, the bigger the . . .*

"Maybe they have a million employees," said Jeremy finally.

"Or a million customers," Summer added.

Sam jumped in, "Let's not get stuck on the million number. The question is—are there at least 10 companies somewhere on this planet who might buy 100,000 copies of the right book at the right price?"

A few heads began to nod as if this might be possible. Courtney continued the thought, "Some companies spend more than that on paper clips."

Michelle put her face in her hands trying to comprehend the magnitude of the idea. "Just think of the logistics. Printing and shipping a million books. And to get it all done in 90 days. Boggles my mind."

Now it was Jeremy's turn. He stood up to address the group. "Ladies, here's where a left-brain male comes in handy." He shot his cuffs like a magician to show that he had nothing up his sleeves. "We don't *print* any books. We don't *ship* any books. We create an *e-book*.^p. 334 Each person gets a personalized, digitized book zipped right into their e-mail box. We sell them for a dollar apiece. Our cost? Next to zero. Our profit? About a buck a book. Voilà." He clapped his hands together like a magician ending a trick. "There's our million."

"Do you know how to do all of that, Jeremy?" asked Michelle.

"Well, I'm a little rusty, but a couple of weeks on the Internet and the team-pair of Jeremy and Summer will figure it out." He held up his palm and Summer gave him a high five.

So that was it! After Sam left, the group spent the morning brainstorming a dozen excellent e-book concepts along with contingency plans.

MENTORED BY A BILLIONAIRE,
BY ROBERT G. ALLEN

When I was 19 years old, I had an experience that made an indelible impression on my young mind. One summer I was working as a driver of a Greyhound Tour Bus based at beautiful Lake Louise in the Canadian Rockies. I was assigned to drive a small group of wealthy tourists from the Philippines consisting of an elderly couple, a Mr. and Mrs. Lopez, and their entourage of about a dozen family members, friends, and business associates. The Lopez family owned many successful businesses in the Philippines, including a television station, radio stations, a newspaper, and a large utility company—certainly over a billion in value by today's standards.

At the end of my tour, the old gentleman graciously invited me to join his entourage as they continued on their journey. I was flabbergasted. The very next day I was part of a billionaire's entourage, with a new set of clothing on my back and extra spending money in my pocket. It was like a fairy tale.

After a brief stop in San Francisco at one of the Lopez family mansions, we flew to Manila, where I began to enjoy all of the benefits of a life of luxury—maids, cooks, chauffeurs. After a few days, I was sent on a tour of the Lopez mansions in various parts of the country, from Davao in the south to Baguio in the north. I saw the mansions and the cars, and was able to experience the wealth firsthand. Impressive!

After several weeks, I continued with the group to Tokyo for another week of sight-seeing, carte blanche. Then I returned home—not before spending three glorious, all-expenses-paid days in Hawaii.

Fast-forward about seven years. I had graduated from Brigham Young University and was in San Francisco on business. I dropped by the Lopez family mansion and was informed that Mr. Lopez had passed away and that the family had suffered a reversal of fortune.

Just as the group was breaking up, Sam's staff brought in two laptop computers—connected to the Internet via a wireless hub—and set them up on the conference table at the far end. Jeremy sat at one of the computers and cracked his knuckles. Then, with Summer looking over his shoulder, he began to work his magic on the keyboard.

83 Days . . .

"We're so happy that you agreed to meet with us for lunch, Tilly."

Michelle and Courtney sat on either side of the older woman, who was seated with them in one of Deer Creek's newer, more gentrified restaurants. It was just before 1 P.M. Twenty minutes earlier, the two of them had met Tilly as the Golden House van dropped her off in front of the Upside Café.

"Oh, I enjoy my little outings." Tilly looked fresh in a blue velour warm-up suit. "Hope I'm dressed okay. At my age, I go for comfort, not style."

"No problem." Both women spoke at the same time and then laughed at themselves.

After the food was ordered the conversation turned to business, which didn't seem to bother Tilly one bit. She immediately launched into her life story, with side trips down some of her more amusing adventures, including an invitation to the Eisenhower White House, during which she'd given Ike an earful about that sharp-chinned vice president of his. Her storytelling was just a few decibels too loud and soon people at nearby tables were leaning in to capture some of the details. Funnier than her political commentary were her reminiscences of failed toys—though few and far between—like My Doggie's Brain Assembly Kit. Some of them reminded Michelle of Gideon's more offbeat ideas.

By the time the food arrived—Chinese chicken salad for the two younger women and a Monte Cristo sandwich for Tilly—the laughter

When President Marcos declared martial law in the Philippines in 1972, he took more than mere power. He seized all of the media outlets—newspaper, TV, radio—and nationalized them (another word for legalized grand larceny). During the ensuing chaos, the president of one of the television stations was kidnapped. The kidnapped man happened to be the son of Mr. Lopez. Mr. Lopez received a phone call shortly thereafter in America and was given a choice: relinquish his rights to all of his Philippine holdings or his son would be killed. I doubt the old man took more than a moment to make his decision. The son was released. The assets were transferred to the Philippine government.

Imagine receiving a telephone call like that—to give up everything you own to spare the life of one of your children. Puts things in perspective, doesn't it?

Over the years, as my fortunes have waxed and waned and waxed again, I have tried to never forget this billion-dollar lesson.

from their table was beginning to ripple into an increasingly large circumference around them. Tilly seemed to relish the attention of the audience. "So, that's how I made 11 million dollars on that one idea," she chuckled as the waiter delivered the meals. Tilly inclined her head to the surrounding tables with all the dignity of the Queen Mother, as if to say, Your attention is no longer required, and began to slice up her sandwich into small pieces.

"So, Tilly," began Michelle. "When I first met you at Golden House, you commented on a gift—a pillow, that I gave my children."

"Yes, and I said that they'd never take a pillow. It would have to be something else—a doll, or a puppet, or maybe a teddy bear— anything but a pillow."

"Who do you mean by 'they'?"

"Why, the toy companies, of course. A pillow would never make it past their new product committees. I've been on those committees before. They see the best ideas in the world—hundreds of them a month. So I know. Toy companies sell toys, not pillows."

"What was it about my gift, then, that caught your attention?"

"Now, that's a good question, my dear. I've seen 10,000 ideas buried in the toy graveyard, many of which I killed myself. And I've seen how precious few of the ones that get past the idea stage get to the shelves, let alone make a plugged nickel for anyone. I think I can safely say I've learned a *few* of the principles that mark the best ones."

"Tell us the principles," Courtney said, polite but direct. She was taking delicate but regular bites. Michelle couldn't eat.

"As you were describing your contraption to your friend, there, I said to myself, 'Now, that's something that I would like to give my own grandchildren.' A little message from Grandma. That's always the sign of the best ideas—they strike you as something you want to use for yourself, you know? I could just imagine my little Caroline— she lives in Atlanta with my daughter and her husband—and wouldn't she like to cuddle a toy and hear her *favorite* grandmother whisper a lovely little message, or read a short bedtime story?"

ONE MINUTE REVIEW OF MENTORING

1. **Every successful person has mentors.** A mentor is a shortcut to perspective, proficiency, and patience.
2. **Mentoring is powerful form of leverage.** Drawing from your mentor's experience is the quickest, safest, and easiest way to climb the Millionaire Mountain.
3. **Mentors are everywhere.** Each person you meet can "accidentally" teach you something to advance your cause.
4. **Mentors don't need to be people.** Anything that causes you to change course in life—a life-threatening disease, losing a job, reading a book, or an encounter with an animal—can serve as a mentor.
5. **Constantly seek out mentoring relationships.** When you find yourself lacking in anything—an attitude, an awareness, a skill, a habit, a technique, or a strategy—seek a mentor to show you the shortcut.
6. **Assemble a Dream Team of your favorite heroes and sheroes, present and past.** Form an imaginary Council of Light consisting of your selected leaders. Imagine being able to counsel with them as if they were communicating with you in person.
7. **Set a goal to search out at least one millionaire a month.** Request an audience, either in person, by phone, or by e-mail to pick your millionaire mentor's brains.
8. **The best kind of mentor is a transformational mentor.** A transformational mentor creates a context in which you experience *ahas*.

Michelle was distracted for a moment, wondering whether the original pillows had made it to Nicky's and Hannah's bedrooms.

Tilly gulped iced tea, none too quietly. "I'm seeing a plush toy . . . something like a teddy bear . . . with a big torso . . . like a minipillow, getting back to the pillow concept . . . comes in all kinds of colors . . . real fun." She paused and stared into the distance with her shiny dark eyes. "Maybe the paw has a little button for the child to press and the recording starts. Back when I was hot stuff in the toy business, those kinds of electronics were hard to find. . . . I bet you're too young to remember Talking Trisha." Tilly laughed and gulped some more iced tea. "The electronics didn't work very well and were expensive, to boot. But I understand that today you can get almost any technology that you want in a toy—fast, cheap, reliable. And all of this flashed through my mind in the 30 seconds that I was listening to you. But *you* didn't seem all that interested." Tilly sniffed, as if affronted by the memory. "So . . ."

Michelle jumped in, "It's not that I wasn't interested, I had just . . . it was an emotionally charged day . . . I'm sorry. I wasn't trying to be rude."

"Tilly," Courtney cleared her throat, "do you think that Michelle's idea—I mean, *her* pillow meets *your* teddy bear—is marketable?" She raised her brows and kept her eyes fixed on the older woman.

"I already told you," Tilly said, just the tiniest bit impatiently, as she daintily wiped cheese off the end of her fingers. "It had *me*, and I'm pretty darn jaded when it comes to ideas for new toys."

"But hasn't this kind of thing been done before? Aren't there toys with recording devices?" Courtney asked.

"Sure, just like there are a billion or so places that serve coffee. So why are there Starbucks on every corner instead of a Joni's Java Joint?"

"I've never heard of Joni's Java," Michelle said.

"My point, dear. With a toy, it's gotta have something a little bit unique. And you've got it—the parent's own voice whispering into

TEAMS

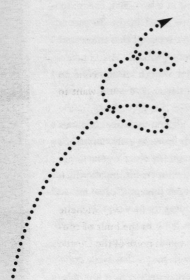

that child's ear. Maybe singing a little nursery rhyme. Something about that gets you right here." Tilly slapped her hand on her heart. "There are a lot of guilty mommies and daddies flying off on trips who will want to leave a piece of themselves home for their kids. If it's marketed right, it could be the next Cabbage Patch doll."

Michelle and Courtney looked at each other in amazement.

"Absolutely," Tilly continued. "I've been on the rocket ride when one of these toys takes off. There's nothing like it. Just picture a line of a hundred mothers wrapped around the block an hour before opening time, ready to pull one another's hair out to get a toy before the store runs out. You think I'm exaggerating, but those Mama Bears can get vicious." Tilly cackled and rubbed her wrinkled hands together.

"Tilly," Michelle began breathlessly, "how much time would it take to get a toy like that on the market, starting from tomorrow?"

"Well, the first hurdle is getting a prototype made. That'd take a couple of weeks. Then we make an appointment to see someone on the new product committee. This is something that you'd want to take to either Hasbro or Mattel—they're the two giants in the industry. Let them fight over it. We'd be lucky to squeeze ourselves in at either place in less than a month from right now, and *that's* only because I know a few people. Then another three weeks to get approvals through the committee, and after that, the contracts, which can take another . . ."

There's no way this can happen in less than six months, Michelle thought, *much less 90 days.* Tilly's voice faded into the buzz of conversation and crockery that was the background noise of the Upside Café. She looked over at Courtney, who had also stopped eating.

"I don't think you girls are grasping my point very well," Tilly reproached them. "I'm telling you that you have a winner toy here."

Michelle took a deep breath. Then she began—as pithily as she could—to explain the circumstances of her bet with her father-in-law. While she talked, Tilly dug under the shoulder of her warm-up

THE POWERFUL LEVERAGE
IN A DREAM TEAM

Success is not a solo project—it needs to be shared. And success is not a competition. There's plenty of it to go around. You have to work with a team that shares the same dream or objective. A team is part of your lever. It makes success quicker and easier. It's all about synergy—the concept of adding 1 plus 1 and getting 11—not 2. People working together can accomplish far more than they can separately.

Incredible power can be released when people work together. Associating with like-minded, success-oriented, joyful individuals—a Dream Team—is one of the most amazing success tools that exists. Anyone who achieves great success—anyone—must have a Dream Team.

Instant solutions exist in Dreamteaming. This process helps you to take your ideas and expand them into greatness.

What characteristics should your Dream Team possess? Successful Dream Teams consist of at least two or more people with a common purpose where both hearts and heads are in harmony with one another. Always be on the lookout for the best people and then ask them to join your team. Attitude is critical; it can make or break your team's success.

Avoid selfish, negative, or egotistical people. This is your team that you're building—don't make exceptions to this. There should be a spirit of joy and contribution within the group. Only dedicated, committed, joyful Dream Teams achieve great success. *Remember, the relationships between you and each member of your Dream Team must be confidential.*

When you have the right Dream Team, its members will help to identify bad habits that are hindering your success, and help you to change them. Your team members will see more in you than you see in yourself. They will be there to cheer you when you become weary.

Enlightened Millionaires have Dream Teams.

suit, apparently adjusting a bra strap. Michelle concluded by telling Tilly that she had a 90-day deadline. "Except that now it's a little less than 83 days."

Tilly gave a brief tug to the other bra strap. "Ninety days or eighty-three, it doesn't really matter. They're both impossible."

The word *impossible* hit Michelle like a sock on the jaw. Then, suddenly, she was back in Sam's garden and hearing the story of the child trapped under the car. Except this time, it was her own children under that car. Then an idea popped into her mind. "Tilly," she began. "Play along with me for a minute. Suppose your granddaughter, Caroline, had been kidnapped and was being held for ransom. You'll never see her again, ever, unless you get this teddy bear to market in 90 days or less."

"Oh, my," gasped Tilly, holding her hand to her bosom. "I wish you wouldn't talk like that."

Michelle forged on. "They're going to take her away forever, Tilly. Unless you do something that's impossible—" Michelle glanced over at Courtney, worried that maybe she was laying it on a bit thick. "But if you get this toy out 83 days from now, they'll release her. Could you do it then?"

Tilly set her jaw. Michelle already knew her to be a woman of imagination and she was sure that Tilly was picturing someone threatening her precious granddaughter. Tilly pursed her lips and closed her eyes. She shook her head every few moments. Then she nodded. Then shook her head again. Followed by another nod.

Finally she spoke. "It'd be tighter than Little Orphan Annie's curls. Every single step would have to flow without a hitch." She looked out into the distance again, her milky dark eyes glazing over.

"We'd have to have buy-in at the very top," she went on after a moment. "See, we'd have to be *so* good that they'd put aside projects that had been on the books for months. I mean literally taking toys off assembly lines. Only the folks at the very top would have the authority to push something like that through."

YOUR DREAM TEAM

The all-wise Providence made us incomplete. You and your team work like a flashlight; it takes two well-charged batteries to effectively function. Teams help you manifest your greater earning power, talents, resources, connections, goals, money, and abilities. Teams make your life brighter. Teamwork leverages you financially, corporately, entrepreneurially, psychologically, spiritually, emotionally, and familially. When you have the right team you are energized, encouraged, empowered, ready and able to accomplish ever more in ever less time. Togetherness creates great strength, power, and possibility for each individual. Together everyone achieves miracles. If you have one arrow it is breakable, but bind together seven arrows and you have an unbreakable force. Greatness depends on two or more people working in harmony, though one or more of the players may be invisible. Search out people to team with you. Dreamteaming starts in one person's mind. The originator involves and enrolls another to join into the on-purpose effort. It's similar to marriage, where two join together to give 100% to the relationship; they become bonded and unstoppable. Choose to form your own group or groups. Attract to your group the best, keenest, brightest, wisest, most cooperative minds available. Pick enthusiastic people with big potential futures who want to grow, glow, discover, and be all they can become. Make sure each team member is aligned with your vision and values. Only admit new members with unanimous consent, after a 90-day probationary period. It's critical to have positive-thinking people in your group. Positive people create a "soul force" that allows each one to plug into the "Invisible Force," sometimes called God. Negative people are like holes in a balloon. How high does a balloon go with a hole in it? Make regular team meetings a life-enhancing priority. Meetings need to be upbeat, enriching, encouraging, helpfully beneficial to each member and the collective group as well. When done properly,

Tilly polished off her iced tea, letting the last drops gurgle in her straw. "Do you know how many toys they look at each year? Hasbro looks at 3,500. About 1,500 pass through for a second look. And of those, only about 10 or 15 get produced—less than 1%. From that point, it can take over a year to hit the stores. . . ." She pulled her bra straps up again, one at a time. "No." She shook her head. "I just don't see how—"

"Think of your granddaughter," Michelle blurted out.

Tilly looked straight at her, lips parted. She thought again for a few long moments. "Well, what choice would I have? Who cares what the odds are. If somebody's got my granddaughter, I guess I'd just have to figure out a way, wouldn't I?"

Michelle began to feel hope flow back into her lungs.

Tilly held up a warning index finger. "I'm not saying I'll help you. Not until I make a few phone calls. Some of my original employees are still at Hasbro. A few of them have moved up the ladder into some pretty influential positions. And of course, the CEO and I go way back." Tilly drummed her nails on the table. The purple manicure from the other day was already chipped. "I'd have to offer him something. They're real big on children's charities. Give millions each year. Are you willing to donate some of your royalties to one of Hasbro's pet projects?"

"Of course." Michelle added hastily, "We're looking for a place to tithe some of the money anyway."pp. 82, 84

Tilly nodded her head, slowly and steadily, and continued to nod as she spoke. "I've got a prototyper who owes me a favor."

Michelle watched Tilly in awe. The shrunken woman was morphing right in front of them. Tilly was sitting up straighter; she was handling her fork with more grace, and her eyes no longer looked so cloudy.

Michelle looked over at Courtney. She wondered if Courtney was appreciating the double magic, too.

"I think I've got one more winner in me," Tilly said, through a

each individual's abilities, talents, and resources exponentially expand; each life instantly improves. Dream Teams are worthwhile, important, and omniprofitable. Enlightenment is awakened awareness.

EXTRAORDINARY DREAM TEAMS

Dreamteaming occurs when two or more individuals come together in the spirit of cooperative harmony to accomplish some goal, activity, or result. Almost all of the great accomplishments and miraculous achievements of history were brought about through the power of this principle.

Jesus used Dreamteaming. He personally selected 12 men and the world has never been the same. Orville and Wilbur Wright did what was said to be impossible by building and flying the first airplane. Andrew Carnegie gathered a team around him and built the world's biggest steel manufacturing company. Carnegie went on to become one of our greatest philanthropists—funding more than 3,000 public libraries throughout the world. Likewise, Bill Gates and Paul Allen started Microsoft and became two of the richest men of all time and are now becoming two of the world's greatest living philanthropists.

Thomas Edison, the world's greatest inventor, had many partners. Edison's most famous Dream Team member was Henry Ford. When Mr. Edison's New Jersey laboratory burned to the ground, Mr. Ford arrived the next morning and handed Edison a check for $750,000 and encouraged him to "start building again." Ford would not accept interest on his loan; he just wanted his friend to get back to work.

Great success is almost always the result of Dreamteaming. *Team* is an acronym that means Together Everyone Achieves Miracles. Can you think of other great teams?

mouthful of the last bite of Monte Cristo. "And it'll be real nice to see if this old gal still has any clout in toy town."

82 Days . . .

Sam gestured toward the apartment building behind her. "Here it is. One of my first major real estate deals."

The members of the group who were working that day were standing in a tight semicircle in front of a hunter-green, two-story building. Michelle could identify the individual units from the pattern of windows: French doors leading to wrought-iron balconies, then a large window that must have been a living room or bedroom, then a small window that must have been a bathroom. The trim was white, striking against the green.

Sam laughed. "The design reminds me of New Orleans, one of my favorite places. But that's not why I bought it."

The sign above the gated entrance read "Sycamore Gardens." It was situated on a quiet boulevard a few blocks from Main Street. Shade from giant sycamore trees along the avenue blocked out the rays of the rising morning sun.

Sam continued, "Up until I bought this building, I was mainly doing little deals—single-family houses, duplexes, the like. Then, a friend in my network told me about this one. Forty units. It was way over my head. I couldn't see how I could come up with the money. So I called my mentor. . . ."

Michelle caught her breath. She couldn't imagine Sam taking advice, let alone instructions, from anyone else. She noticed that the others looked similarly surprised.

Sam picked up on this. "Yes, I had a mentor.[p. 128] Just like you will all be mentors some day." Sam straightened her caftan and continued, "Anyway, as we were grilling the Realtor®, it came out that the owner had recently been turned down on his application to convert this building from apartments into condominiums.[pp. 190, 276]

Walt Disney and his brother Roy. Helen Keller and Annie Sullivan. Michael Jordan and Phil Jackson. Lily Tomlin and Jane Wagner. Steven Spielberg and George Lucas. Jack Canfield and Mark Victor Hansen combined, activated, and accentuated each other's talent to create the phenomenally successful *Chicken Soup for the Soul* series, which has sold more than 80 million books worldwide, with 29 bestselling licensed products, including calendars, greeting cards, and games.

Your greatness lies in your ability to create an extraordinary Dream Team. Begin your team now—whether you are ready or not. Start with people you know. Search out an associate whom you trust, respect, and admire—someone who wants to work with you to accomplish great things and who has core competencies that are strong where you are weak, and vice versa. As you grow and develop, add more team members and/or form new Dream Teams.

Something magical happens when two or more people combine their single dream to form a Dream Team. List the names of the people you would like on your ideal Dream Team. Then, pare this list down to half a dozen who agree to play on your team.

_____   _____   _____

_____   _____   _____

_____   _____   _____

_____   _____   _____

_____   _____   _____

_____   _____   _____

'Aha,' said my mentor, 'Big money is always hidden behind a big rejection.'"

Sam shot a subtle smile in Michelle's direction.

"What he meant was that so many people quit digging when they're just inches from the gold vein. So we did some more research. Turns out some of the more liberal members of the city council didn't want to see some rich developer come in and make a killing on this project while depriving the city of affordable rental housing.

"Now we knew what their objection was. So together we designed a strategy."

"Who was—is—this mentor?" Michelle asked.

Sam shook her head. "Not really relevant at the moment, Butterfly. He likes to keep a low profile. But I will say that if any of you ever need to go into Denver for some serious disease, though of course I pray you don't, you might end up in a hospital wing that has his name on it."

"Real low profile," Jeremy mumbled.

Sam, if she heard (and Michelle was willing to bet that she did), ignored Jeremy's remark and went on to describe the deal. "Don't worry about taking notes. We'll go over the numbers later. Anyway, as apartments, these units were worth $25,000 apiece. But as separate condominium units, they were worth $75,000 apiece. There was a $50,000 difference in value. On 40 units, that was two million dollars, my friends. My mentor and I decided that there had to be a way to 'liberate' this profit."

The first step was to make an offer to buy the building. Sam offered full price—no dickering—but she negotiated to close the deal in 90 days. The next step was to visit every tenant in the building and make each of them an offer they couldn't refuse: She offered to let each tenant stay in his or her own unit as an owner instead of a renter. The purchase price was to be $50,000—a full $25,000 below market. Sam had already arranged for a mortgage for

AN ALIGNED TEAM

Most people's lives are a direct reflection of their peer groups.

ANTHONY ROBBINS

As mentioned earlier, there is tremendous advantage in not pursuing your goal on your own. No matter how talented you are, you cannot "synergize" on your own. An aligned team always outperforms an individual. That is why your Dream Team is so important.

However, there can be a downside when you invite people onto your team. Granted, they bring their gifts and perspectives that are key components to creating synergy. But they also bring their values.

Values are the core beliefs that rudder your life. They define the very essence of your being. These values must be aligned on your Dream Team. The team's results are meaningful only when the path to their creation is in sync with shared values. No matter how much money is made, without shared values, disruption, dysfunction, and disappointment will be the result. Failure to live your values is not a setback; it is *real* failure.

We mentioned earlier that each new member of your Dream Team needs to be on a three-month probation. During that time you can observe the new member's behavior. Does this person have the integrity, the passion, the love and commitment needed? If not, is he or she willing to change? Not everyone is going to be in touch with these values or even understand their importance. Often the context of your values clearly stated and acted upon will mold members' thinking. New team members learn and incorporate your values into their behavior. When this happens you will have very strong allies and great Dream Team members.

If a person does not embrace your core values, he or she needs to be removed. Such an action, tough as it may be, will ultimately benefit everyone. You keep the rudder of your team strong and your journey on course,

them—they were already approved. All they had to do was sign the papers. There would be no down payment. Their monthly payments would actually be less than what they had been paying for rent. Without spending a penny, these tenants would become instant owners sitting on a profit of $25,000.

Sam finished her story with a question: "If that offer were made to you, would you say yes or yes?"

"I sure wouldn't say no." Jeremy laughed out loud.

"It took three weeks to contact and convince each of these tenants how everyone could win. At the next city council meeting, the chambers were packed with people. One by one, the tenants approached the mike to voice their approval of the deal. After about 10 people had spoken, a blind gentleman was brought to the mike. He'd been living in the complex for years and knew every corner and stairwell. He said his greatest fear wasn't being forced to find a new place, even though he couldn't afford increasing rents—his greatest fear was having to learn his way around a new building. But under the proposed plan, he would become an owner. His monthly payments would be fixed for 25 years, and then he'd own it outright. He'd *never* have to move.

"The city council was faced with a dilemma. They could vote yes and convert 40 renters into very happy homeowners, tripling the tax revenue from this one property. Or they could vote no and face the wrath of 40 angry voters and their extended families. It was unanimous—they voted yes.

"With the building now approved for condominium conversion, it was worth three times my purchase price, so my bank approved a quick loan so I could pay off the seller before my 90-day deadline. Over the next two months, we completed the conversion and my mentor and I netted about a million dollars in profit."

Sam paused as a motorcycle roared past them down the street. "This was an enlightened transaction.[p. xvi] Everybody won. The tenants, the city, the bank."

and you liberate that person to find another group that is more aligned with his or her values.

We recommend you use our Enlightened Millionaire Values Survey. Please go to www.oneminutemillionaire.com and log on to the Enlightened Millionaire Values Survey and follow the instructions. It is a short but critical diagnostic instrument that reveals your values. It can also provide you with similar information on potential (or actual) team members.

CREATING YOUR DREAM TEAM

All it takes is a dream, a team, and a theme to create a stream
of perpetual income

We all have the capacity to be creative and capable. However, as mentioned earlier, with a Dream Team you create synergy, where the sum of the parts is far greater than the whole. Aligned people working together accomplish far more than anyone can working alone. With a great team you have better ideas, plans, and execution.

One method to create the best Dream Team is to use objective instruments as part of your evaluation process. A number of popular tests and profiles are available to help you. Most of them identify personality traits and recommend ways to improve your weak areas.

For your Dream Team we suggest you do the opposite. We ask you to stay just the way you are. We want to measure *you* to find your strengths and capitalize on them.

It's best to start with yourself. This allows you to determine what your work strengths are. Once you understand your strengths, then look

Sam continued, "Being an Enlightened Millionaire doesn't mean that you don't earn a profit. It just means that you try to find situations where you can help solve a problem in a win-win way."

Sam began talking about the characteristics of a person who makes "enlightened" money, asking questions and inviting comments as she went along. She elucidated for them how being en*light*ened resulted in a "lighter" kind of wealth—money earned for noble purposes—as opposed to selfish wealth, or money earned strictly for selfish purposes.

"Enlightened wealth is *honest* wealth—earned with integrity," Sam said. "It's *principled* wealth—because there are some things you won't do, no matter how much money is thrown at you. It is *added-value* wealth—money earned where both sides can win. It is *balanced* wealth—because all the wealth in the world isn't worth ruining your own family for. It is *leveraged* wealth—because when the visible and infinite networks are fully activated—when the 'light' of all of that cumulative experience and wisdom is focused on one specific task—the result always flows lighter, easier, faster. The En*light*ened Way is the *only* way to go, eagles."

Michelle felt the smugness of having learned some of this already at various sessions at the Rock, while also being humble enough to appreciate the review.

Summer asked, "I'm curious, what happened to the blind man?"

Sam pointed to one of the lower-right condo units. "He still lives right there." A number of flourishing plants crowded the balcony.

"Now, enough field trip. Let's get back to my office. I have a lot planned before lunch."

"I'm afraid I can't join you," Courtney said. "As the saying goes, who's minding the store? The store is mine and I have to get back to it. I'll catch up with you later."

Michelle felt an moment's unjustifiable hurt.

But Sam was unruffled. "We'll tape the discussion for you."

for others who have complementary abilities. This way you can hand off your "weakness work" to someone who has strength in that area.

We recommend the HOTS team process to select your Dream Team. HOTS is a short diagnostic instrument, found on our website, that reveals your strengths. It can also provide you with similar information on potential (or actual) team members. The key is to have each team member do what she or he does best and to make sure the Dream Team has strengths in each area needed for success. When this is done, you have a high-impact team that produces maximum results with minimum effort.

Please go to www.oneminutemillionaire.com and log on to the HOTS process and follow the instructions. This is a critical step in creating your Dream Team. Study this information very carefully. If you already have teammates, have them go through the HOTS process, too.

Once you discover your strengths you will know what other types of people you will need on your team. This way you will be designing your Dream Team based on objective data, based on highly reliable research. When this is done, you will know who you should ask to do specific activities. The benefits of using everyone's strengths and avoiding their weaknesses speed your ability to manifest riches.

An aligned team will always outperform an individual. We are providing you with a predictable process to do that: to have an aligned Dream Team. When this is properly done, you will be unstoppable.

By the way, if you're wondering what *HOTS* stands for, we'll show you on page 176.

"Why do you think I had you meet me at Sycamore Gardens this morning?" Sam turned to the flip chart in her conference room. She wrote the number *1* and turned to wait for her apprentices to answer.

"You wanted to show us what to look for," Jeremy answered.

Sam wrote, *Increase Awareness.*

"To show it's possible to make lot of cash in a short period of time?" Summer said.

Sam nodded and wrote, *2. Build Belief.*

"To show us how making money can be win-win," said Michelle.

Sam wrote, *3. Enlightened Wealth.*

Then she tossed the marker into the tray of the easel. "There are several ways to make quick cash in real estate. Like Sycamore Gardens, where we converted a property from one use to another. Can anyone think of another way?"

"Fixing up a property," Renee answered quickly. "My husband and I have done a few of those over the years, working weekends. He's very handy, and it's a lucky thing, because *my* salary doesn't go very far."

"It's amazing, isn't it?" Sam said. "You can put five grand into painting and a little landscaping and increase the value of the property by 20 grand or more. Are there any other ways?"

Renee was able to showcase her own real estate experience. "Property values jumped dramatically about 10 years ago when they announced the building of a new ski resort near Deer Creek. Dick and I missed that one, though."

"Yes, that can happen. Anything else?"

"So many questions," Jeremy said irritably. "Why don't you just tell us the answer?"

"Good question, Jeremy," Sam chuckled. "Why do you think?"

Michelle squared her shoulders. It was nice to see Sam put someone else on the grill for a change.

THE FOUR TYPES OF WORK

According to the wonderful research of Allen Fahden and Marie West, most project-oriented work breaks down into four categories.

Solutions Brainstorming options and ideas to solve problems and take advantage of opportunities

Strategies Picking the highest-priority ideas and making a plan of action

Analysis Figuring out what can go wrong with your solutions

Results Converting the plan of action into a concrete system. Then getting it done

Four types of workers correlate with these four types of work.

Hares Idea people who think randomly. They love to come up with ideas. They usually get bored with the idea once they've thought it through. They're creative. Others may complain that they don't have a lot of follow-through.

Owls These people love to prioritize and plan a strategy for success. When you tell them an idea, they instantly tell you the next steps to make it happen. They are go-getters who like to make connections and create action plans.

Turtles These people believe that slow and steady wins the race. They are naysayers, who are suspicious of new ideas. They believe in tradition, proven solutions, and not doing anything risky. They are good at pointing out problems and seeing around corners to know what might go wrong. They allow the team to simulate most failure at the concept stage, thus saving time and money.

Squirrels These detail-oriented people are great at step-by-step work. They think and act in a methodical, logical way. They keep

"Well?" Sam waited.

"I guess because you want us to figure it out for ourselves," Jeremy replied, a little sulkily.

"Why would I want that?" Sam asked, but this time, perhaps sensing that she had pressed up against Jeremy's limits, she answered her own question. "Because when you discover it for yourself, you get an *aha* . . . and you learn it at a deeper level."

"But it's *slower* that way," Jeremy pointed out, as if saying, Got you there.

"I call it the speed of going slow."

"Well . . . I'll mull that over for a bit."

"Let's get back to real estate, shall we?" Sam continued. "One of the most popular ways to make money in real estate is to look for bargains—foreclosures, distressed sales, and so on.[p. 274] I call that buying wholesale. A good example is this building we're in right now. I bought it three years ago. The owner was involved in several other projects and was floundering. He needed some quick cash and was willing to substantially discount the price of this building to raise the money he needed."

Sam went back to the flip chart to draw out the deal. "He had about $1,000,000 in equity. I offered him $500,000 cash and he was glad to take it. He could have lost everything. He took the money, solved his other problems, got back on his feet, and is doing very well. I still see him around town and every time I see him he thanks me. The point is I made $500,000 and doubled my money all in one day."

"Yeah, but *we* don't have that kind of cash," Jeremy objected.

Michelle winced. She had taken off her rubber band some time ago, but she remembered the pang of the snap when she heard a Yabut.[p. 32] Still, at the same time she was amused at the thought of how Sam would react.

"You don't think I used *my* cash, do you, Jeremy? Of course not. I use OPM—other people's money. That's the easy part. Finding the deal is the hard part."

things organized and running smoothly. Give them their exact steps and expectations and they perform beautifully.

You need to have at least one of each work style on your team. Most people have one predominant work style and one backup. If you have a team of only two people, you should ideally have either one Hare/Owl and one Turtle/Squirrel or one Hare/Turtle and one Owl/Squirrel. This way you will have someone who is good at each kind of work.

Your team can break down in any number of ways, as long as you have people representing each work style. Without one, you're in danger. Without two, you face disaster.

Which are you? A Hare? A Squirrel? An Owl? Or a Turtle?

PUTTING YOUR
DREAM TEAM TOGETHER

No man becomes rich unless he enriches others.

ANDREW CARNEGIE

After your team members have completed the HOTS diagnostic online, place each name in the column on page 166 that matches their dominant work style. A person may have two dominant styles. If so, list the person under both columns.

"Hmmm," Jeremy said, flipping a pencil between his index and middle fingers.

"So here's what I want you to get from this example." Sam returned to the subject. "In every market, there are distressed sellers. People who need to sell immediately. They're overextended on other payments, or they're divorcing and need to divide up the equity in their house or other properties. I call them *highly motivated* sellers.[p. 278]

"Now, in the 50-mile radius around us right now," Sam took her finger and traced a circle like a lasso above her head, "there are thousands of properties for sale. Thousands. But maybe only one in a thousand of them is owned by a highly motivated seller. Right now, I'd guess there are 10, maybe 20 incredible deals in our target territory. The trick is finding them."

"Like looking for a needle in a haystack," said Summer, sounding very proud of her analogy.

"Exactly. Plus, other investors are looking for the same needle, so 'you snooze, you lose.'"

"I'm uncomfortable with this," Michelle began tentatively. "It doesn't seem very enlightened to look for people with problems and take advantage of them."

"That's what happened to my mother when my father died," Summer said, sounding less cheerful than she had a moment ago.

"Give us the details, then," Sam suggested.

"She couldn't afford the house payments, so she put an ad in the paper to sell the house. Somebody offered her some cash so she could walk away. Mom thought she should get more so she turned him down. But two months later, she still hadn't sold it and was two months behind in her payments."

"So what happened?"

"Someone came along and offered Mom even less, and this time, she took it. At the time she was happy to get rid of the house. She says, looking back, she should have taken the first offer. Mom would have netted a lot more money and saved herself two months of grief."

SELECT A MIX OF HOTS FOR YOUR DREAM TEAM

Hares	**Owls**	**Turtles**	**Squirrels**
Idea Makers	Strategists	Analyzers	Detail Workers
_____	_____	_____	_____
_____	_____	_____	_____
_____	_____	_____	_____
_____	_____	_____	_____

If any of these work styles are missing on your Dream Team, they need to be filled.

If you only have Idea Hares and Strategy Owls, then your team will have lots of ideas and no follow-through. Have you ever been on a team where there is a lot of enthusiasm for new ideas, and people even begin to work on them, then nothing happens? These teams need Turtles to slow them down in order to make a reasonable plan. They also need Squirrels to efficiently fulfill the plan.

A team of Analysis Turtles and Detail Squirrels can run a good system, yet they will lack the innovative ideas or products to move forward.

If you only have Idea Hares and Analysis Turtles, you have two sides engaging in endless debate. Turtles think Hares are out of control, with harebrained ideas. Hares feel like Turtles are just critical jerks. The Turtles will constantly overrule the Hares' ideas. While working together, they will feel frustrated, morale will suffer, and little action will take place.

One particularly creative Hare became vice president of an advertising agency that had a few Hares, many Turtles, and only one Owl. The company was having difficulty instigating fresh campaigns and attracting new business. The vice president brought in outside Owls to work on projects.

Sam picked up the thread. "If my drain gets clogged, I hire a plumber. If I get sued, I hire an attorney. If my appendix bursts, I hire a doctor. These professionals get paid to solve my problems. You get paid to solve real estate problems. Therefore, you look for people who have problems. Just remember to be fair, and you'll be all right. Do you all think I was fair with the condo conversion?

"To summarize, then, keep your eye out for situations that contain the seeds of quick profit.[p. 274] At this point, I just need you to be bird dogs. Bring me the leads, and I'll show you how to turn them into money. If you're diligent, I'm confident we can uncover one or two deals we can flip for a nice chunk of cash."

She held the marker up in the air. "What makes it a little tougher, of course, is that we don't have a lot of time."

81 Days . . .

Ringggggg.

A phone was ringing somewhere. Awakening from an exhausted sleep, Michelle groped to find the receiver.

Ringggggg.

She squinted at the cheap clock on the nightstand. Six-thirty A.M. Ordinarily, Michelle and Sam would have been up before this, standing on the point shouting out their Manifestations.

Ringggggg.

But Sam had stayed over in Denver and Michelle had decided to play hooky from the early class of "millionaire school" this morning.

Riii—Michelle caught the phone just as it was ringing for the fourth time. "Hello," she said in her throaty, just-awake voice.

"Hello. Michelle? Can you hear me? Hello." It was Tilly.

"Hi, Tilly. You're up early this morning." *And on my one day to sleep in—maybe forget the stress for an extra hour.* Michelle rubbed her face with her free hand.

"Early bird gets the worm," Tilly chirped.

The company's revenue went from $7,000,000 to $29,700,000 to $44,000,000 in successive years.

Having a balanced team is an essential step on the journey of the One Minute Millionaire.

DREAM TEAM SPEED

So now that you have this fabulous team, what do you do to optimize it? You delegate the work that they don't do well.

You may think this is impossible. "Won't someone get stuck with all the dirty work?" you might ask. No, because every member of your balanced HOTS team likes work that someone else on the team doesn't like.

For example: What about those expense reports the Hare never turns in? The Squirrel gets a sense of accomplishment from filling in those neat little columns and having it all balance. And what about the sales meetings that paralyze the Squirrel? Your Owl loves doing this activity.

There is no dirty work, just the wrong person doing the wrong work. So it's time for a work swap. Everyone delegates his or her "dirty work" to someone else who loves it. This is win/win at its best. This can triple what gets done, because what we hate to do bores us, and what bores us slows us down. Speed is the new currency of business. Here is how you dramatically increase your team's speed:

1. Have all team members list all their daily basics.
2. Label each task Hare, Owl, Turtle, or Squirrel by putting an *H*, *O*, *T*, or *S* next to each one.

But the second mouse gets the cheese. "What's happening?" Michelle sat up and gathered the blanket around her. It was the middle of September and the nights were getting colder.

"You know, folks my age are usually up early. That's not a problem. The problem is that I hardly slept all night. Couldn't get the image of those kidnappers out of my mind. Thanks to you, dear. Anyway, I thought you'd like to know what I did yesterday. Called that prototyper I told you about. Joanie."

Michelle shifted the receiver to the other ear. Her heart quickened.

"I told her what I wanted and she's dropping everything to make something for me. We brainstormed some clever ideas. She's going to make three models, two designs for girls, one for boys. She'll have them overnighted. We'll have the prototypes in record time—the day after tomorrow."

"Oh, Tilly." Michelle was fully awake now, her face flushed. "Thank you *so* much!"

"Never you mind, it's just the first step. We're a long way from a yes. I also put in a call with some of my contacts on the inside at Hasbro. Haven't heard back yet, but I expect it won't be long. I'll get back to you when I hear something."

Michelle flashed on the Plan A/Plan B session in the conference room a few days earlier. "Say, Tilly. What's our Plan B? What if Hasbro or the other big company doesn't take it?"

There was silence at the other end.

"Tilly?"

Tilly had already hung up.

Michelle got up and jumped into her jogging suit. Within 20 minutes she was at the Rock shouting out the Manifestation for that day:

"I am a money magnet! I like money and MONEY LIKES ME!"[p. 120]

3. Take all the labeled tasks that are not part of your profile and trade them with the appropriate someone whose HOTS profile (not their job description) matches the label you've given the task.
4. Continue this trading process until the tasks of your job match your personal profile.

How far off the profiles were from the tasks demanded determines the gains in productivity.

Doing tasks this way will allow everyone to work faster and be happier and, in the long run, become richer.

THE SPEED MEETING: HOW TO GET MAXIMUM BENEFITS FROM YOUR TEAM

Most people hate meetings. They find them unproductive and frustrating. At the end of a meeting people often complain they feel tired and defeated, certain no action will result. Every great idea is born drowning. This means that the best ideas have plenty of things wrong with them. This doesn't mean they should be dismissed. Yet in most meetings or collaborations, an idea with anything wrong with it gets shot down as unworkable. Just as it is born, someone else, often a Turtle, points out its faults and it dies.

An idea must have time to grow, to be supported. Then, when its time has come, it can be selected and perfected. This means that those cautious, risk-averse Turtles get to express their concerns. And the nimble-minded Hares in turn get to come up with solutions that will fix the problems and make the idea stronger than ever.

When she arrived in Sam's conference room, there were only two people there: Jeremy and Summer. They were sitting side by side operating two different computers. The glow from the screens reflected off their intent faces.

"How's it going?" Michelle asked.

"Oh, hi, Michelle," Jeremy responded, after a shake of the head that indicated that his concentration had been broken. "Summer and I have made some incredible progress."

Jeremy got up from his computer and went to the head of the room, where a large flip chart displayed a neat headline in bold red letters:

LOOKING FOR ADDICTS P. 326

"It's no secret that I'm a recovering gambling addict. Anyway, this might sound a little sick, but I remember what it was like to be addicted. It started with day trading. I was hooked on getting all the information I could get—about the markets, about new trading systems, about a hot stock tip. I was a scavenger shark feeding my jones for information. I bought books, seminars, newsletters. Dropping $25, $50, $100 was nothing to me. I devoured three or four books in a week, looking for just that one tidbit that would be my fix for a few hours. Then it would start all over again. I was *insatiable*. Do you know what I mean?"

Michelle looked a little worried that this process had triggered a relapse into his addiction. Jeremy seemed to read her thoughts.

"No, don't worry. I'm okay. Thank God for 12-Step programs. But I should have been able to learn something from my experience. Anyway, it just dawned on me, 'Aha! Everybody is addicted to *something*.' Everybody. Think of it: golfers, bridge players, doll collectors, fitness nuts, racing fans, movie buffs, TV couch potatoes. We're a nation of addicts."

"Okay," Michelle said. "We get the cultural commentary."

"So, I'm thinking that when it comes to the Internet, we need to

The secret is in timing. There is a time to create, to imagine, and to dream. Initially, ideas should get nothing but support. Only after that has happened should the naysayers have a chance to bring in their fears and foreboding. This way your Dream Team can support its own brilliance, instead of talking itself out of it.

1. **Conduct a Positive Brainstorming Session.** Everyone involved in the project gets to play. Except for the Owl, the whole group spends 10 minutes writing down all of their ideas for solving the problem, helping the client, or whatever the task. Next, every person in the group shares all the ideas on his or her list. No one is allowed to say a negative or judgmental thing at this time. Participants can only make statements that support or further the idea.

2. **Determining the Process.** Once the list is complete everyone leaves the room except the Owl. The Owl has a special instinct for priorities and what will practically work. Owls recognize brilliance. They have an innate ability to see the gems in different ideas and combine them into something even greater. The Owl selects those ideas that have the most potential and promise. The other ideas are collected and put in an idea bank for future brainstorming.

3. **Identify the Drawbacks.** The Turtles join the Owl (without the Hares or Squirrels present) and are asked to use their strengths to blow holes in the idea. You give Turtles their greatest dream by asking, "Tell me everything that could go wrong with this idea." Usually no one welcomes their well-intentioned warnings of doom. Turtles share with the Owl every problem they have with the idea. Then they leave.

4. **Problem Solve.** Now the Hares come back into the room to join the Owl. They are asked to solve these problems. This step is repeated as many times as necessary for the Hares to satisfactorily solve what the Owl agrees are all the major problems with the idea.

For a more detailed description on how to run a HOTS meeting, log on to Speed Meeting at the OMM website.

find the addicts. People who are insatiable for their particular kind of information. If we want leverage, we have to find people who will buy without thinking or stewing or weighing the pros and cons or consulting with their partners. Addicts—like me—buy quickly and more often, and they talk to other addicts."

"I have to admit that I'm uncomfortable with the addict analogy," Michelle said.

"Well, I can see why. . . ." Jeremy frowned, then brightened. "How about 'passionate people'?"

Summer had been listening to the conversation, having swiveled her chair away from her computer screen. Now she put in, "I'm that way about shoes."

"I guess I was that way about quilting," Michelle said, feeling better about the whole concept. "Not quite to the extent you describe," she added, "but if I saw a quilt book in a store, I'd grab it—even if it was 50 bucks. Otherwise, I'd *never* spend that kind of money on a book."

"That's what we're looking for," Jeremy said. "We need whole groups of these kinds of people, and the information they're hooked on. And here's what Summer and I are finding . . . there are hundreds of online groups like these, like quilters or scrapbookers or wine lovers. The Internet has made it possible for people to connect on a whole new level—which means that *we* can connect with them, too." He held a fist up for emphasis.

Jeremy's fever-pitch excitement made Michelle uneasy. But was it any different from her own crazy scheme to market and get rich on a new toy in three months? Michelle looked over at Summer, trying to get a read on her reaction. But Summer had just put a stick of gum in her mouth and was chewing absently, with a contented if spacey stare in Jeremy's general direction. No feedback there.

Michelle asked, "Why is that so different from the way business is done every day?"

THE FOURTH MANIFESTATION

"I attract my Dream Team."

T

TOGETHER

To become super successful, I attract the perfect Dream Team.
With the right dream and the right team,
I know I can accomplish miracles.

E

EVERYONE

I know where I'm weak and where I'm unique.
I attract people who are unique where I am weak.
My Dream Team is composed of individuals
who are dedicated to the same goals.
We are like-minded. We respect, depend on,
and trust one another.

A

ACCOMPLISHES

My Dream Team has access to all
the resources we need: the capital, the
information, the markets,
the insights, and the contacts.
We work together seamlessly
with effortless effort.

M

MIRACLES

I am supported.
I feel supported from the top down and inside out.
Because I positively and correctly support myself and others,
all others lovingly, correctly, and completely support me.
My life works. It's full of miracles.
I am a reverse paranoid: I expect everyone to benefit me.
I savor my relationships, friendships, and family.
I just keep getting better all the time.

"Because"—Jeremy impatiently raked his fingers through his hair—"most businesses create a product first and then go looking for addicts. We go find the addicts first and then create the product. Why? Because if our LIFE depends on it and we only have 90 DAYS, we don't have time to guess what they want. We need to have this product work the first time out of the gate.

"So, using that as a guideline, Summer and I brainstormed lists of the most highly addictive *positive* activities that people get hooked on." He directed a look at Summer, who was now twirling a lock of blond hair. "Summer." This second, sharper mention of her name got her attention and she sat up straighter. Then Jeremy turned the page of the first flip chart to reveal their list:[p. 334]

Exercise	Dieting	Money
Golf	Hobbies	Games
Sports	Pregnancy facts	Coffee
Collectibles	Spiritual needs	
Food	Chocolate	

"There are thousands of groups with anywhere from 10 members to a few million members. People wanting to discuss the nature of God and people who want to build better bomb shelters for the end of the world."

Summer giggled. "My favorite was a chocolate group called Addicted to Chocolate. Their motto was, *'After I'm dead, I don't want to be wishing that I'd eaten more chocolate.'*"

Jeremy rapped his hand on the flip chart. "But we don't want to sell products to these people. We want to sell information. It's cheaper. It's faster. It can be digitized. And wait for the best part. We can have all this information for free."

"How so?" Michelle asked.

"The Internet is full of information that is available to anyone who wants to use it. Like public domain stuff. So we can create it,

THE WIN/WIN REAL ESTATE COMPANY

Marshall Thurber came to San Francisco in the late sixties to attend law school. He was immediately taken with the classic beauty of the city's Victorian buildings.

While still in law school, Marshall borrowed $10,000 from his grandmother and purchased his first run-down Victorian in the Haight Ashbury district. Taking his cue from the free spirits in the neighborhood, he transformed the exterior by using bright, high-contrasting colors. Immediately he sold it for a large profit.

Suddenly it hit him: Why not make San Francisco more beautiful by transforming its Victorians into "painted ladies"? Being a dreamer, Marshall knew he couldn't do this alone; he needed a Dream Team. He found the perfect pair in Rob Cassil and Bill Raymond. United in vision and mission, the three formed Hawthorne/Stone Real Estate and Investments.

In the next three years they transformed over a hundred buildings. The purchase criteria were always the same: If they couldn't add value immediately, they didn't buy.

One project was a 287-unit apartment building in Ventura, California. By buying the complex as apartments and converting them into condominiums, they were able to sell each unit to the tenants at substantially below market value. Initially, the conversion application was rejected by the city's planning department. Upon appeal, however, that decision was unanimously overturned by the city's board of supervisors because hundreds of "tenants" attended the hearing demanding the right to transform themselves from renters to condominium owners.

The tenants bought their units at far below market value (win), the city got an increase in its tax base (win), the salesperson who found the project got part of the increased value (win), and the Hawthorne/Stone partners turned a $100,000 investment into $3,000,000 in 90 days!

market it, and deliver it for free, which gives us . . ." He turned toward the two women with arms outstretched and took a bow. "A 99% profit margin."

Michelle sucked in a deep breath. It was still sounding a little off-the-wall—but certainly seductive. "It's important that we deliver positive, helpful information."

"I'm with you all the way on that," Jeremy insisted.

He went on to explain the practical details of his approach. A couple of weeks both to identify the groups and to forge relationships with the owners of the lists. Then another couple of weeks to research the market: to discover what information was needed; how much were people willing to pay? How would they pay? How quickly did they need it? What format did they prefer to receive it in? After that, he figured, about 30 days to create "an irresistible bundle of stuff."

Jeremy panted melodramatically, waving his hand in front of his face in a caricature of someone trying to revive someone—in this case, himself—from a faint. "You can see I'm pretty optimistic. Michelle, I'm sorry I've been hogging all this. How's your toy project coming along?"

"That's what we all want to know!"

It was Sam, just in from Denver, coming through the doorway, in a stunning saffron-and-amber-patterned African robe. By this time Michelle had perched on the edge of the conference table and was swinging her legs. She certainly did not want to lie, but at the moment her intuition was telling her not to launch into a long and hyper speech. Everyone already knew about Tilly's background, and about her interest in Michelle's initial idea, so Michelle merely added that they had persuaded Tilly to join them, but success was still a long way off.

As Michelle was concluding, Renee came hustling in. "Whew! Have I missed much? I took a day off from school, but I've spent all of it so far in the field." She was as worked up as everyone else.

ONE MINUTE REVIEW OF DREAM TEAMS

1. **You need a team to obtain your dream.** Success is not a solo project.
2. **Synergy is combining one plus one and getting eleven.** The synergy of a team gives you maximum leverage.
3. **Values are the core beliefs that *rudder* your life.** No matter how much money is made, without shared values, disruption, dysfunction, and disappointment will be the result. Failure to live your values is not a setback; it is a *real* failure.
4. **Take the Enlightened Millionaire Values Survey.** Go to **www. oneminutemillionaire.com** and discover your core values.
5. **Each new member of your Dream Team must be on three-month probation.** If a team member doesn't share your core values, he or she needs to be removed.
6. **Determine what your natural strengths are.** Then look for others who have complementary abilities. This way you can hand off your "weakness work" to someone who has strength in that area.
7. **Determine if you are a Hare, an Owl, a Turtle, or a Squirrel.** Go to **www.oneminutemillionaire.com** and take the HOTS Survey to determine your natural strengths. This is a critical step in creating your Dream Team.
8. **There is no dirty work, just the wrong person doing the wrong work.** Approach each team task with the HOTS Survey results in mind.
9. **Every great idea is born drowning.** Initially, all ideas should be supported. After that has happened the naysayers are given a chance to express their fears and foreboding. This way your Dream Team supports its brilliance rather than talking itself out of it. Conduct Speed Meetings for maximum results.

"Have I got a lot to tell!" Courtney came in just a few seconds behind her—she had hired some extra help for the store to give herself more time for their million-dollar project.

Sam took a chair at the table next to Michelle. "Well, my little eaglets, sounds like it's very busy in the nest."

She gestured for them to gather around the conference room table. "My assistant, Stephanie, will be bringing in some truly fine Cajun food that Mama eagle brought back from a new Cajun restaurant in Denver. I figured you deserved a little treat. Before I share my own news, I'd like to get a progress report from each pair. Who wants to go first?"

Jeremy, still hyped up, raised his hand and then began to explain to Sam and Renee what he and Summer had been working on. Sam seemed pleased but reined him in after a while. Then she turned to Michelle and Courtney.

Now Michelle knew that the time was right. She let Courtney describe in her dispassionate way the lunch with Tilly. Then Michelle joyfully told them all about her early morning phone call and about the prototypes that were on the way.

There were "wow"s all around. Except for the key "wow." Michelle anxiously watched Sam's impassive face.

"Michelle," Sam spoke after a moment. "I have to admit that I've gotten a little concerned about this toy project. These major companies move like molasses on frame-by-frame advance. I'd hate to spend precious time on something that might not pan out."

Was this a test of her commitment? Michelle rapped her fingers nervously on the table's edge. "Well, you're the one who taught us about the Infinite Network.[p. 216] We've been sending out signals, and these people started showing up. What are the odds that I'd happen to bump into someone with so much experience and so many contacts in the toy business?"

Sam still looked skeptical.

"Okay, so she sold her business 10 years ago," Michelle admitted.

NETWORKS

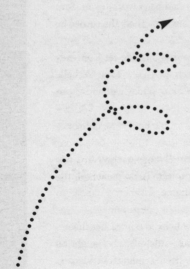

"But she was consulting with companies all over the world up until last year. I know the time is tight and the probabilities are really small, but I just have a feeling that something's gonna happen here. I just feel it"—she tapped the left side of her chest—"right here."

Sam's face relaxed. "All right. But as you're working with Tilly and her contacts, I want you to really, really tune in to any other possibilities that might create some quick cash. What I've discovered with hunches is that often the thing I thought was supposed to happen didn't, but in the process of pursuing the lead that I thought I was supposed to pursue, another opportunity revealed itself. *That* was the lead I was *destined* to follow . . . a path that was perpendicular to the path I was pursuing. Hunches aren't logical. One thing leads to another totally unrelated contact who leads you to another offbeat opportunity that happens to be owned by the brother-in-law of the person you eventually end up with.

"You've already got the explanation: the Infinite Network. It knows what you need and is using the six degrees of separation to nudge you in the right direction. You may end up with the *result* you imagined, just not *in the way* you imagined. As long as you get there, it shouldn't matter which route you take, right?" Sam paused. "What I'm saying is that *my* hunch is a little different from your hunch, but maybe we both need to go with that Infinite Network. Just remember that it's often down these side passages where the gold is hidden. Does that make sense?"

Michelle nodded slowly, just as Stephanie, a tall, sturdy woman, pushed the conference room door open with a cart laden with an aromatic mix of red beans, rice, blackened redfish, and crabcakes.

The whole group descended gratefully on the food. Michelle was ravenous and for a few moments thought of nothing but those first few bites, which she had to stop herself from cramming into her mouth. But even their shared hunger did not distract the group from the business at hand.

Renee spoke through a mouthful of rice. "Sam, that thing you

THE POWERFUL LEVERAGE
IN A NETWORK

Since a relationship involves two members investing in it,
its value increases twice as fast as one's investment.
KEVIN KELLY, *NEW RULES FOR THE NEW ECONOMY*

Your network of relationships increases your leverage. The more connections you have, the more leverage you possess.

Whatever the investment made by two people in a relationship, there is stickiness to it. This is because ending the relationship means both parties lose not only what they put into the relationship but also lose what the other person put into it.

One principle for extending your network lever is "weak ties." Most people intuitively feel it is their close friendships and strong ties that are most important. In fact, in most cases it is just the opposite. Your *weak* ties are more important.

For example, when you are seeking new information, you'll soon discover that you have a lot in common with your close relations. These people have enjoyed a lot of the same experiences and share similar viewpoints with you and with one another. Most information they possess you are likely to already know. Your weak ties, by the very fact that they are weak in nature, occupy a different world than you. They are much more likely to know something unknown to you or your close friends. Cultivating a network of weak, or loose, ties is an enormous advantage to you, particularly since we live in an information economy.

Malcolm Gladwell, in his book *The Tipping Point*, writes about "Connectors." These are people who know an extraordinary number of people. Connectors are masters of the weak tie. They possess a curiosity,

were talking about, that's exactly what happened yesterday for me. I just dove into the multiple listings at the real estate office that I have my license with. I'm a bit rusty since I haven't used that license in about two years, but then I started getting my legs back. There was another agent there, an old friend, Brendan, who helped."

"And who just happened to be there," Jeremy said, wiggling his eyebrows, Groucho-style, and clearly about to add, "Woo-woo."

Renee had bent over and now slung her briefcase on the table just beyond her paper plate. She flipped open the briefcase and pulled out several file folders. "Sam, I did several passes through the listings. I eliminated all of the houses priced above a million—those properties don't sell as quickly, because there are fewer people chasing fewer properties."

She was speaking too fast for Michelle to absorb all the details, but Renee was as unstoppable as a bullet.

"I screened what was left over to give me just the properties that had low mortgage balances where the seller had a lot of equity. That gave me 155 properties to look at. Then I read through every one of those to find any hints that the seller might be flexible."

"Words like . . . ," Sam prompted, very much in teacher mode.

Renee rattled her file folders. "Words such as *transferred, must sell, seller might consider a trade, owner might be willing to carry some financing.*"

Sam nodded.

"Okay, so there weren't many clues there, but 10 of them indicated some flexibility. Then last night I tried to reach the agents representing each of these sellers. I figured if the agent was willing to indicate some flexibility on the listing form, that was more a mind-set of the agent than the seller. I figured that the most creative agents in the area would have their fingers on the pulse of some of the most motivated sellers."

"And what did you discover?" Sam asked.

"Well, I only reached four of them. I left messages with the

self-confidence, sociability, and energy that make them powerhouses in creating large networks. Their special gift is bringing the world together.

In the late 1960s Stanley Milgram did a wonderful experiment to determine how closely humans are connected and linked together. Out of his experiment emerged the general concept of six degrees of separation. This means that all of us, through our social networks, are within five or six connections to anyone on the planet.

Most people do not instinctively cultivate "weak-tie" relationships. However, to make large sums of money quickly you need to hone this skill. You must master the strength of the weak tie.

Remember: The bigger your network, the more leverage you have.

NETWORK YOUR WAY RICH!

You can network your way to riches. Every rich person who has gone before you has built a million-dollar Rolodex and you can, too. Networkers develop and nurture contacts for information, support, advice, referrals, and resource utilization as well as to reach out and connect with whomever they want, whenever they want.

To make vast sums of money fast you need to have relationships with those who generate successful results fast, competently, and consistently. When Lee Iaccoca became chairman of the essentially bankrupt Chrysler Corporation, he brought with him a list of 200 individuals whom he had kept track of in the auto industry. Lee knew whom to call to get Chrysler back on the fast track again. His Rolodex was the key to achieving superlative results immediately. Like Lee, you can start to build a Rolodex to grow rich in your niche.

Each industry has only a handful of superstars. You need to study them—read their books, listen to their speeches, watch their videos—

other six. But what I found was very exciting. I told each of them exactly what I was looking for—properties I could flip for quick cash in 90 days or less. Turns out that my hunch was right . . . none of the properties that I earmarked from the listing service would fit into our narrow parameters. But one of the Realtors® thinks he has a client who is willing to substantially discount his price if we can cash him out quickly."

Jeremy, who had been concentrating on his food, looked up at the mention of the word *cash*. "Sam, I'm glad we have this division of labor, because I'm not tracking a lot of this. But there's one word I've always understood pretty well, and that's *cash*. Can you *share* with me where all of this cash that *we're* supposed to come up with is coming from? If anybody were to look at my finances, they'd run the other way."

"That's a common assumption of beginning investors," Sam pointed out. "They think that they will be using their own cash, their own credit. . . ."

"If anybody looks at my credit, the deal is DOA," Jeremy reiterated.

"Mine, too," Michelle mirrored him. *As if everyone doesn't know already.*

"It's just that attitude," continued Sam, "that keeps people from buying real estate. As I was trying to teach you, before I was interrupted"—quick glances at the offending parties—"imagine what it would be like to have a credit line of $10,000,000 in cash . . ." Now she looked directly at Jeremy. ". . . that you could use to buy as much wholesale real estate as you can find. How confident would you be in your negotiations?"

"It'd make me feel, oh . . . maybe a *little* more confident." Jeremy's sarcasm indicated that it would in fact make him feel extremely confident.

"That's the point. Right now, when you try to negotiate, your posture is weak. You feel dishonest. You know you don't have the wherewithal to afford the property—no credit, no cash, no steady

befriend them, and be close to them to be part of the action. You can meet them at national trade association meetings. Offer to do some task or assignment that they need done. Outperform yourself and show your stuff. Every current superstar apprenticed eagerly to some industry giant. It's your objective to match and surpass their greatness. While you are apprenticing, collect the names, addresses, and phone numbers of all the people you meet.

Make yourself eminently likable. Develop an above-average handshake, a magnetic eye contact, and a radiant presence. Choose to serve greatly for the sake of serving. Help everyone whom you can help. Always go the extra mile and put the Universe in your debt. Create relationships, the hinges of which never rust, but get deeper and more meaningful over time. Stay in touch personally, by phone and fax. Have outings, parties, events, or seminars to which you remember to invite your clients and friends. Mark annually renews his marriage vows with his wife of over 20 years. They invite 500 friends, relatives, and clients to an unforgettable wedding theme party every year.

Cavett Robert, the dean of American speakers, said: "You have to make contacts to get contracts." You are the center of your network. Your network creates your net worth, because at some level all business is done through people. You will see the truth of this in every biography and autobiography that you study. As you build a superb network, your MQ (Motivation Quotient) goes up, because you're constantly inspired and excited to be an insider's insider.

Create a list of the 200 people you want to meet, study, grow with, talk to, spend time with, and imitate until you can emulate, match, and surpass. You will be astounded how fast you synchronize in time and space with these folks. You will automatically become part of the *Who's Who* by association. In networking, it's who you know, who they know, and also, who knows you. Choose to make yourself well known. Get a reputation that everyone likes, trusts, respects, and admires you. You are here to make a significant contribution and you can do so more easily with a strong and well-established network. Start at once whether you are ready or not.

income stream. You know that when it gets time to qualify for a bank loan, you'll be discovered. And all of these thoughts are being broadcast subliminally through your body language, your posture, your words, your eyes. You're a walking billboard screaming, 'I'm a deadbeat!' Jeremy, before you make an offer, you've got to be confident. *Confidence* is like having the cash in the bank. So where do you find this cash? It's all around you, right now. Billions of dollars sitting in other people's bank accounts just itching to be put to work at higher than the measly 3% or 4% they're earning. That's how I do my deals, Jeremy. I don't use my money. I don't use my credit. I use other people's money. That's leverage."p. 112

"Great." Jeremy's sarcasm remained. "Where do we find all these people who are going to be falling all over people like us, wanting to give us all this cash?"

"I'm not going to tell you right now. But once one of you finds me a deal worth shouting about, believe me, the cash is just a phone call away."

"I'm sure interested in *that* phone number," Jeremy commented.

Michelle wondered, did Jeremy think that Sam was making this up to keep them working? A nonexistent carrot to be followed by an all-too-real stick? *Do I think that myself?*

"Here's the formula," Sam continued. "'Find it, Fund it, Flip it.'p. 278 First you find the great deal. Then, you find the money to fund it. And finally, you flip it for a profit."

Renee reentered the conversation. "Well, I think I'm close to finding the first part of the equation. My Realtor®, Brendan, is a whiz, and he knows exactly what I'm looking for. He's beating the bushes for me, right now."

It was harder *not* to believe in an Infinite Network, Michelle reflected, hearing how these pieces were fitting together.

"In my mind," Sam said, "we've got about 30 to 45 days to beat the bushes, as you say, to flush out several potential real estate deals. That will leave us about six weeks to flip them. It'll be close,

NETWORKS OF NETWORKS

Someday this will be true for all of us:
Our network will equal our networth.

TIM SANDERS

A traditional way to grow your social network is one person at a time. This, however, is very slow. In a networked world, those who "network the networks" gain the most leverage. They affiliate with larger social networks.

These network affiliations provide loose affiliations similar to the "weak ties." There are a myriad of existing networks, and their web of connections is huge.

What are your interests and experiences? Inventory the topics you can intelligently talk about. Once you have this, search for networks that relate to your list. Go beyond the obvious professional networks. Search engines on the Internet offer an efficient way to look for these networks. Typing in key words related to your interests/experiences will turn up networks you never knew existed.

As an experiment, go to your favorite search engine and type in the five letters *LOHAS*. See what you find. (Hint: *LOHAS* is an acronym for Lifestyles of Health and Sustainability.) Did you know there was a growing network related to this? This network is a large, rapidly growing market in the United States and an even larger one in Europe, made up of consumers who make their buying decisions based on their values of environmental and social justice issues. Do you have any connection to those who affiliate with this network? Would it be useful to affiliate with it? These are the networking questions you need to continually ask. These "weak-tie networks" become enormously useful in terms of access to people and information normally outside of your close networks.

but we should find at least one or two, maximum three, deals to flip . . . at $50,000 to $100,000 each, it'll add to the old stew pot."

"Do you really believe that we can make as much as a quarter of a million dollars in 90 days?" Summer asked, breathlessly.

"Ordinarily, no," Sam answered. "Most people don't pursue their dreams as if their life depended on it or"—she shot a glance at Michelle—"as if the lives of their children depended on it. Most people have a 'let's-try-this-let's-dabble-in-that' attitude. They're ready to pull the plug at any hint of trouble—not to mention to blame bad luck or other people if they don't make it. I got into this to help Michelle, but the truth is that I've lived my whole life as if my life depended on it, because my life does depend on it." She grinned. "If you follow."

Michelle pushed her plate away. She'd eaten her fill.

Apparently Sam had, too. She stood and flipped another page on another chart. Then she wrote in big red letters:

A deadline
A consequence
No other options

"Michelle has a deadline, a consequence, and no other options. These are the kinds of situations where you can no longer count on yourself . . . you have to bring in other forces to help you. Why are we so willing to help her right now? Because she doesn't have any choice. This brings out the best in people. Not everyone will rally around you, but the right people will. They'll join the team because you're playing a big game."

"Sam," Jeremy interrupted. "You said you had some news for us about something."

"Yes, I do. The rest of you put your forks down, because I need your full attention."

Sam gave them the background. She had called her friend at the

One way to strengthen your weak-tie networks is to give something away for free that is valuable to network members. "Givers Gain" is the networking motto. It brings attention to you and it builds trust. Do not expect reciprocity. Those who are excellent network builders don't expect a specific return. The return is name recognition and trust. With recognition and trust in place, you can mine the network when needed.

Two excellent books to read about how to build and maintain a powerful network are *Networking with Millionaires*, by Thomas J. Stanley, and *Love Is the Killer App: How to Win Business and Influence Friends*, by Tim Sanders.

Once you have created a network, do whatever it takes to maintain it. The Golden Rule of Networking is: "Be very quick to build connections and extremely slow to break them."

YOUR MILLION-DOLLAR ROLODEX

Metcalf's Law: The value of a network grows in proportion to the square of the number of users.

Where are your acres of diamonds? Certainly you will find them hidden all around you—in your own talents, skills, and opportunities. You'll also find them right in your own Rolodex. That's why we call it your million-dollar Rolodex.

The average person knows at least 250 people. Remember, each of these 250 people also lives in the middle of his or her own acres of diamonds. Then, each of these 250 people also knows another 250 people. So instantly, you have access to 62,500 people (250 × 250) who also are living in the middle of their own acres of diamonds!

planning commission, who was not an elected official but a county employee. The plans for all the major projects that were being developed came through his office before they went on to the county commissioners for final approval. There was a vote scheduled on a major new shopping mall.

"Some of this has already been reported in the papers, but my friend tells me that even though there has been a lot of political pressure on the commission to turn it down, he has heard the scuttlebutt that it will probably pass. If it does, there is going to be a massive amount of activity surrounding that part of town. Lots of construction. It's going to affect property values in a major way. All residential properties on the streets adjoining the mall will now be ripe for conversion to office space. Up to now, there was no reason for commercial zoning, but now, with commercial zoning across the street, there will be a lot of conversion possibilities.

"Let me give you a quick example. Suppose a 1,000-square-foot apartment is renting for $1,000 a month. As a small office space, the same area will rent for between $2,000 and $3,000 a month. That effectively doubles or even triples the value of the property. Although there has already been some speculation in property values there, I just feel that there will be some sleeper deals available if we focus on that target territory. So, Michelle, while you're waiting for the next call from Tilly, I want you to go down to the courthouse and get copies of the plat maps in the 10-square-block area around the proposed area for the mall. Bring 'em back here, tape them together, and put them up on the wall." Sam pointed to a place where some Monet reproductions hung. "I'll have my staff pull this artwork down and you can tape up the maps. Then I want you to systematically contact every owner of any property. Go knocking on doors if you have to. Most owners will be aware of the rezoning issue and will ask for top dollar for their properties. I want us to find the four or five properties out of a thousand in this area that are owned by people who have a need to sell at a lower price."

The possibilities are endless. That is why it is so important to build *and* nurture your million-dollar Rolodex. Here's how.

First, set a goal to build your Rolodex, working on it weekly, if not daily. Add at least one name a day of someone you want to work with, grow with, and get rich with. Your goal is to have multiple contacts in multiple fields.

- ▲ Stay in touch at least twice a year by e-mail blast, phone call, letter, or face-to-face.
- ▲ Rate each person in your Rolodex with a letter from A to D.
- ▲ A's are those with the largest databases and the greatest potential for opportunity.
- ▲ Spend the most time cultivating your relationships with A's.
- ▲ Narrow your list to your 100 "Eagles"—your "A" list of top contacts.

Your Rolodex is where all of the money is . . . because it forms the beginning of your business database. One of the highest forms of marketing leverage is to contact the owner of a large database and have him or her agree to endorse your product or service to the entire database. The fastest way to market a product is to focus exclusively on the owners of databases (networks of networks), as opposed to building your own customer list.

The person with the largest network of Rolodexes wins.

Michelle nodded her agreement, although she wondered exactly how she would do it.

"Now, listen up, eagles," Sam continued. "Things are going to start to get chaotic as we put out more and more feelers through our networks[p. 194] looking for highly motivated sellers.[p. 278] Renee has already got a few lines going with Realtors®. We need to run our own ads in the paper. We're going to start phone campaigns, direct mail campaigns, visiting the courthouse . . . we've barely just begun. It's like a big funnel. At the top are all of the possible deals that are going to flow our way. Of them, 95% will not pan out . . . only 1 in 20 will be worth looking at. The goal is to evaluate 1,000 properties in the next 30 days. There are going to be hundreds of leads to follow up. This is grunt work. Lots of little failures. A few promising successes that peter out. Then one or two deals that will make it all worthwhile. The phone is going to start to ring. People will be popping in. It's going to be like Grand Central Station around here."

Renee sat up straight as if she'd just had a small electric shock. "I set my cell phone to vibrate," she explained as everyone looked her way. She already had the phone out, and when she looked at the display, she said, "I think this is my Realtor® calling. I'll just step out and take it in the hallway."

As Renee was leaving, Sam gave the group their marching orders. Jeremy and Summer were to continue their search for their million-dollar needle in the Internet haystack. Michelle was to be dispatched off to the courthouse. Sam herself was going to write and place an ad in the Classifieds section of the local paper. As the group was breaking up, Renee came back into the room.

"We've got a hot lead on a foreclosure," she said excitedly. "Michelle, do you want to come with me? I'll drive you by the courthouse after we check out this one property."

THE FIFTH MANIFESTATION

"I am a millionaire!"

I am a millionaire. I think like a millionaire. I talk like a millionaire.
I walk like a millionaire. I believe, feel, and act like a millionaire.

Like a radio that's tuned to one frequency, I am tuned to the millionaire's frequency.
I continually condition my mind to think rich, abundant, prosperous thoughts.
I talk about the endless possibilities to all who will listen.
I read what millionaires read.
I soak up biographies and autobiographies of millionaires and billionaires.
I drink in their wisdom, insights, and deep understandings.

I think about creating valuable million-dollar business enterprises during the day.
I dream about them at night.
I enjoy creating million-dollar enterprises.
I am creating multiple millions—honestly, ethically, and morally.
I am a wise steward over my money.
I master my money. My money does not master me.

I love to serve. I realize that it is the quantity and quality of my services rendered
with a positive mental attitude that grants me unlimited, overflowing, ever-flowing
compensation. I am constantly rendering increasingly better service. The better I
serve, the more I make.

I love challenges. I conquer my wealth-building mountains with glee and joy in my
heart. There is a banquet of prosperity ready and waiting for each of us. I cheerfully
help others on their journey to wealth, riches, and true spiritual abundance.

Being a millionaire means I live the abundant, balanced life—growing, serving,
sharing. It's great to be a millionaire.

79 Days . . .

Michelle and Sam were headed for the Rock. It had been several days since they had been down there together. But now on this crisp early morning in the middle of autumn, they could see the trees across the hillside turning their beautiful oranges and reds. It was a breathtaking scene. After going through their usual ritual of calling out their goals and Manifestations, Sam and Michelle sat down side by side.

Michelle couldn't wait to share with Sam some of her major concerns. It seemed that they were going into so many brand-new areas that Michelle had never imagined before. And it was over-whelming. It was as if the pathways to her brain were jammed with information that she did not have time to assimilate. Toys, real estate, and the Internet, all mixing together. She felt as if she was the central focal point of it, the fulcrum of the entire process. As a fulcrum she needed to be strong, and she did not feel strong at all. She felt as if she was putting all these people at risk, wasting their time and squandering their hopes.

She knew Sam would understand and yet would have some kind of answer for her. Sam sat next to her and dangled her feet over the Rock and began to talk as she looked out over the beautiful mountain peaks dusted with clouds.

"Your husband had a very interesting name—Gideon. Do you know what it means?"

"No, not really."

"It means 'one who cuts down the enemy.'"

Michelle wrinkled her brow, "Where did you learn that?"

"I was browsing in the Bible a few nights ago and stumbled across the story about an Old Testament hero named Gideon."

"Hmmm."

"Gideon lived at a time when the nation of Israel was under the control of the Midianites—a nation to the south, about where Saudi

A STICK-TO-IT-IVENESS STORY

One day in 1948, a machine shop manager and inventor named George de Mestral went on a hike with his dog near his home in the Swiss Alps. They came back covered with burrs. At first annoyed while plucking them off, he became intrigued. He wondered what made them stick so well to cloth.

Placing a burr under his microscope, he saw small hooks that burrowed into the little loops within the clothing fabric. The idea of a "hook and loop fastener" was born. However, commercial production of hook-and-loop tape turned out to be no easy task. He set out for Lyon, France, to present the concept to textile experts. They laughed at him. But one weaver there took an interest in de Mestral's idea. The two began working together and succeeded in producing a workable prototype.

De Mestral then found a Swiss loom manufacturer who agreed to manufacture their product. But it proved to be too difficult, prompting the manufacturer to give up.

De Mestral was forced to take on the task alone. For months he carried out various experiments. Months went by. Still no solution. He had lost all of his backers' support. He went broke. Desperate, de Mestral retreated to a mountain cabin to think the problem over.

Upon his return he recontacted his friend the weaver to discuss a new approach. The two built a special loom that worked. An investor agreed to finance the venture. De Mestral named the new fastener Velcro—*vel* for velvet, *cro* for crochet. He patented it in 1955 and by 1959 was selling more than 60 million yards of the material per year. Last year the company had total annual sales over $250,000,000, and it employed 3,300 people.

George de Mestral's eight years of perseverance paid off handsomely.

Arabia is today. For seven years the Israelites lived in such oppression and abject poverty that they cried out to the Lord in prayer. One day a young man, Gideon, was threshing a meager supply of wheat when an angel appeared to him." (Judges 6–7)

"I'll bet that was a shock," Michelle remarked.

Sam chuckled. "The angel spoke to this poor farmer and said, 'The Lord is with you, mighty warrior.' Gideon looked around and said, 'Who, me?' 'Yes, you,' said the angel, 'Go and save your country.' Gideon said, 'How can I save my country? Mine is the weakest family in our tribe and I am the least son in my father's house.' The angel said, 'Go in the strength you have and destroy the Midianites. I will be with you.'"

"What did he do?" asked Michelle, suddenly interested.

"That's the best part of the story. After Gideon gathered an army of 32,000 men, the angel said, 'Your army is too big. When you beat the Midianites, I don't want you boasting that you did it yourself. Tell those who are afraid that they can go home.' And 22,000 men went home. That left an army of 10,000."

Michelle looked shocked.

Sam held up an index finger. "'But,' said the angel, 'there are still too many. Take them down to the river and separate those who scoop the water up to their mouths with their hands from those who get down on their knees to drink.' That was to show who was the most battle-ready. This left just 300 men out of 10,000. With these 300 men, the angel promised to deliver the enemy into Gideon's hands."

Sam paused. "This is how he did it. In the middle of the night, Gideon and his men surrounded the armies of Midianites in the valley below—the enemy soldiers were thick as locusts and their camels could no more be counted than the sand on the seashore. Each of Gideon's men was armed with only a trumpet and a clay vessel with a torch inside. On Gideon's signal, each man smashed the vessel and blew his trumpet and shouted, 'The sword of the Lord and of

ONE MINUTE REVIEW OF NETWORKING

1. **A network of relationships increases your leverage.** The more connections you have, the more leverage you possess.

2. **One principle for extending your network lever is "weak ties."** Most people intuitively feel it is their close friendships and strong ties that are most important. In fact, in most cases, your *weak* ties are more important.

3. **You must master the strength of the weak tie.** Most people do not instinctively cultivate "weak-tie" relationships. However, to make large sums of money quickly, you need to hone this skill.

4. **Those who "network the networks" gain the most leverage.** The value of your network is the square of the number of people in it.

5. **"Givers Gain" is your networking motto.** Give something away for free that is valuable to network members. It brings attention to you and it builds trust. Do not expect reciprocity.

6. **Once you have created a network, do whatever it takes to maintain it.** The Golden Rule of Networking is: "Be very quick to build connections and extremely slow to break them."

Gideon.' The sleeping men in the enemy camp below were awakened by the trumpets and stumbled out of their tents to see the valley ringed with torches. Confused, they began fighting *one another*—talk about friendly fire! Those who weren't killed fled and were later routed. A hundred and twenty thousand Midianites died that day."

"Wow," said Michelle.

"I think I know why you're feeling overwhelmed, Butterfly. Like Gideon, you've wondered, 'How can one weak woman defeat an Army of Ericksens?'"

This caused Michelle to smile.

"But remember who Gideon had as his partner. You and God can do anything. But without that spiritual foundation—even if you're as strong as the Midianites—your troops end up fighting amongst themselves, your army is scattered, and the battle is lost."

"Hmmm," Michelle pondered out loud.

"I call it spiritual math.[p. 84] You're either with God—multiplied by infinity. Or without God—multiplied by zero. One times infinity equals infinity. But a million times zero still equals zero. That's why I tithe. I want God on *my* side."

Michelle sat there in deep contemplation. More than anything, she was moved by the new meaning she had discovered for her late husband's name.

A few minutes later, Sam pulled her up by the hands. "C'mon," Sam said, "I've planned a fun exercise for the team to do this morning. We don't want to be late."

78 Days . . .

Michelle sat down at the conference table. In front of her she found a small white box wrapped in purple and yellow ribbons. There was an identical box in front of each team member.

"Go ahead," said Sam, smiling. "Open them."

Inside, each team member found 500 crisp white business cards

INFINITE
NETWORKS

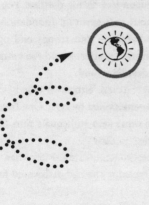

with their own names embossed in raised gold lettering. Under the name was the title *Millionaire Eagle*.

"Very impressive, Sam," Jeremy said. "Thank you."

"Look on the back," she encouraged.

Each person flipped over the card to find the amount *$1,000* printed in black.

"What does this mean?" Summer asked.

"I'm glad you asked," countered their mentor. "When you hand this business card to someone, they will probably ask you the same question, 'What does this mean?'"

Each of them nodded expectantly.

"Here is what you say: 'This card is worth $1,000, so don't lose it. I'm a real estate investor. If you ever hear of someone who is desperate to sell their property, give me a call. If I buy the property, I'll give you $1,000 in cash for the lead.'"

"Whoa! That's a lot of money," said Courtney.

"But," Sam responded, "it's nothing compared to the profit *you'll* make — because you won't even consider buying a property unless you can earn at least $25,000. Shouldn't you share a little of the windfall with the person who told you about it?"

Courtney had to agree.

"Now, here is your assignment," continued Sam. "We need to get more feelers into the area. The faster we can spread the message, the better. So, wherever you go—to the grocery store, to the restaurant, to the cleaners, to the gas station, in a bank line—make contact with at least one person. Get his or her business card and give them your own card with instructions. Break out of your normal routine. Go to different places each day so you can meet new people. Give out 5 to 10 cards a day. We can never tell where one of these cards might end up."

"Sam, isn't this a bit extreme? What are people going to think?" Renee countered.

"Well, look at it this way. Suppose I gave you a $100 bill for

THE POWERFUL LEVERAGE OF
THE INFINITE NETWORK

*You can rest assured that if you devote your time and attention to
the highest advantage of others, the Universe will support you,
always and only in the nick of time.*

R. BUCKMINSTER FULLER

Enlightened Millionaires realize that there is a spiritual dimension to
wealth. They understand that this unseen world is the source of infinite
abundance. When you unite with the source of infinite abundance, you
also become infinitely abundant.

How do you tap into this Infinite Network of abundance? In the Twenty-
first and Twenty-second Millionaire Ahas, we already shared with you our
belief about the power of tithing. Tithing expands, multiplies, and adds
value to all that you do.

Another way you tap into the Infinite Network is to simply maintain
your integrity. It is this integrity that ensures your long-term success.

Knowing and acknowledging the spiritual dimension makes your life
far less stressful. Moreover, as your success gracefully unfolds, a deep sense
of gratitude will permeate your being.

Embracing the spiritual component of wealth and recognizing the
existence of the Infinite Network is the single most important and most
powerful form of leverage.

All Enlightened Millionaires humbly acknowledge their reliance on the
Infinite Network.

every one of these cards you properly placed by the end of the day today."

"You mean, I hand out 10 cards and you give me $1,000 in cash?"

"Yes," said Sam. "Now do you care what people think?"

"If you put it that way, no . . . and I won't stop at 10." She smiled.

Jeremy offered under his breath, "I'll talk to every person I see."

"Here's one of my favorite sayings," Sam said. "You'd be a lot less worried about what people think of you . . . if you realized how *little* they do." Sam followed this with one of her hearty laughs.

"Are you saying that each card we hand out makes us $100?" Michelle wondered out loud.

"Let's suppose that 500 well-placed cards eventually lead us to one excellent property that nets us a $50,000 profit. That breaks down to $100 for every card we gave out. So, in essence, every time you hand out a card it's like getting back a $100 bill in future money, isn't it? Eventually, these contacts begin to pay off. Cast your bread on the waters and eventually you get a sandwich back."

"Hmmm . . . ," several of the group responded at the same time.

"The same holds true for calling ads in the newspapers," continued Sam.

"I've got to admit," replied Summer, "I don't know why, but I hate to call on the ads in the paper. . . . I feel like I won't know how to respond if they ask *me* a question."

"Okay, Summer. There's a newspaper." Sam pointed to a newspaper on the conference table. "And there's a telephone. Suppose I gave you a $100 bill for every ad you called from the real estate classifieds . . . but only for the next hour. How many calls would you make?"

"As many as I could."

"Would you care if someone made you feel like a fool because you couldn't answer their questions?"

"Not if you gave me $100 a call."

TAPPING INTO THE POWER
OF THE UNIVERSE

*"What senses do we lack that we cannot see or
hear another world all around us?"*

FROM *DUNE*, BY FRANK HERBERT

The 1981 Oscar-winning movie *Chariots of Fire* tells the story of two British runners in the 1924 Olympics: Harold Abrahams, a Jew driven to compete by anti-Semitism, and Eric Liddell, a Christian missionary who feels God's presence when he runs. Did you know that the title of the movie was inspired by one of the most remarkable stories from ancient scripture?

In this story, the King of Syria is angry with the Jewish prophet Elisha and sends a great army to capture him. Elisha's servant awakes one morning to find that their city is surrounded with a huge Syrian army "both with horses and chariots." (II Kings 6:15–17).

He runs to tell Elisha. "Alas, my master! What shall we do?"

Elisha responds, "Don't be afraid. Those who are with us are more than those who are with them."

We can only imagine what the servant was thinking when he heard this: *How ridiculous! There are thousands of them and only two of us!* Then Elisha prays and says, "O Lord, open his eyes so he may see." Then the Lord opens the servant's eyes, and he looks and sees the hills full of horses and *chariots of fire* all around Elisha.

If *your* eyes were "opened," what would *you* see?

If you've ever been snorkeling near a tropical reef, you've experienced what it's like to peer into another world. As soon as you put your mask in the water, a brilliant new dimension of bright-colored fish and strange creatures explodes into sight. We're not accustomed to seeing such brilliant color in our normally drab existence, but that doesn't mean it doesn't

"Besides, how are they going to know it's you?" Jeremy chuckled.

"Thank you, Jeremy." Sam smiled at him. "Every contact we make this month, every ad we call on, every offer we write, is *future money* in the bank. So let's go out and make some future money today. It's Saturday, so I'm suggesting that rather than spend another minute in this stuffy conference room, we split into teams and hit the streets for three hours."

"Are you serious?" Jeremy said.

Sam produced two $100 bills and slapped them in the center of the table. "The team that hands out the most cards in the next three hours wins. But you can't just leave a stack in a dry-cleaner's, folks. You have to hand the card to someone. And you get an extra point if the person you talk to will give you one of their business cards in return." Sam looked at her watch. "This contest officially ends at 12:30 at the diner downtown. My treat for lunch."

For a moment, no one moved. The eaglets all looked at one another as if their mentor had gone off the deep end. Then Michelle looked at Courtney and raised her eyebrows.

"I'm game," said Courtney, who got up, grabbed her purse, and headed for the door.

Within 15 seconds the conference room was empty.

Sam and Renee were already seated in a corner booth as the two other teams came in the front entrance together laughing. It was 12:45 P.M.

"That was incredible, Sam," Summer said as she plopped herself down in the corner booth, next to Michelle. "I met more people in this past three hours than I did in the past three months. A few people looked at me funny, but for the most part, people were really nice."

"I agree," Michelle seconded. "Although the manager of one restaurant did ask us to leave."

exist. To use Wayne Dyer's analogy, this physical world is only one room of a thousand-room mansion. There is so much more for us to explore beyond our physical senses.

Call it what you will—the "other side," the "other world," or "the world of spirits"—most of us admit to a system of spiritual beliefs. Is there another world all around us right now—an invisible world? Is there a thin curtain that separates us from this invisible world? Are dozens of unseen beings anxiously waiting to do our bidding, to help us? Are chariots of fire around *you*? And if not chariots, is an angel or two cheering you on?

Yes, this may seem far-fetched, but what if it was true? In the Jewish tradition, every blade of grass has an angel standing over it, encouraging it: Grow! Grow! Wouldn't it be nice to know that you are not alone—that there might be a powerful support system surrounding you?

We believe there is such an invisible world—a world just waiting to help you fulfill your congruent desires—summoned to your side "with horses and chariots of fire."

YOUR INFINITE NETWORK

If only God would give me some clear sign!
Like making a deposit in my name in a Swiss bank account.
WOODY ALLEN

To grow and maximize your leverage, you need to work with several expanding bandwidths from the broadcast station called *you*.

The infinite is infinite. You are the center of the world, metaphorically speaking. Think of your mind and brain as a radio station that outputs your chosen messages. Your imagination creates the broadcast that

"But *even he* took one of our cards," said Michelle's partner, Courtney. "And here is his business card to prove it." She slapped the card down on the table with a flourish.

"Okay, eaglets," Sam said. "Let's have a tally."

The team of Sam and Renee had given away 35 cards and had received 23 business cards in return, for a total of 58 points. Michelle and Courtney had gathered 18 business cards while handing out 30 cards, for a total of 48 points. Jeremy and Summer had purposefully waited until last to report their results. When Summer reached into her purse and pulled out a huge pile of business cards, everyone gasped.

Jeremy announced their tally. "Five hundred and sixty-three points. If we'd have had another two hours, we could have gone through our entire box of cards."

"It was Jeremy's idea," Summer began. "We started out by asking ourselves where we could find the greatest concentrations of people. Jeremy said he used to work at the Mariposa Plaza, so we went there first and arrived just as three conferences took their midmorning break. So there were hundreds of people milling around in the halls and foyer. We bumped into a seminar leader who was holding a real estate seminar. We told him that we were real estate investors with millions of dollars to invest." Summer looked at her mentor expectantly. "That's what you told us, wasn't it, Sam?"

Sam nodded her agreement.

Jeremy jumped in to complete the story, "I took you at your word, Sam, that you'd show us how to find as much money as we wanted with one telephone call. The seminar leader was happy to introduce us to his audience. We told the group that we would come up with the cash and partner with them if the deal was right, or that we would simply give them a $1,000 finder's fee if we bought a property from a lead they gave us. It was like finding an entire room full of bird dogs. Everybody was very happy."

Summer jumped in excitedly. "I was kinda nervous. I'd never

originates your future. If you send the wrong outbound messages, you get the wrong results. If you broadcast the right messages consistently and persistently, you will get the right results, right here and right now.

First, as we've established, you need a mentor, a guide, and someone to share with you the shortcuts to instant success in an endeavor or enterprise. All successful people whom we have ever encountered have had a great and inspiring mentor with whom they were attuned and who wanted to personally help them become who they were capable of becoming.

The second circle out from your broadcasting station is your Dream Team. It starts with you and at least one other person. Miracles only happen when you have a dedicated Dream Team. Greatness only happens to and through teams.

Third, your alliances and networks will geometrically expand from your association with your Dream Team. It's as if the "brothers of serendipity" arrive just in time with the right people. Your million-dollar Rolodex will source and serve you in ever-expanding ways.

The Universe is forever testing you and giving you feedback. The messages that you have been sending create an echo effect. The problem is that the feedback is not instantaneous, so it is sometimes difficult to observe and understand the cause-and-effect relationship.

Alone, you and your task have a one-to-one relationship; your task will be slow, arduous, and painful drudgery. With your mentor, team, and network in place, your power is greatly multiplied and your Infinite Network comes into serious play. You have witnessed its presence and its superlative results, though it was not previously named or popularized. The Spiritual Internet kicks in when a team has a big purposeful dream, and everyone stays positive about its accomplishment.

It is impossible to obtain these results in any other way.

spoken to a group that big before. There had to be 250 people in the room. But we were able to hand out 250 cards—one to every person—and got back 175 cards from them. And that was just one group. At this point, we split up to cover more territory. Jeremy concentrated on the other hotels, and I hit the malls and restaurants. After a while, it didn't bother me at all to walk up to a total stranger."

"What did you say?" asked Michelle, who was completely amazed to hear her shy friend describe how she had broken out of her cocoon.

"I struggled with what to say at first, but then I just decided to tell them the truth—that we were trying to make a million dollars in 90 days. I told them about being mentored by a millionaire." She looked over at Sam. "I didn't tell them your name, Sam."

Sam nodded to Summer as if to thank her.

"But as soon as I started saying that, I had a hard time ending the conversation with most people. They wanted to know more. But I was running out of time. So I told them that if they gave me their business card, I would get back to them after the 90 days and tell them what happened." Summer took a pause for effect. "Get this, I even had one guy offer to pay *me* $1,000 if I would spend two days with him, one on one, showing him how we did it."[p. 334]

"Well, Summer," Courtney interjected, "that might have had something to do with the fact that you're a not-so-unattractive blonde. . . ."

Everyone laughed.

"I disagree," Summer countered, mildly offended. "He was with his wife, and they both wanted me to teach them. Can you believe that? Somebody was willing to *pay me* $1,000 bucks."

"Sorry, Summer, I didn't mean—"

"That's it!" Jeremy exploded, cutting short Courtney's apology. Now he had everyone's attention. He was staring into the distance, speaking half to himself, half to his partners.

THE SIXTH MANIFESTATION

"I am a giver."

In this life, there are givers and takers.

I am a giver.

I like to give.

I love to give.

Giving is my way of life.

I give away my ideas to great causes that I care deeply about.

I give money where it is needed, is wanted, and can do enormous amounts of good.

My giving always creates more.

I inspire others to give and like doing it.

It is my subtle mission to give and motivate other rich people to give so that human dignity is re-created on Spaceship Earth.

Giving is God's way.

It is the way that I now understand is the truth of the Universe.

Giving multiplies me and makes me feel complete and fulfilled.

Giving makes me feel that I make a real and important difference.

Giving is one of the main reasons that I enjoy being a millionaire.

I make millions.

I save millions.

I invest millions.

I give millions away.

"For over a week, I've been surfing the Internet for our million-dollar idea . . . and it was right there . . . in front of my face . . . the whole time."

"What are you talking about, Jeremy?"

"Oh, my gosh . . ." Jeremy spoke as the *aha* broke brighter over his face.

"Jeremy?" Summer tried to bring him back.

"Sorry, guys. I've got to test something out."

With that, he bolted from the booth, leaving his partners staring at him as he ran out the door.

77 Days . . .

Michelle rushed eagerly into the Golden House lounge, where she found Tilly, alone, sitting in her wheelchair, clutching the remote, and staring fixedly at the big-screen television. "There you are!" Michelle cried when she saw her.

"Oh, dear, this isn't the best time." Tilly frowned. "My drama is on."

Michelle crouched beside Tilly's wheelchair. "I've been worried about you! I've been leaving messages all morning and Summer said you weren't in your room. I finally decided just to come track you down."

Tilly looked down at the control panel of her wheelchair. "I'm not sure where you thought I had gone to, dear."

Michelle refrained from pointing out that Tilly was at an age where sudden departures were not uncommon. "Well, but Summer—"

"Michelle, I'm sorry, but this is the one program I'm hooked on. You are just going to have to wait for the commercial."

Michelle sighed and sat down on the couch behind Tilly. She watched as patiently as she could while two heavily made-up blond women argued about a man who had amnesia.

ONE MINUTE REVIEW OF THE INFINITE NETWORK

1. **Embrace the spiritual.** Embracing the spiritual side of wealth is the single most important and most powerful form of leverage for Enlightened Millionaires.

2. **The unseen world is the source of infinite abundance.** When you unite with the source of infinite abundance, you also become infinitely abundant.

3. **Integrity is key to tap into the infinitely abundant Infinite Network.** It is this integrity that ensures your long-term success.

4. **Tithing works.** Regardless of your income, acknowledge your relationship with the Infinite Network by giving 10% of your income to your church, community, or favorite humanitarian cause. Just as a wise gardener prunes a growing tree to balance it and prepare it for greater growth, God encourages us to prune back our money trees by tithing.

5. **Acknowledging the spiritual dimension makes your life far less stressful.** Moreover, as your success gracefully unfolds, a deep sense of gratitude will permeate your being.

6. **Dream impossible dreams.** The Spiritual Internet has God as the mainframe computer, with individuals as miniframes off the mainframe. The Spiritual Internet works when a team has a big, purposeful dream, and everyone stays positive about its accomplishment.

Finally the commercial came on. Tilly maneuvered her wheelchair sideways to talk to Michelle. "Actually, I was at my son's house all day yesterday. He has the most adorable—but never mind, we'd better get down to business. I received the prototype yesterday morning and it's just not acceptable."

"Oh, Tilly."

"Yes, I was quite disappointed myself."

"Couldn't we just use it anyway?"

Tilly clicked her tongue. "No, you have one opportunity with these higher-ups. It's got to be perfect."

"So what do we do now?"

"Well, that's why I went to my son's house, but first I took the van down to the fabric store. His wife's got a nice sewing room set up and, well, I used to do all of the prototypes myself, back in the old days."

"You're creating the prototype yourself?"

"Well, not exactly. Another Golden House resident and I are putting a couple of them together right now. Eleanor is still a fine seamstress, though her hearing is not what it used to be. We should be finished by tonight. Just because you caught me in front of the television doesn't mean I haven't been working hard."

"I never meant to say—"

"By the way, I was eating dinner with another resident last night, Jack Morris—he was an attorney for many years, on the boards of several corporations, you know. I've been telling everyone about our 'talking bear,' and that includes him. Jack thinks it would be a great fund-raising item for charities. One of his other buddies down the hall has also had a lot of experience in the charitable area. He calls it philantropism—a cross between *capitalism and philanthropy.*p. 318 Get it? You provide the product at the lowest wholesale price, and then you and the charity split the profits. Everybody wins." Tilly smiled. "Think your friend Sam would approve?"

Michelle sat back. "I know she would. I'm impressed. Thanks, Tilly."

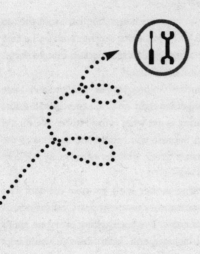

SKILLS AND TOOLS

"And then another one of my friends who lives down the hall, her son is an expert in import/export. He's got contacts in Hong Kong who will give us a real good deal on the electronics, if we need it."

"So what do you want me to do?"

"Don't you worry. You just keep up your prayers and leave little Tilly to work her magic. I haven't had this much fun in 10 years. Except for that darn sewing machine. These newfangled ones— they're all computerized these days. It took me an hour just to read the doggone instructions."

"Any word from your folks inside of Hasbro yet?"

Tilly shook her head. "With all the ways people have of getting in touch now, it's even harder than it used to be. Don't you find that amusing? We've been trading messages, but I'm confident that they'll come through for us."

"Tilly, you are the very best." Michelle grasped Tilly's hand, but the commercial had ended, and with that, so did their conversation.

❧

76 Days . . .

Jeremy had asked all the team members to meet in the conference room for "an announcement of earth-shattering intensity" at 7:00 A.M. Everyone was able to attend, even Renee, although she would have to leave by 7:45 to get to school on time.

Michelle smiled to herself when she walked in the conference room. Jeremy and Summer had started with two computer terminals on a sideboard at the far end, but their territory of flip charts and books was extending not so gradually toward the center of the room.

Jeremy had arranged the conference table chairs in a semicircle around his end of the room. "Everyone here? Okay, okay, quiet on the set." Jeremy paced like a tiger in a cage. Michelle noticed that

THE SKILLS AND TOOLS OF
THE ONE MINUTE MILLIONAIRE

With the advent of the Industrial Revolution, the business dynamic dramatically changed. The means of production (Karl Marx's famous words) became too expensive and too complicated to be maintained individually. A person could build a table alone, yet building an automobile required many more resources.

Now we live in the information economy. The means of production are back in your hands. An inexpensive greeting card with a computer chip contains more production power than a room-sized computer of the 1950s. With a properly configured computer, a printer, and a phone line to the Internet you have enormous power. As the IBM ads say, when offering its smaller computers, "It might not make you a giant conglomerate, but it sure can scare one."

On the World Wide Web there are few barriers to entry. You can almost instantly open a storefront that is open 24 hours a day, seven days a week, to anyone who has Internet access. Daniel H. Pink calls this "digital Marxism." You, the individual, now have the power. As Pink points out in *Free Agent Nation*, "In the age of inexpensive computers, wireless handheld devices, and ubiquitous low cost connections to a global communications network, workers can now own the means of production."

You must own and know how to use each of these tools. Computers, handheld devices, and modems are all part of your Enlightened Millionaire lever. Having these items (the tools) and knowing how to use them (the skills) is critical to your success. It is the glue that tightly connects you to all the other elements of your millionaire lever. Your team, your mentor, your mastermind group are all exponentially strengthened when you own these information tools and have the skills to use them.

his once-awkward gait had become more assured and graceful. He was sporting a new haircut and actually wearing a sport coat. *When he walks in here with a tie I'm going to need to take a nitroglycerin pill,* she thought.

Michelle obediently took her seat, as did the others, except Sam, who hoisted herself on the edge of the table. They all knew that Jeremy had been working hard and that he was excited about his presentation. Michelle hoped that he could deliver something to equal his excitement.

He glanced down at Summer, who was examining a broken fingernail, then began. "Everyone all been to the bathroom? I'm just asking for 15 minutes of your time, then you can harass me with any questions you want or just tell me I'm crazy. Though I don't think you will.

"Last time I updated you all together I was working on finding free information, information that's in the public domain, to package and resell online.

"Let me give you a little background. I know, I know, a lot of you don't need it, but I want us all on the same webpage, if you catch my drift.

"The first step that Summer and I took was to start building our lists. Companies spend years putting together those customer lists. Used to be direct mail—now more and more it's e-mail. Summer and I figured right out of the gate that we didn't have time to do that."

"I'm no math genius," Summer interrupted. "But even *I* know that two years doesn't go into 90 days."

Jeremy seemed irritated at this comment, which puzzled Michelle, but she let it slide. Jeremy went on. "I have been on this project 24/7. I'm even keeping my bathroom breaks to a minimum. But—" he tapped the side of his head "—as the result of this unprecedented dedication, we have managed to acquire a group of e-mail lists totaling almost *one million names.*"

Michelle led the applause.

Did you go to work today on horseback? Did you listen to a 78 record? Of course not! The world changed and you changed. You had no vote. To succeed you had to learn how to drive a car and how to play (if not burn) a CD.

The same requirement is true with computers, handheld devices, and modems. You have no vote. You *must* have both the tools and the skills to use them.

Let's look at the story of Betty Fox. Her husband died at 33, leaving her with little money and two boys. She worked as a bank teller and then as a clerk in a boys' shirt company until it went bankrupt. Betty then lived on unemployment until she found a job for a small billing company. That company moved when she was 67 and she was once again unemployed.

Her son got her connected to WebTV, a service that uses the TV set to surf the Internet. Less than a year later she started her own website, called GrandmaBetty.com. The site became so popular that GrandmaBetty.com was purchased by iGrandparents for more money than she ever dreamed.

If Betty Fox, at 67, could master both the tools and skills, what is the probability that you can, too?

PERSUASION

The person who chooses to master the skill of persuasion can positively affect millions around the world. You are such a person or you wouldn't be reading this book.

Master teachers and leaders have always used storytelling to effectively communicate their point of view and illustrate their arguments. Stories paint an irresistibly compelling word picture that communicates heart to heart and soul to soul.

"How in the name of Pete did you pull that off?" Renee asked.

"I'd like to say 'Easy,' and it does seem that way, now that it's done." His grin was broad and self-satisfied. "But let me back up a little first.

"While we were acquiring these lists, we were also looking for some terrific information that we could package and sell. I was checking out some government websites because—" he coughed quickly into his fist "—well, I have a little outstanding debt with Uncle Sam, but I'm working to pay it off. Now—coincidence? You be the judge. But wait till you see what I found."

He lifted the top, blank page of the nearest flip chart to reveal a list of several titles:

How to Get a Great Deal on a New Car
Marketing Strategies for Growing Businesses
9 Ways to Lower Your Auto Insurance Costs
12 Ways to Lower Your Homeowners Insurance Costs
Power$mart: Easy Tips to Save Money and the Planet
Clean Up Your Own Credit: How to Dispute Credit Report Errors
66 Ways to Save Money: Practical Ways to Cut Everyday Costs
Investment Swindles: How They Work and How to Avoid Them
10 Questions to Ask When Choosing a Financial Planner

"These articles are available to anyone who wants them, without cost. That is, free. Gratis, gratuit. Do you know why?" He didn't wait for an answer. "Because they were compiled at taxpayer expense. They're public domain. That means that anyone can use this information in any way they wish. Including Jeremy Cavalieri and the intrepid Millionaire Eagles."

"So what's your plan?" Michelle couldn't help but ask. "To copy these reports and sell them?" She remembered their earlier conversation about groups with special interests and his idea to sell information to the members of those groups.

In a story, context is everything. Consider the following archetypal scenario: Two associate pastors are seeking the permission of the senior pastor and ask essentially the same question in different ways and get totally different answers. Associate pastor number one requests: "May I eat when I am praying?" The senior pastor responds, "No, that would be a sacrilege of the highest order. Absolutely not."

A few hours later the second associate pastor asks: "May I pray while I am eating?" The senior pastor responds: "Of course, you are to 'pray without ceasing,' as the Apostle Paul said, so by all means keep praying."

Both pastors were asking to do the same thing, eat and pray at the same time. Yet one gets a yes, the other receives a no. The only difference is the context of the question. One asked the question of eating in the context of praying. In that "context," eating detracts from praying. The other asked the question in the context of eating. He got a yes because praying adds to the context of eating. The most persuasive individuals are careful to present questions in a context that is more likely to get a favorable response.

Another persuasive tool is the rhetorical question. It presumes the answer by the way the question is asked, like "You do want to be a millionaire, don't you?" It subtly stimulates the listener to agreement, especially if the persuader is gently nodding his or her head up and down and smiling to obtain consent.

Messages on the wings of humor are also very powerful. For example, in the Douglas-Lincoln presidential debates, Douglas called Lincoln "two-faced." Lincoln in his rebuttal gently smiled, chortled, and said to the audience: "Ladies and gentlemen, if I had two faces, do you think I would wear this one?" Insightful, self-deprecating humor helped Honest Abe become president. As president, Lincoln persuaded America that slavery was wrong, immoral, and had to be abolished. His persuasive communication and deep conviction that slavery was bad for the Union made way for the Emancipation Proclamation that abolished slavery.

Management consultant Marshall Thurber says his three secrets to persuasion are brightness, darkness, and frequency. Paint bright word pictures that describe the positive, exciting future that awaits if a person follows your recommended course of action. Paint dark word pictures

"That was more or less the original idea," Jeremy replied, looking at his list with love. "It's still part of it. This is just a taste of the financial info we found.

"Once we found these articles, it clicked for me right away. Money is our theme. You remember, we were joking about targeting chocoholics. But money is the probably the single area of greatest interest to most people. Except maybe sex."

"I'm not sure about that," Renee said uncomfortably.

"Being around all these women has turned his head," Summer commented, rather dryly.

"Let the boy go on," Sam said.

"It just made sense," Jeremy said to Summer. "We're learning how to make a million dollars. Why not target people who are as passionate about making money as we are.

"So we started compiling a *very* useful little book, *Money Loves You,* that we could sell over the Internet."

"How do you find people like that?" Michelle wondered aloud.

"There are thousands of e-zines devoted to money subjects," Jeremy answered.

"Tell us about e-zines," Sam said, "just in case anyone feels embarrassed about asking."

"An e-zine is an electronic magazine sent out via e-mail. The 'magazine' comparison is a little grandiose, but here's how it usually works: I go check out a website, and they offer to put me on their e-mail list for a free subscription to their online newsletter. Then, on a weekly or sometimes even daily basis, I get an e-mail from them. It might just be an inspirational message or it might constitute an entire newsletter."

"I get a few of those," Courtney said. "I just didn't know what they were called. I get them from small business associations I belong to."

"Exactly," Jeremy continued. "Summer and I have contacted the owners of dozens of these e-zines and have made arrangements to joint-venture with them."

that describe the gloomy and frightening future that awaits if a person doesn't follow your recommendations. You then repeat the message (like advertising does—again and again) until your audience gets it and automatically does what you have suggested.

You can learn to persuade. You can learn to sculpt your words and phrases into masterpieces that evoke the response you want.

EVERYBODY WANTS SOMETHING

To be a millionaire is to be a student of what motivates people—learning to discern the wants behind the behaviors of the masses. Motivational speaker Zig Ziglar says: "You can have everything you want if you help enough other people get what they want." Everybody wants something. You just need to find out what they want and give it to them.

Effective listening is a rare skill. Your quest is to listen with your outer and inner ear to discover what people truly want. You may get your answer by asking them directly—oftentimes the direct approach does work. Other times you need to probe deeper and talk to their personal assistants, secretaries, associates, friends, or relatives. As you ask direct and indirect questions and keep pondering the idea of what they need, want, and desire, you'll be amazed how fast you will discover it.

Occasionally, you'll need help. A friend of ours hired a consultant to help him resolve a conflict with his publisher. He wanted his publisher to produce electronic versions of his books but the publisher was resisting. One day, while on their morning walk, his consultant stopped him in his tracks, and said: "Close your eyes and pretend to be your publisher for a minute—why do you object to electronic publishing?" He answered, "Because I have a $20,000,000 investment in my printing presses and I

"Why would they let you use their mailing lists?" Michelle asked.

"Well . . . I was working on that one. Then our Queen Eagle here"—he bowed toward Sam—"took us out for that little card-distributing adventure. D'you remember how someone offered *Summer* a thousand bucks to mentor with her?"

Summer puckered.

"When she said that, when we were at that booth at the diner, everything fell into place in a nanosecond. Here we were, going to sell some kind of book for, say, $10 apiece. But to generate a million dollars we would have to sell 100,000 copies.

"So, instead, what we're going to do is to sell 'Seminars with Sam.' The actual title is Enlightened Millionaire Coaching. It's a powerful two-day seminar with the Queen herself. The price is a mere thousand dollars. Sam is donating her time in exchange for our tithing 10% to Sam's designated charity."

"So you've just dropped the idea of the money book?" Renee frowned, looking at her watch.

"No way! Here's how it works. We have a million names from a total of about 20 e-zines that deal one way or the other with small businesses or financial planning or just personal money management. Over the next week, for a share of the profits, all of those e-zines are going to offer our book, *Money Loves You*, for free, to anyone who goes to our website.

"We expect, conservatively, that we'll get 25,000 to 50,000 people to download the free book. Then, with viral marketing . . . it could double or triple that number. Our goal is to gather 100,000 names. And we'll send them all the free book, of course. But then that 100,000 becomes *our* mailing list. Within two days we e-mail each and every one of them with the irresistible offer to work with our very own Samantha Ann Munroe. At a thousand bucks a pop, we only need 1,000 of those 100,000 to say yes. That's only 1%. A thousand people at a thousand dollars each is one million bucks."[p. 348]

have 168 employees who are depending on me." Voilà! Our friend positioned himself in such a way that he could understand why his publisher was so resistant; eventually they were able to come to terms. Sometimes, we need to get private, get quiet, and see things from the other person's point of view to discover an omni-favorable solution.

I recently called the executive officer of a major company to set up a meeting, along with Bob, to explore business possibilities. At first, the executive was abrupt and arrogant. But I listened deeply and behind his words heard exactly what he wanted—to do business with billion-dollar entrepreneurial companies primed to go global. I said, "If we could help you make that happen, would you meet with us when we are next in New York?" We did, and our "power breakfast" was vastly successful. He introduced us to the power brokers of the city. It was incredible.

But this meeting would never have taken place if I wasn't listening with my "inner ear" to what this gentleman wanted.

Just remember, everybody wants something. Your task is to discover it.

SEVEN MONEY SKILLS OF EXTREMELY PROSPEROUS PEOPLE

Why do some people earn 10 times more money in their lifetime than the rest of us? Do they work 10 times harder? Are they 10 times smarter? Of course not. The bottom line is that wealthy people are good at the seven following money skills. Anyone can learn them.

▲ **MoneySkill #1—Value.** They value each dollar bill as a money seed. Just like a tiny acorn contains the power to grow into a mighty oak

"Whew!" Renee whistled. "I like those odds. Listen, gang, I have to run to work. I'll catch up with everyone after school." She slung her purse over her shoulder and headed out the door.

School, Michelle thought, her heart aching. And just a few doors down from Renee's students were her own . . .

"I'm good at keeping a secret, aren't I?" Sam grinned. "Jeremy and I are thinking beyond the original seminars idea, too. We're going to offer a year of mentoring with yours truly for $5,000. I think there'll be a few takers."

"Sam, don't be so modest," Jeremy said. "It'll be a life-changing experience and worth far more than we're charging. You see?" Jeremy spread out his hands. "It's the simplest solution. It's Occam's razor."

75 Days . . .

The office building of the second-largest toy company in the world was located in a suburb of a small city just outside of Providence, Rhode Island. It was a two-story brick building in the style of the early 60s, with clean straight lines.

To Michelle it looked like the Emerald City at the end of the Yellow Brick Road. She had arrived with Tilly after a tiring trip. Even though Denver was a hub, they had had to change planes in Chicago. And Michelle had never fully appreciated the challenges one faces when one is confined to a wheelchair, in spite of helpful airport personnel and the prevalence of wheelchair ramps. Tilly, however, had remained cheerful throughout. "Isn't it nice to get on first?" she had said to Michelle as a gate agent pushed her down the jetway. Tilly's mechanical wheelchair would not easily fold for travel.

Now Michelle said a prayer of thanks for the Americans with Disabilities Act as she pressed the large button that would keep the automatic door open while she pushed Tilly into the building. At the front desk they both received adhesive visitor's badges. As she

tree, each dollar has the power to grow into a mighty money tree. If you destroy an acorn, the oak tree inside also dies. So, too, with a money seed. Wealthy people know that a dollar a day can grow into a million dollars. So they are very respectful of every dollar they spend.

▲ **MoneySkill #2—Control.** They control their money down to the penny. Prosperous people take a few extra steps every time they spend money: (1) They shop for the best value, (2) they ask for and expect a discount, (3) they examine their receipt for mistakes, (4) they attempt to turn each expenditure into a legitimate tax-deductible business expense, (5) they balance their checkbook to the penny, and (6) they file their receipts upon returning to their home or office. These activities only take an extra minute of time but build long-term financial peace of mind.

▲ **MoneySkill #3—Save.** Wealthy people love to save money by spending wisely. But they don't stop there. They save at least 10% of what they earn.

▲ **MoneySkill #4—Invest.** They have a system for investing their money. Imagine a series of buckets where money is siphoned from your main bank account. The first bucket is your emergency bucket. Let your 10% savings flow there first until you have at least three months' living expenses saved in an insured bank account. Once this first bucket is filled up, the stream of 10% overflows into one of three additional buckets—conservative investments, moderately aggressive investments, and very aggressive investments. Contact a reputable investment adviser to help you put your savings into these three types of mutual funds. The money should be automatically deducted from your bank account so you never forget.

▲ **MoneySkill #5—Earn.** They have Multiple Streams of Income (MSIs) outside their job. This entire book is dedicated to showing you how to dramatically increase your earning power.

▲ **MoneySkill #6—Shield.** They protect themselves with trusts, corporations, limited partnerships, LLCs, and other legal entites. In truth, you don't want to be a millionaire. You want to *live like a millionaire* but have very few assets in your own name.

stuck hers on the lapel of her black suit, Michelle regarded her friend with affection. Tilly had put spots of blush on her papery cheeks, spots that weren't very well blended in, and she had applied red lipstick to her thin lips. In her lap she protectively held the prototype that she and her friend Eleanor had made. What it lacked in elegance it made up for in impact—at least Michelle thought so. It was a bright purple bear with an abnormally large torso, even for a teddy, and the seams were strikingly crooked. But there was so much love on its crudely sewn face with the black buttons for eyes that Michelle felt a twinge every time she looked at it. Nevertheless, it was also clear to her that they never would have gotten this meeting had it not been for Tilly's connections in the company.

In the end Jeremy had helped with the electronics part, and Michelle's nervousness receded when she thought of the moment when they would play the message that Courtney had recorded to her own son in her soothing contralto.

Down to the right of the lobby about 100 feet was a conference room. Tilly knew the way and Michelle followed her. When Michelle held the door for Tilly again, she was surprised to find the room smaller and simpler than what she had imagined: It was furnished with just a table and chairs, a television, and a VCR. There wasn't even anything on the walls.

Inside they were greeted by two members of the executive committee who were already waiting—Jill Ranson, a petite woman in her 50s, head of the game division, and Paul Marshall, a young man in his late 30s, in charge of international toy acquisition. As others came in, many gave Tilly a hug. Everyone there had either worked with her in some capacity or had heard of her since coming on board. Their warm welcome confirmed what Tilly so matter-of-factly said about herself: that her reputation preceded her. If she said a toy was going to be a winner, 9 times out of 10 it was.

Several of the top executives were late from various different meetings so there was a good 20 minutes of gossip and catching-up.

▲ **MoneySkill #7—Share it.** They are very generous, donating at least 10% of their income. The secret is that money multiplies fastest when it's divided. When you share freely, you prime the pump of the Universe. We encourage you to establish a legacy that will outlive you. Plant money trees from which others will harvest the fruit. This is true prosperity.

NEGOTIATING FROM ABUNDANCE

The Enlightened Millionaire pursues a principled approach to negotiation. Its context is one of abundance rather than scarcity. This means that in every transaction where there is negotiation, the Enlightened Millionaire intends to work cooperatively with the party to expand the situation so that everyone wins. There can never be a loss for anyone in the transaction.

This means that every "negotiation" is an act of creation coming from the "Ocean of Abundance." From this context the Enlightened Millionaire creates only abundance, never scarcity. This means all Enlightened Millionaire negotiations are ethical, honest, and win/win events.

An Enlightened Millionaire negotiates from a place of stewardship. That is, the Enlightened Millionaire negotiates to create wealth that improves the lives of everyone. The goal is to enrich oneself while enriching others. The goal of negotiation is not to win at someone else's expense. Rather, it is to expand what is possible. Success is defined by how much bigger the pie is after the negotiation than before.

Negotiation thus becomes a blessing for all involved.

Michelle didn't talk much; unlike Tilly, she didn't know anyone, but most of all, her nervousness was returning. How could Tilly be so relaxed? It was mean-spirited to think that it was only because the custody of *her* children didn't ride on this. After all, Tilly had worked as hard as anyone on Michelle's team.

With the arrival of the woman in charge of new product development, the CEO of the company gave Tilly a brief introduction and turned the meeting over to her.

Tilly held up the teddy bear as if it were her new grandchild. "Ladies and gentlemen—and I must say I'm glad to see more ladies now than I did 50 years ago—"

Michelle closed her eyes.

"—I've wondered for the last decade if I had one more toy in me and it looks like I do. Here it is."

Michelle opened her eyes again. Even in the unflattering fluorescent light, Tilly glowed, as if the very frailty of her skin were letting her soul shine through. No longer a shriveled, disabled woman, she was manifesting on the outside what Michelle had come to see on the inside.

"You all know that I've always wanted to bring toys to the market that would not just make money but would benefit children and their parents. You've seen a whole heck of a lot of stuffed animals, and in the past few years you've seen every mechanical gizmo we ever could have imagined—why, my granddaughter has a little CD that will teach her chess—but this is something special."

Tilly cradled the bear next to her cheek and gave it a squeeze, as if on impulse. And from the inside of the creature came the gentle sound of Courtney's voice. "Honey, I'm thinking of you right now. I hope you're going to have sweet, sweet dreams. . . ."

A hush fell over the room as the rest of the message played. Although Courtney was not the actual mother of anyone present, she had read it with her own son in mind, and the evident love of a mother for her child permeated the room like a pleasant fragrance.

ACTIVITY MANAGEMENT

An Enlightened Millionaire values time. The following 10 tips can give you more opportunity to add additional activities to your day.

- ▲ **Tip #1—Focus on the Critical Few.** Eighty-five percent of the things you do account for only 15% of your results. And vice versa. Therefore, only work on the critical things and you'll get there faster and with less effort.

- ▲ **Tip #2—Learn how to procrastinate!** Procrastination is absolutely essential to your success. Just make sure you procrastinate the right things. Put off the 85% and tackle the 15%. Losers do just the opposite. They tackle the 85% and put off the 15%.

- ▲ **Tip #3—Throw away your "to-do" list.** Create instead an 85/15 list. Write the top-priority items at the top in the 15% box. Write the lower-priority items at the bottom. Only work on the top of your list.

- ▲ **Tip #4—Reward yourself for doing the right things.** There's a great book by Michael LeBoeuf, called *GMP: The Greatest Management Principle in the World*. Here's the book in a nutshell: The Things That Get Rewarded Get Done. If you reward yourself for your most positive actions, you will get more of them done . . . almost effortlessly.

- ▲ **Tip #5—Do your FTF: Feared Things First.** Which activity on your list do you fear the most? That's your FTF. When you start your day, ask yourself, "What's my FTF today?" Start your day with that activity. By training yourself to do your FTF, you unconsciously urge yourself to tackle tougher tasks.

- ▲ **Tip #6—Do a daily Power Hour.** Take a few minutes every day—it doesn't need to be an hour—for planning. Planning is like a rehearsal. Every great actor rehearses many times before stepping on the stage. Don't step on the stage of life without rehearsing your performance.

After a perfectly timed pause, Tilly continued on in a more practical vein, describing the benefits. The design of the teddy bear was unique, colorful, and fun. The body was shaped like a pillow so a child could take it to bed. But the combination of stuffed animal and personalized message was what put it over the top. She helped the committee members imagine what it would be like to be able to leave a special message for their small son or daughter, who would be able to listen to it over and over again. A story, a poem, a song, a prayer.

She told them about the new rage of picture frames that grandparents from all over the world had been buying by the millions. Picture frames that were talking because a grandparent can leave a message for the family with a picture of Grandma or Grandpa. This was even more powerful, because a small child can't *hug* a picture frame.

"If any one of you here has young children, and I mean children who haven't turned into teenagers and discovered that you're not really the sun and the moon after all, then I'll bet you have to leave them at home to travel once in a while. Every day you just have to leave them when you go to work. Imagine your child missing you desperately and all she needed to do was press a little button, and there you were."

One of the older men present chuckled. "I'm flattered by the implication, Tilly. But heck, my kids are in their 30s."

Tilly looked at him sharply. "Think about your grandchildren, then."

In the brief silence that followed, Michelle discreetly scanned all the faces in the room. They were mesmerized. But Tilly had warned Michelle that this was only the first, if crucial, stage. They would have to anticipate and draw out any objections that might come down the line—because if they weren't voiced here and now, they would be voiced later, either by the committee, by the wholesalers, by the retailers—or the consumers.

▲ **Tip #7—Exercise.** It helps you work harder, longer, and think more clearly. It increases your health span and your life span. While we exercise, we also listen to our tapes so that we can layer those two activities together. And therefore, we're not only exercising our bodies, but our brains at the same time. Speaking of that . . .

▲ **Tip #8—Layer your activities.** Use your waiting time productively. Do two things at once. Listen to tapes while exercising, driving, or standing in line. Constantly ask yourself this question: "Is this the most productive use of my time?"

▲ **Tip #9—Write out your goals daily.** We learned this from Brian Tracy, who writes out his top goals each and every day. See the Twelfth Aha, page 54, for more information. (By the way, an excellent book on time management is Brian's book, *Eat That Frog*. Bon appétit!)

▲ **Tip #10—Just say "No!"** Don't let other people dump their "monkeys" on you. Sometimes you just have to say no.

Tilly began by raising and answering some possible objections. This got the committee rolling. The woman who was in charge of new product development raised her hand to speak up. "You know, I've always had this feeling that things like this are almost kind of like mind control. Maybe I'm the only person who thinks this way, but I'm just a little concerned about that."

Michelle said another prayer of thanks, this time for how well Tilly had prepared her. She jumped in with an answer. "If you want to talk about mind control, think about the fact that children on average in this country spend over 50 hours per week sitting in front of the television. Now, that's mind control. Don't you think that parents should be able to control at least one minute of their child's life? A minute that they record? It's time for parents to regain control of the programming and it starts with this minute that they record for their children."

A gentleman in a bright yellow tie with miniature Mr. Potato Heads on it commented, "Some studies I've seen suggest that women are reluctant to record messages on devices like these. They're perfectionists about anything to do with being a mom, and they don't want to do it unless it's absolutely perfect. It's almost like writer's block."

"Let the dads do it, then," another man joked, though all it got him were a few annoyed glances from the women present.

Tilly ignored the joke and the glances, while responding to the concern. "We're going to include with the toy a booklet of one minute scripts that parents can use. It covers just about every blessed thing." The booklet would contain one minute bedtime stories, modern and classic; words to favorite songs for those daring enough to sing; and, perhaps most important, a number of scripts aimed at common childhood fears such as the dark, disasters, and death, and common difficulties such as bedwetting and shyness. Tilly assured them that this last category had been prepared by nationally known psychologists.

ONE MINUTE REVIEW OF SKILLS AND TOOLS

1. **You, the individual, now have the power.** In the age of inexpensive computers, wireless handheld devices, and ubiquitous low-cost connections to a global communications network, you now own or can own the means of production.

2. **You must own and know how to use each of these tools.** Computers, handheld devices, and modems are all part of your Enlightened Millionaire lever. Having these items (the tools) and knowing how to use them (the skills) is critical to your success. This is the glue that tightly connects you to all the other elements of your millionaire lever.

3. **Master the power of persuasion.** The person who chooses to master the skill of persuasion can positively affect millions around the world. You can learn to persuade. You can learn to sculpt your words and phrases into masterpieces that evoke the response you want. People want someone to persuade and lead them in the right direction; you can be that someone.

4. **Wealthy people are good at the seven money skills.**
   - ▲ MoneySkill #1—Value: Each dollar bill as a money seed.
   - ▲ MoneySkill #2—Control: Control your money to the penny.
   - ▲ MoneySkill #3—Save: Save at least 10% of the money you earn.
   - ▲ MoneySkill #4—Invest: Have a system for investing your money.
   - ▲ MoneySkill #5—Earn: Have MSIs outside your job.
   - ▲ MoneySkill #6—Shield: Protect yourself with legal entities.
   - ▲ MoneySkill #7—Share: Donate at least 10% of your income.

5. **The Enlightened Millionaire pursues a principled approach to negotiation.** Its context is one of abundance rather than scarcity. The Enlightened Millionaire intends to work cooperatively with the other(s) to expand the situation so that everyone wins. There can never be a loss for anyone in the interaction.

6. **An Enlightened Millionaire values time.** Eighty-five percent of the things you do account for only 15% of your results. And vice versa. Therefore, only work on the critical things, and you'll get there faster and with less effort.

Michelle pressed her lips together to keep from smiling; they were still in the idea stage with the psychologists. Tilly was forging ahead brightly. "We'll have even more scripts available on the website. The parent can go online and download them for free." She winked.

Another woman, a sharp-featured brunette, expressed concern that it might be a little too technically advanced for some parents who were electronically challenged.

Michelle was ready again. "I know that it used to be difficult for people to record their own voices on various different machines. But the way we designed this is much easier than an answering machine, and 10 times easier than programming the voicemail message on your cell phone, which almost everybody has to do these days. With the touch of just one button, a person can record and erase a message easily and simply."

The brunette seemed only partly mollified. "What about kids going into the store and recording a message on the toys that are available on the shelves? Because I imagine you're going to want to have the ability for a parent to try this out, aren't you?"

But another gentleman, who had introduced himself earlier as being in the product development department, spoke up. "That's something that we have a lot of experience with. We've learned our lessons there, and what we do is basically provide a simple 10-second message that a parent can listen to in a demo mode." He looked around the table, "You probably already know what Amy's worried about   teenagers coming through and recording nasty messages on the bears. That's not going to happen with Hasbro toys. And, even after purchase, we can make it so that parents will be able to control and lock in the messages that they want so that nobody else can change them."

The brainstorming went on for a while, with Michelle and Tilly throwing out as many objections as the committee. As these concerns were raised and dispensed of, the level of excitement rose palpably.

SYSTEMS

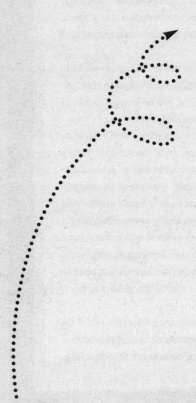

Michelle realized on a more visceral level that she was in a room full of seasoned professionals, as the ideas for marketing, packaging, and design bounced across the table like tennis balls.

Somehow, invisibly, the meeting moved from a discussion of "if" to "when." But when Tilly told them that this bear needed to be in production for availability in less than 90 days, the man in the yellow tie told her that for once she really was crazy, and everyone else enthusiastically agreed. "Twelve to eighteen months is our normal time."

Tilly took this part in stride. She had already told Michelle that she knew the people in the company who had what Sam would call "Make-It-Happen" power. If the word came down from above that this was a toy that needed to be fast-tracked, then it would happen. None of them in the room could remember a toy that had been fast-tracked in less than four months, but Tilly appeared confident that she would be able to prevail.

In this mood of triumph, the final part of the meeting was spent brainstorming the name. They went though hundreds of rhyming words until Michelle, who'd been quiet for this part, feeling that the professionals could take over, blurted out: "The Always Together Bear."

There was lots of noisy chatter and heads nodding in agreement before she continued talking. "When my husband had to leave home on business, which he did all too often, he'd always kiss the children and say to them, 'Don't worry, even though you can't see me, just know that I'm always there.'"

Although it was bittersweet for her to say it, Michelle did: "The toy will remind the child that Mom or Dad will always be there, no matter where they may be." *And Nicky and Hannah, I'll be with you soon.*

73 Days . . .

After returning from the meeting with Hasbro, Michelle had taken on the assignment to go down to the county courthouse to research who

SYSTEMS THINKING

Picture this situation. It is late afternoon and you are tired. You have an important dinner engagement that evening so you decide to take an hour nap. Instead of setting your alarm you ask a friend who is visiting to wake you in an hour. He agrees.

Two hours later, your friend wakes you. You ask, "Why didn't you wake me after one hour?" He replies that he thought you asked him to wake you in two hours and that is what he did. You then have to run around and get ready quickly, muttering to yourself about how you should have set the alarm rather than asking your friend to wake you. Had you done that, you would not have been so rushed to get ready.

Your conclusion is correct. Your analysis of what happened looked at the system you used. Your friend's failure to wake you resulted from a miscommunication. Either he didn't hear you correctly or you misspoke.

As we mentioned earlier, blaming others or yourself is not operating from above the line. Looking at the situation from the point of view of being personally responsible is always better than blaming yourself or another. So how do you best be "responsible" in this situation? The answer is found in systems thinking.

Dr. W. Edwards Deming is the American statistician who is credited with bringing the quality practices to Japan. Before his arrival in that country in 1950, the label "made in Japan" was synonymous with inferior quality. Now the same "made in Japan" label is synonymous with high quality.

So what did Dr. Deming teach the Japanese that made such a difference to the quality of their products? The answer is quite simple, yet profound. Based on years of statistical analysis, Deming was able to validate that 94% of all failures are not because people don't want to do a good job. The fact is that most people want to do a good job.

had defaulted on the payments of their mortgages. Michelle found that literally dozens and dozens of defaults had occurred in the previous 30 days. It was amazing to her. Why would people not make the payments on their homes? And then she remembered how she had not been able to keep the payments current on her own home. With this in mind she continued looking through the list with greater empathy.

Whatever the problems that had caused the owners to fall behind, their properties were certainly diverse. She saw expensive homes, inexpensive homes, condominiums, vacant lots, and town homes.

After about a half an hour of writing down the names and addresses of all these properties, she decided to use her intuition. It felt like an odd leap to take, but she knew that she had to tap into the Infinite Network—there was really no *logical* way to sort through this much information. So she went down the pages one by one by one, surrendering as much critical thinking as possible. She skipped many properties with good numbers, simply because they didn't feel right.

In the end, she took down the information on three properties out of a total of about 200 different defaults. In turn, one property seemed to stand out among the others.

The mortgage on it was $35,000 and, since the payments were two months behind, the deadline for the foreclosure was only about two weeks away. Michelle copied down the address; it was in a fairly good neighborhood. She decided that she would drive by to see if it was in good condition, too, and to try to assess what equity there might be.

Later, when Renee asked her how she chose that particular property, she found it almost impossible to put into words. The closest she could come to describing her process was that somehow she saw past the numbers to the story behind them. She did not exactly picture the owner and yet somehow she heard someone calling for help.

The owner turned out to be a widow named Jane Jasko. The property was a town home located in the south part of Riverdale in a neatly landscaped development. The units were in excellent condition,

What, then, is the cause if it's not the people?

It's the system. The system failed in 94% of the cases, not the people.

If you've ever failed to make money in a venture and blamed yourself, perhaps you'd better rethink the root cause. The probability of creating financial freedom depends on the system you are using.

Enlightened Millionaires search for successful systems before they launch their moneymaking vehicles. Having the right system gives you enormous leverage.

This is the essence of systems thinking.

SPECIALIZED WEALTH SYSTEMS

There are dozens of systems for making money. The word *system* forms an acronym:

$$\text{S}_{\text{ave}} \, \text{Y}_{\text{our}} \, \text{S}_{\text{elf}} \, \text{T}_{\text{ime}} \, \text{E}_{\text{nergy}} \, \text{M}_{\text{oney}}^{\text{™}}$$

It's true. When you have a system, it saves you time, energy, and money. In the beginning, if you don't have a system, it's almost impossible to succeed.

Bob once illustrated this point to a small seminar audience. On a table he placed a blue-velvet jeweler's pad. In the center, he placed a jeweler's magnifying glass, a pair of special tweezers, and a pile of 50 sparkling diamonds.

He explained, "These sparkling stones are not diamonds. In this pile, there are 49 cubic zirconians (fake diamonds) and only one real, but very valuable diamond. If you can find the real diamond, I'll give it to you. Would anyone like a chance to try?"

or at least appeared to be from the outside. She noticed "For Sale" signs in several windows.

She checked her notes again for confirmation—there was the $35,000 first mortgage but no other encumbrances. Therefore, whoever owned this unit was two weeks away from losing a substantial amount of equity in their property.

Michelle approached the front door with some trepidation. She remembered how difficult it had been for her to lose the house after Gideon died, and she remembered the negative experience Summer's mother had in selling her home.

She rang the doorbell, then straightened her blouse and skirt while she waited. After a full minute she rang the bell again. Finally the door opened to reveal a petite white-haired woman, slightly stooped, a bewildered and somewhat cantankerous look on her face. She looked a little younger than Tilly, but the ancient housecoat she wore and the moldy smells from within the house revealed a life less organized and probably a mind less sharp.

Michelle spoke slowly (and perhaps a little too loudly), "Good afternoon, ma'am. My name is Michelle Ericksen." She quickly produced a driver's license, which the woman ignored. "Are you Mrs Jasko? Forgive me for bothering you here this afternoon, but I was doing some research down at the county courthouse and I found that your home was listed as a property that is about ready to be foreclosed on."

Mrs. Jasko spoke in the gravelly voice of a longtime smoker, although Michelle neither smelled nor saw any evidence of tobacco use. "You're about the tenth person that's come to tell me that. And I keep telling every one of them that they must be mistaken. I put most of my savings down on this little house when I bought it, and the first thing I do when I get my husband's pension check is to make my monthly payment." She plucked with gnarled fingers at the collar of her housecoat. "So you see, there is no possibility of my home going into foreclosure."

Everyone volunteered. "There is only one catch; you only have 60 seconds to find it."

One by one, they tried to find the real diamond, but with such a short time frame, they all failed. Then Bob agreed to show them the system. With the clock running, he proceeded to turn each of the stones on its flat face, its faceted side straight upward. It took Bob 55 seconds to arrange all of the stones in this manner. Then, with a few seconds remaining, he looked down on the stones from above and was able to spot the real diamond from among the fakes with only his naked eye. Once things are set up properly, it is extraordinarily easy to spot the real diamond every time.

Why? Because all the cubic zirconians are exactly the same, flawless and perfect. Only the diamond has a flaw in it—a tiny fleck of carbon, called an inclusion—which refracts light slightly differently than the other stones. This difference is obvious, even to the naked eye.

Now, with the system (or secret) revealed, everyone wanted another try at finding the real diamond.

"No," Bob explained, "you had your chance. Since you didn't know the system, you got nothing. I, on the other hand, know the system. So I get the diamond every time."

All wealthy people have systems—or "cookie cutters"—that they have developed through years of trial and error to cut real "dough" out of the market.

In the next few pages, we are going to share with you proven million-dollar systems.

One of these systems is going to work for you.

But first we need some simple benchmarks for keeping score.

That's the first rejection, Michelle said to herself. "Forgive me, ma'am, I don't blame you for being annoyed at these intrusions, but I truly would hate to see you lose your home because of some misunderstanding. Are you absolutely certain you've been making the payments? Can you show me any canceled checks?"

"I'm not going to let you into my house." Mrs. Jasko scowled. She started to close the door.

The second rejection. But how to get past this one? Michelle opened her file folder, even as she gently pressed her foot against the bottom of the door. "Ma'am, forgive me, but I have the paperwork right here. I just want to verify that this is your address. Would you please just look at these documents that I have here from the county courthouse?"

"I don't have my glasses." Mrs. Jasko looked at the door, as if puzzled that it wasn't closing.

"Mrs. Jasko, please. Go get your glasses. You need to look at this, because you're going to be in serious trouble if you don't do something about it."

Michelle didn't know why this finally turned Mrs. Jasko around. Perhaps she saw it as her best shot at getting rid of Michelle. She made a point of closing the door, but after a few minutes—during which time Michelle worried that she might have had the last word after all—Mrs. Jasko returned with a pair of tortoiseshell reading glasses on her nose. She took the paperwork from Michelle with slightly trembling hands and scanned it, her lips moving as she read. *But of course she doesn't understand.* The legalese would be beyond her. So Michelle produced a yellow highlighter from her purse and quickly marked a few key phrases, like *default notice, delinquent,* and *forfeiture.*

As the ominous words penetrated Mrs. Jasko's understanding she looked up and said, her gravelly voice rather plaintive now, "Are you absolutely certain that this is an official government document? I've been warned that people will try to fool seniors with fake documents."

MILLION-DOLLAR BENCHMARKS

In becoming a millionaire, you will cross many benchmarks.

Are you a salaried employee? Which benchmarks have you crossed?

Your lifetime net income exceeds $1,000,000.
The total value of everything you own exceeds $1,000,000.
The net value of everything you own exceeds $1,000,000.
Your yearly net income exceeds $1,000,000.

Are you a commissioned salesperson? Which benchmarks have you crossed?

Your total lifetime sales exceed $1,000,000.
Your lifetime net income exceeds $1,000,000.
Your total yearly sales exceed $1,000,000.
Your yearly net income exceeds $1,000,000.
The total value of everything you own exceeds $1,000,000.
The net value of everything you own exceeds $1,000,000.

Are you the owner of one of the 6,000,000 businesses in North America? If so, which of the following benchmarks have you crossed?

Your total lifetime business revenue exceeds $1,000,000.
Your lifetime net profit exceeds $1,000,000.
Your total yearly business revenue exceeds $1,000,000.
Your yearly net profit exceeds $1,000,000.
Your monthly gross income exceeds $1,000,000.
Your monthly net income exceeds $1,000,000.
The total value of everything you own exceeds $1,000,000.
The net value of everything you own exceeds $1,000,000.

Michelle spoke from her heart. "I'm absolutely certain, ma'am. We're talking about your home, here, and I truly want to help you."

Mrs. Jasko put crooked fingers to her forehead. "I just don't understand how this could be."

Michelle had a guess. Now that Mrs. Jasko seemed a little less mistrustful of her, she renewed her request. "Could I see your records?"

This time Mrs. Jasko let her into the house. On the inside, Michelle discovered further signs of neglect: Glancing at the kitchen, off to her right, she saw greasy walls and peeling linoleum. And as they entered the living room she observed the stained carpet, the dirty drapes, and a layer of dust thick enough to make snowmen.

Mrs. Jasko took Michelle to a card table covered with a series of piles of papers. On closer inspection Michelle saw that an entire peak of this mountain range was composed of unopened envelopes. She lifted a dozen or so of them off the top and randomly checked some postmarks in the middle of the pile. It looked as though Mrs. Jasko had not been taking care of business for at least a few months.

With Mrs. Jasko's permission she took some time to confirm her suspicions. After a few minutes Michelle sighed, placed her palms on the table in front of her, and then did her best to explain the situation to Mrs. Jasko. Since her loan was seriously delinquent, the only sure way to prevent foreclosure was for Mrs. Jasko to pay off the loan in full. Michelle suspected from reviewing Mrs. Jasko's mail that while she had some income, she wouldn't have anything close to $35,000 in liquid assets.

She couched her words carefully, being honest that the cause of the problem was Mrs. Jasko's lapse, but not confronting her directly with the likelihood that she was in the beginning stages of senility. In any case, Michelle now had an agenda that went beyond the profit she also hoped to make.

She concluded with an honest plea. "Ma'am, I'd like to help you resolve this situation somehow."

FIVE CHARACTERISTICS OF
THE IDEAL MONEYMAKING SYSTEM

Ideal Multiple Streams of Income (MSIs) have these five characteristics:

1. **Zero cash.** Zero cash is required. Not necessarily no cash, just not your cash. As you may have read in Robert Allen's classic book, *Nothing Down*, there are dozens of techniques for buying real estate with little or no money down. Business masters in all ages have been masters of the "creative nonuse of cash." The great billionaire Andrew Carnegie bought many of his major businesses with nothing down. Even the discovery of America was a nothing down deal. Columbus borrowed the money he needed from the king and queen of Spain. You can learn how to do the same.

2. **Zero risk.** If you don't have a lot of your own money in the deal, you dramatically lower your risk. The more successful you become, the more risk averse you will become. You will cover your assets. You will learn to use corporations, LLCs, and other legal entities to lower your liability. The goal is to be risk free.

3. **Zero time.** Zero time does not mean that you invest "no time"; it merely means that once your project is up and running, it should operate on automatic pilot. It is like writing a book; your goal is to write it, market it, and get it to automatic pilot as quickly as possible. Then you can concentrate on the next project or task. You focus your thinking and creative energy to design a self-perpetuating system. The ultimate goal is ongoing massive, passive cash flow with little or no investment of your time.

4. **Zero management.** Management is an endless "to-do" list that absorbs your time. The objective is to outsource and delegate your work effort. Operate from your highest and best thinking. Simulate yourself as the president of the United States, complete with all the

Mrs. Jasko had her fingers on her forehead again. "I'm so bewildered. I don't know what to do. Would you really help me? No one else who came to the door offered to help. One of them had a very frightening beard."

Michelle touched her reassuringly on the arm. "Yes, I will. I promise."

Mrs. Jasko insisted on making Michelle a cup of tea before they talked further. "You're such a kind person," she said as she handed Michelle a cup, rattling in its saucer. "I could tell from the first moment I laid eyes on you."

Michelle looked into the cup. There were flecks of something floating in the brown liquid. She didn't know what they were, but she was certain they weren't tea leaves. "But what will I do?" Mrs. Jasko whimpered. "I don't have $35,000. I have no family, none. Where will I go? What will I do?" Her whimper became a sob.

Michelle sat down on the folding chair next to the card table and took Mrs. Jasko's free hand with her own. "Will you trust me now to help you?" She looked straight into Mrs. Jasko's red-rimmed blue eyes, praying that the other woman would use her own intuition.

"Can you? Will you?" Mrs. Jasko begged. "I don't know anyone who can help me."

Michelle let out a breath. She felt that she had probably cleared the first hurdle. She had a win/win plan, but of course she needed Mrs. Jasko to agree. Over tea—or at least, over the cups—Michelle did her best to explain. Michelle would pay off the $35,000, and then help Mrs. Jasko move to Golden House. She wouldn't have to worry about cooking or cleaning anymore, let alone the bills, all of which was clearly beyond her now. (Michelle had noticed several rather stale utility bills and guessed that Mrs. Jasko wasn't far from losing her phone and electricity—not that it would matter if she lost her home first.) "One of my best friends works there," she said. "She'll take good care of you. They take field trips twice a week and there's a library—or volunteers come in, they'll read to you. . . ."

resources, talent, connections, and money that you could possibly use to realize your desires.

5. **Zero energy.** Life is energy. Your invested energy is your life. You want the greatest possible returns per unit of energy invested. When your life is over, will you feel rewarded or regretful? Energy well invested will give you a great return on your investment.

You want high profits for your high thinking and high service. It's available. Rare is the person who thinks through these critical concepts with regard to his or her own future and fortune. Every business giant has done this "rare" thinking and that's why we recommend the reading of business biographies and autobiographies.

Learn to "zero out" your life.

MAKING MONEY WHILE YOU SLEEP

Prosperous people have always known two truths:

1. **Truth Number One: The Importance of Having Multiple Streams of Income.** Smart people recognize the need to cultivate a *portfolio of income streams*—not one or two, but many streams from completely different and diversified sources. If one stream goes dry, it doesn't bother them. They have time to adjust. They're stable, safe.

   Do you have MSIs flowing into your life at this time?

2. **Truth Number Two: The Power of Residual Income.** Residual income—that's a fancy term for a "recurring" stream of income that continues to flow whether you're there or not. In other words, making money while you sleep. For example, when you earn interest on the

Mrs. Jasko's lips parted. She looked as though Michelle were describing heaven. "But my little house here . . ."

"I know, I know." Michelle patted Mrs. Jasko's hand. "What I would do is fix it up so that we could get the best price—I'll pay for that—and then, after I sell it, we'll split the profits 50-50."

"Would you really do that for me?" Mrs. Jasko asked.

"Yes, absolutely," said Michelle. "I'll put it in writing and we'll both sign it, in case . . . Well, it's just an extra way to reassure you that I'll do my part." Michelle guiltily admitted to herself that she wanted to make sure that Mrs. Jasko did hers, too.

"Oh, thank you," said the woman. "Thank you so much."

That had been three days ago. The property did indeed appraise for around $100,000 and it was going to take at least $3,000 to do the fix-up and another $2,000 to bring the paint up to Michelle's standards.

"So, Sam." Sitting in Sam's private office, Michelle took out a notepad and pen from her briefcase. "Now is the time for you to share your big secret. How do I get the $35,000 in cash to be able to pay off the original mortgage holder, plus the extra $5,000 to fix it up? You've been telling us for the last several weeks that all the money we ever needed is just a phone call away.^{pp. 284, 302} I'm ready now for that phone number." She made a show of waving her pen over the notepad.

Sam put her hands behind her head and tilted her chair back. "Butterfly, no matter where you are in the country, there is cash available for the right kind of deal, and it can happen quickly. Go out to the reception area and bring back the *Denver Post*. We put a fresh copy out every morning."

Michelle did as she was told and returned in a moment with the newspaper.

money in your bank account, that's residual income. It flows into your account 24 hours a day without any added effort on your part.

What percentage of your income is residual? With residual income you work hard once, and it unleashes a steady flow of income for months or even years. You get paid over and over again for the same effort. Wouldn't it be nice to be compensated hundreds of times for every hour you work?

Have you seen that tiny battery tester on the Duracell battery? The inventor presented his idea to the big battery companies. Most turned him down, but Duracell saw the genius of it and agreed to pay just a few pennies per battery pack for his idea. And now he makes millions, because those residual pennies add up. And the best part about it—HE DOESN'T HAVE TO BE THERE! It flows without him.

You see, the trick is to get money working for you instead of you working for money. Here are a few places where you could put your money to work for you to create streams of income while you sleep:

Savings and certificates of deposit
Bonds
Investments that generate dividends
Stocks that have potential for long-term growth appreciation
Your own house appreciation
Real estate investments: single family, multi-unit, commercial
Owning your own business
Commissions
Franchising Fees
Marketing consulting—% of revenues generated
Celebrity endorsements
Database owner: rent and sell lists and related intelligence
Royalties: books, tapes, CDs, videos, seminars, films, software, games,
     inventions, patents, agenting, brokering
A website that sells 24 hours a day
Network marketing

"Open it to the classifieds." Sam came around her desk as Michelle sat cross-legged on the floor and spread the paper out on the coffee table.

"I want you to look for a section of the paper called 'Real Estate Wanted' or 'Money to Lend.' Either one will probably do," Sam said.

The first of the categories Michelle found was "Money to Lend." It was a column with about a dozen ads in it, placed by various different types of lenders. There appeared to be larger lending institutions, smaller lending institutions, and ads run by private individuals.

Sam explained, "This is one of the fastest ways to find cash. You just look in the newspaper to find those people who are willing to lend it."

Well, duh. "But," Michelle objected, "I can't qualify for a loan. My credit is terrible. You already know that." She frowned. "And when you first brought this up, Jeremy and I made that pretty plain—"

"That's the beauty of dealing with these people in the paper," Sam interrupted. "They don't care about your credit rating, they only care what the property looks like and whether it can carry the loan balance. In this particular instance, the loan balance is less than half of the value of the property. Many of these people will be happy to loan you the money."

"Not to be cynical about human beings or anything, but what's in it for them?"

"That's easy. They're going to charge a high interest rate and they're going to charge you fees up front. We call them points. As you make your phone calls here you'll find that the interest rate is going to be between 10 and 20 percent and they are going to charge you between 10 to 20 points for the privilege of using their money."

"What's a point?"

"A point is 1% of the value of the money that you are borrowing. You need to borrow $40,000 for this property, right? So they're going to probably take 10 points as a fee. So if you're borrowing $40,000, the fees would be $4,000."

THE SEVENTH MANIFESTATION

"I attract Multiple Sources of Income"

I

realize

that I need more

than one source of income.

I choose a new and wiser financial path.

*It is called the wisdom of **Multiple Sources of Income**.*

My first stream of income is my PSI, my primary source of income.

I focus on my PSI until it is stable and almost permanent.

I treat my PSI with respect, love, care, and delight.

Then, I add new MSIs—one at a time.

Each MSI is a joy to my heart.

I create them in my mind

and instantly record

them on

paper.

Because I seek them, I find them—find so many MSIs that I have to prioritize them.

I schedule the launch of each MSI sequentially after writing a "wow" of a business plan.

I involve my Dream Team to help me pull together the resources to create a successful MSI.

Multiple Sources of Income are pouring into my life, and from all over the world.

I am under the spout where all the good things pour out.

"Four thousand dollars!" Michelle put her hand on the classifieds as if it were the money she had been asked to part with.

"All depends on your point of view, Butterfly." Sam chuckled. "The alternative is you won't be able to buy the property at all and therefore you'll lose out on a $60,000 profit—or should we say the $30,000, which is your share of the deal you made with Mrs. J."

"Hmmm." Michelle looked back down at the ads.

"These folks aren't called hard-money lenders for nothing. This is *not* the way you finance your kids' college education. What helps make it work for you is that you won't have this borrowed money for very long. Like here, what you'll probably want to do is borrow $45,000 against this property, which you should be able to do without any trouble at all. That's the money you have to pay back—but the lender will only give you $40,500. The extra $4,500 is the points. That's okay, because you're going to take the $40,000, immediately pay off the delinquent first mortgage, and use the balance to fix the property to get it into good condition."

Michelle was indeed looking at the transaction in a new light. "So, somebody would actually lend me money so that I could buy this property."

"That *is* what I've been trying to tell you." Sam briefly regarded her new nail tips, painted in a rich plum color. "It's another win-win, if you think about it. Figure out the rate of return these lenders are getting. When you add it all up, they earn approximately 24% on their money. Not bad, hmm? It's even better if they foreclose, because then they get an extra $60,000 profit."

"So much for *my* win."

"You win if you do what you're supposed to do. You couldn't buy it any other way."

Michelle looked back down at the classifieds column. She was playing with the big boys now, and she was just a little scared. A *little*? Then she had an idea. "Hey, Sam, why don't you be my hard-money lender? Talk about win-win. If I'm going to pay those fees

ONE MINUTE REVIEW OF SYSTEMS

1. **Ninety-four percent of failure is caused by the system, not the people.** Most people want to do a good job. Ninety-four percent of all failures are not because people don't *want* to do a good job. It's because the system they were using failed.

2. **All wealthy people have systems.** These systems, developed through years of trial and error, now have predictable outcomes. Enlightened Millionaires search out the most predictable systems.

3. **Million-dollar benchmarks.** On the way to your first million-dollar net worth, you will cross several million-dollar benchmarks. Are you tracking these benchmarks?

4. **Ideal Moneymaking systems have five characteristics:**
   - ▲ Zero cash
   - ▲ Zero risk
   - ▲ Zero time
   - ▲ Zero management
   - ▲ Zero energy

5. **Prosperous people have always known two truths:**
   - ▲ Truth Number One: The Importance of Having Multiple Streams of Income
   - ▲ Truth Number Two: The Power of Residual Income

I'd much rather pay them to you." *And maybe you'd shave off a couple of those points.*

"Little eagle, you've got to get out of the nest pretty soon. The best thing for you is to learn how to play the real estate game in the real world without falling back on me too much. That way, when I can't be here with you for whatever reason, you'll be able to go to any city in the United States, start from scratch, and build up another fortune.

"There's one more thing." Sam put her arm loosely around Michelle's shoulder. Their faces were very close together. "I want to tell you that you've made me proud. You're not a millionaire yet, but I believe you will be, because you are taking the enlightened path, and the Universe will support you. From what you told me, it sounds like you're helping this woman even more than she's helping you. Instead of getting more and more isolated and then losing everything and ending up God knows where, she's going to have a new life."

Michelle couldn't bring herself to raise her eyes. "Thank you," she said humbly.

The escrow officer came to Golden House with the paperwork for Michelle and Mrs. Jasko to sign. Mrs. Jasko seemed less confused since her move and, though she signed the papers with trembling hands, when the officer handed her her check, she fully understood its meaning. "Michelle, you've saved my life," she said. "I'm so happy here."

Michelle was touched, but she was too distracted by the sight of her own check—her share of the profits—to give her full attention to Mrs. Jasko. She had never once in her life seen a check this large. But there it was, in black ink against a pale green background: $29,014.62. It was a long way from a million. But it was a start. And it was all about leverage. If, on the next deal, she could find a

REAL ESTATE

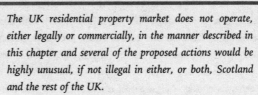

The UK residential property market does not operate, either legally or commercially, in the manner described in this chapter and several of the proposed actions would be highly unusual, if not illegal in either, or both, Scotland and the rest of the UK.

Nevertheless, while accepting this limitation, the author's fundamental premise that a property transaction can constitute a financial opportunity remains just as true here as in the US.

bigger property in trouble, she could make even more in the same period of time.

Meanwhile, this first $30,000 was already spoken for, and the first 10% of it was going to tithing. With Sam's prompting, Michelle had decided to split her first tithing check—half going to a local church and half to the Horatio Alger Foundation, to provide college scholarships to deserving, underprivileged students. Another portion of the check would go to reimburse Sam for some of the expenses she had incurred in helping them get started. The rest would help finance another property that she had already taken steps to acquire.

As Sam kept emphasizing, it was a numbers game. "The more lines we can get in the water," she said, "the greater the chance we'll get a bite. We'll try to reach them in every way we can think of—ads in the paper, direct mail, trips to the county courthouse, out-of-state owners, banks, foreclosure sales. We've got to circulate if we want to percolate."

And so, one night, the whole team had gathered in the tiny living room of her bungalow to stuff and stamp almost 300 envelopes addressed to the owners of properties that had gone into default.

Michelle had written the letter. It was a form letter, to be sure, but one that she had composed carefully to convey the team's genuine concern for the mortgagee's problems. After all, it hadn't been long since Michelle had been in the same situation.

It had been Michelle's idea as well to include a photo of the team. Sam had a digital camera and they asked Sam's assistant, Stephanie, to shoot them outside, under a tree. They all dressed informally. Jeremy wanted to stand behind Summer and make donkey ears, but Sam drew the line there. "They want to see that we're real people, not crazy people," she said tartly.

TRACKS UP
THE MILLIONAIRE MOUNTAIN

Okay. You're congruent. You're motivated. Which Millionaire Mountain should you climb? We've already shared with you that there are only a few Millionaire Mountains.

But each of these Millionaire Mountains has several routes or tracks to the top. Each individual track is a unique, systematic way of creating wealth. If you're not aware of these business tracks, you can't use them. (Just like if you had never seen an automobile before, you wouldn't be able to imagine how useful it could be to you.) Just showing you these various wealth vehicles might ignite your imagination.

Let's begin with real estate. . . .

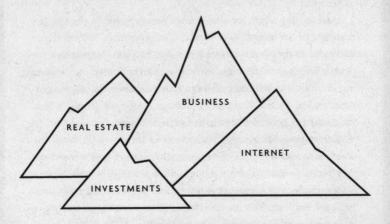

"I've never sent out letters like this before," Renee said. "What kind of response do you think we might get?"

Michelle guessed, "Maybe 20 or 30."

Sam chuckled. "In your dreams, maybe. If we get one or two good deals out of these 300, we should be doing back flips. These people will have already received five or six letters, and some of them will have already resolved their financial crisis. That's why it's worth our time to hand address these envelopes. That alone is going to get a much higher percentage opened. Now, I want to see you all use your best penmanship!"

And so the party labored on into the evening, comforted by a fire in the fireplace and soothed by classical music from hidden speakers.

Sam was right: The return on their mass mailing was small. Out of the inquiries they did receive, though, Michelle and Renee had no trouble choosing their next project. It started as a call from a woman in response to their letter. She was the single mother of five children. When she and her husband had divorced, she had bought him out of his share of their home, so that her children would have the stability of staying in the same place and continuing at the same schools. Also, it was a large home, which is what she needed for her large family.

To buy her husband out she had refinanced, leaving her with payments that were a bit of a stretch, but still within reach, given her salary. Then the hospital where she worked had financial problems and downsized. She lost her job and then missed a payment.

Letters began to flood her mailbox, offering to buy her home at a substantial discount—her reward being that her credit would not be ruined. But most had a threatening tone. Then she opened Michelle's, saw the photo of her eclectic team, and read a letter that was sensitive to her situation. "That's why I called you," she told Michelle, near tears. "What I need to do is to move into an apartment, but I don't even have money for the move. And if I don't do

A HANDFUL OF PROPERTIES
CAN MAKE YOU A MILLIONAIRE

Let's assume that you want to make the most amount of money from the least number of properties in the shortest possible time. Is it possible to make a million dollars from one property in one year? Highly unlikely, but possible. It certainly has been done. To see how to pull it off, let's refer back to the Millionaire Map (see page vii). You'll need to be driven by a clear and powerful DREAM. You'll need to attract an excellent TEAM of mentors who will lend you the resources you need—money, credit, expertise, and so on. Then you'll need to focus, like a laser beam, to find the right kind of property. It may even require that you broaden your horizons to include properties in other states or provinces. But let us ask you: Do you think there are a handful of bargain properties—one to five—somewhere in your county that could generate a million dollars of profit to you this year? Absolutely!

As Warren Buffett says, to be a successful investor, you must either find value or create value. Here is what you're looking for.

A. DISCOUNT SITUATIONS

- ▲ Look for sellers who are forced to liquidate their real estate to solve a cash need.
- ▲ Look for mortgage holders who are anxious to liquidate their mortgages at a discount to solve an immediate cash need.

something PDQ, I'm going to miss the second payment. If my credit's ruined, I'll have a hard time coming back from that."

Michelle and Renee met with the woman and offered to help in any way they could. She was confident that she'd get a new job before too long, but the ongoing maintenance of a house would put her over the top. "The kids can share rooms," she said. "I've got to keep my priorities straight. I was trying so hard to make it the same as it was before Derrick left, but we all have to face facts."

She needed physical and financial help moving and an extra $1,500 to catch up on bills that she'd been unable to pay since being laid off. Michelle and Renee agreed immediately.

"I'm going to ask you a personal favor, too," the woman said, looking both relieved and a little anxious at the same time. "I know you're professional real estate investors. Will you keep on the lookout for me for another house, something a little smaller with smaller payments, that I could back into, maybe sometime next year when I have a little saved up?"

To which Michelle replied, "You can trust us to make every effort on your behalf. It's the least we can do."

They drew up paperwork the next day. And Michelle walked out of the escrow office the proud owner of $50,000 in equity.

It remained to turn this equity into cash. The mom had left the house impeccable, so all Michelle and Renee had to do was shampoo the carpets, paint the front door, and put a "For Sale" sign on the building. Within two weeks they got an offer of $35,000 for a quick closing. Suddenly Michelle had $60,000 in the bank. She began to think about what colors she would paint Nicky's and Hannah's new rooms.

B. DISTRESSED PROPERTIES

▲ Look for sellers who are anxious to unload properties that are "in crisis"—problem tenants, natural disasters, floods, fire, and so on. To them, peace of mind is more important than ownership.

▲ Look for properties that are run-down and need a major fix-up. Often a total face-lift will give you the ability to dramatically increase rents, thus dramatically increasing the property value.

C. CONVERSION OPPORTUNITIES

▲ Look for properties that are ripe for conversion to another use: apartments to condominiums, apartments to office space, office space to retail space, vacant farm land to building lots or commercially zoned acreage. When you convert something from one use to another, it can often dramatically increase its value.

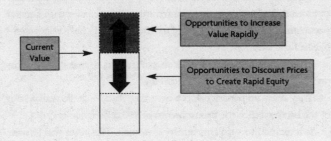

Michelle's euphoria did not last long. It was that very evening that Tilly called to tell her that the Hasbro deal had fallen through.

Michelle couldn't think of anything to say until she finally sputtered, "What?"

"The committee had told me it was a sure thing. Well, wouldn't you know that the kibosh came from the one executive who hadn't been at our presentation. He pointed out that a similar toy had been produced by a small competitor and hadn't done very well."

Michelle finished Tilly's thought. "So he wasn't there to raise his objection and hear it overcome."

"We certainly would have overcome it," Tilly said peevishly. "I know the piece of junk he's talking about, and the Always Together Bear is not only better, it's different. I pointed that out to the young man who called, but he thought it would be too difficult to reassemble the committee."

"Tilly, we've got to consider that the first rejection."

Tilly chuckled. "I thought you might say something like that, dear. I have to admit I was pretty down when I first got the news. That's why you haven't heard from me sooner. I took ol' Betsy"— her nickname for her wheelchair—"down to the garden here for a little stroll. I just can't take it for a final no. Sometimes people in these companies get to talking in their little groups and it becomes an almost informal committee meeting where they do reconsider."

"No," Michelle said firmly. "That sounds good, but it also sounds too slow. We have to get this thing going *now*. Tell me, Tilly, there must be another way. How about taking it to another company?"

"Well . . ." Tilly hesitated. "There *is* Hasbro's main competitor, but I've never had as much luck with them and I don't have the same contacts there."

"So?" Michelle was getting excited now; her intuition was telling her that she was on the right road. "Our goal isn't necessarily even to get a deal with the competitor."

BUY LOW/SELL HIGH REAL ESTATE

How do *you* go from zero to millions using the vehicle of real estate? As complicated as real estate investing may seem, it really boils down to becoming proficient in three specific skills:

- ▲ Finding deals: How to find real estate bargains
- ▲ Funding deals: Qualifying for mortgages and finding down payments
- ▲ Flipping deals: How to remarket the property quickly and profitably

This process includes the following seven steps:

1. **Only buy residential property within 50 miles of your home.** Single-family homes, apartment buildings, condominiums, are easier to sell, to rent, and to finance. Stay away from anything else.
2. **Pick a target territory about one mile square and become an expert there.** Within these boundaries there will be 3 to 10 excellent bargains per year. Be there first.
3. **Use one of nine methods to locate motivated sellers.** People become flexible in the selling of their property for numerous reasons:

   Management, money problems
   Out of area, out of work, out of luck, out of time, out of money
   Transfer
   Illness, inheritance, ignorance
   Vacancy
   Area in decline, attorney problems (lawsuits, liens, bankruptcies)
   Tax problems
   Estate and probate problems, emergency, early retirement
   Delinquent payments, divorce, death, debts, dissolution of partnership

"Of course not!" Tilly said brightly, understanding Michelle all at once. "Our goal is to get Hasbro to know that there's another toy company interested.

"Don't you fret, now, dear. Those executives were wrapped around our fingers at that meeting and we've got 20 fingers between us waiting to snare them again."

68 Days . . .

If Michelle had ever doubted Sam's belief in negative and positive precession,[pp. xiii–xv] she certainly believed in it passionately now. *Look,* she thought proudly as she surveyed the buzzing headquarters of the Millionaire Eagles—the place formerly known as Samantha Ann Munroe's conference room—everyone here on a Saturday, working their derrieres off. Jeremy was the only one of the team not present. He found it hard to concentrate when this many of them were in the same room together and had gone home to work from his computer there.

Michelle congratulated herself that she had worked with integrity, always putting that ahead of short-term profits, and that it had led to positive results. Tilly was preparing to do her best to get the Always Together Bear produced, and if Michelle's real estate profits continued at the same exponential rate, she would be a millionairess many times over.

The idyll ended only a moment later, when Jeremy burst into the conference room, looking like a mad scientist from a Grade B horror film, his hair sticking out in wild tufts. "It's crashed," he moaned.

Michelle had the horrible fantasy that maybe he was talking about the NASDAQ. Except that it was Saturday. What about the Nikkei?

"Our website." Jeremy plunked in the nearest chair, and let his head sink between his knees. After a moment he raised it. "It's worse than you think."

Here are nine of the many ways to find motivated sellers: (1) classified ads, (2) run your own paid ads, (3) Realtors®, (4) canvass a target territory, (5) friends and contacts, (6) banks, (7) the county courthouse, (8) investment clubs, (9) professionals (accountants, attorneys, etc.).

Start immediately with your local newspaper. Begin reading every classified ad to find clues to motivated sellers. Read ads in Houses for Sale, Condos for Sale, Investment Properties for Sale, Houses for Rent or Lease, Houses for Lease Option. Circle those ads that sound flexible. You don't want problem properties. You want excellent properties owned by people with problems. Then rotate through each of the other eight ways of finding bargains until you locate a highly motivated seller.

4. **Analyze each potential deal by asking five key questions:**

	Poor	Average	Excellent
What is the price?	1	2	3
What is the property condition?	1	2	3
What are the terms?	1	2	3
How about the location?	1	2	3
Is the seller highly motivated to sell?	1	2	3
		Total:	_____

Whether you are calling on the phone or face-to-face, ask the preceding five questions of the property owner or agent. Score each answer with a 1 to 3. For example, if the price is below the market value, give it an excellent score of 3 points. If the price and value are equal, score it average with 2 points. If the price is above the market value, give it a score of 1. The scoring should be done on the phone, before looking at a property. Each score is just an "informed guess." Total up the scores from all five questions. If the total is 10 or less, move on. If the property scores 11 or higher, go see the property. If a property still scores well after inspection, you may consider writing an offer to purchase.

5. **Determine which Nothing Down technique to use.** Nothing Down is an attitude. Quite simply it means that you want to use OPR—Other

"Why don't you tell us?" Michelle asked. Her voice sounded distant in her own ears.

"I went to log on and it kept telling me, 'Page requested not available.' To make a long story short, I finally found out that our stupid Internet service provider decided to upgrade to new servers, right? They crashed out a whole bunch of web pages, including ours. My first thought was that *they* must have backed everything up, but no dice."

"Jeremy," Michelle began, *"you* backed everything up, didn't you?"

Jeremy put his head back in his hands.

"Oh, boy." Summer slapped her hand against her forehead. "I can't believe you could be so dumb."

"Me!" Jeremy shouted, and jumped to his feet. "Me! Listen to her! Summer, you have been riding on my coattails since we started this project. You spend half your time gabbing to your sister in Phoenix and the other half doing your freaking nails, and then when we make a presentation, you stand up there like you did 70% of the work on good looks alone. Even that day we were passing out business cards—"

"How dare you!" Summer leapt up as well. "You have been hogging all the glory from Day One. While we're on the subject of taking credit, how about *Money Loves You*? You showed everyone that list of government articles 'cause that was the stuff *you* found, and somehow you just didn't bother to show all the stuff *I* found! How many times have I said to you, 'I don't know that much about computers, you have to help me help you'? But no, you've acted like what you're doing is *man's* work. You're a chauvinist pig!"

Michelle glanced at the others. Courtney and Renee looked very uncomfortable, but Sam was calm. "That's enough, you two," she said, her voice steady but loud enough to shout the combatants down. "I'm not having any of this negativity in my place."

Michelle was ashamed to admit that her more immediate concern was the website, not Jeremy and Summer's feud.

People's Resources—whenever possible. When Bob was dropped in San Francisco with only $100 in his pocket, he was able to buy six properties in 57 hours using these techniques. Other people provided everything he needed to be successful—he just had to find them. So, his challenge was not to have adequate credit, cash flow, or collateral— but to find other people willing to lend them to him. And the same holds true for you. Eventually, you will run out of money before you run out of good deals. Even if you're as rich as Donald Trump, you need to find partners to fill in the gap of your lack. That's why you first look for motivated sellers. They might be willing to sell the property to you without all of the traditional hurdles that banks and Realtors® put in your way. Then if a conventional mortgage is required, you turn to your partners to qualify for loans and/or provide the necessary down payments. Your main responsibility is to be the bargain finder—for which you receive a handsome share of the profit. If the deal is good enough, *you may not have to come up with any cash.*

See pages 286–306 for a primer on the top Nothing Down techniques.

6. **Write offers on all properties that score 12 or more.** Once you have a few creative ways to buy the property, make your offer in writing.

7. **Buy it! Keep it or flip it.** As a beginner, you may need to make as many as 50 offers before you find a seller willing to accept your creative offer. The more experienced you become, the more your ratio will improve—one in ten, one in five, one in three, and so on.

"And what exactly are you going to do about it?" Jeremy challenged Sam, folding his arms across his chest.

Michelle saw the other women cringe—but not Sam. She gazed steadily at Jeremy until he visibly wilted. "Mr. Cavalieri, you sit yourself down right now and take a few deep breaths. The first thing *you* have to do is take some responsibility for what's happened. What about it?"

"What about the way he's been treating me?" Summer wailed.

"Missy, you sit down and wait your turn," Sam said. "One thing at a time. Jeremy, who didn't back up the data?"

"The ISP," he replied defiantly. Then, under Sam's continued gaze, "And me."

"Right. Now, what can you learn from that?"[p. 24]

Jeremy mumbled, like a guilty schoolboy, "To back up the data." He shuffled his feet a little. Then he went on, in a slightly different tone, "I mean, it's still a big drag, but rebuilding the website won't be like totally starting from scratch, since I've learned so much."

Summer was sitting with her arms folded across her chest and her legs crossed. Her foot bobbed impatiently in the air. "Great," she said. "So I guess this is everybody's way of acknowledging that I've had no part in this."

"No one said that." Sam was grave, but she lightened up almost immediately with a gesture toward Michelle. "I'd like to turn the proceedings over to Michelle."

Me? Michelle gulped. She was about to demur, but then she knew that it was a challenge that Sam wanted her to accept. It felt like an important one. She knew that the day was coming when Sam would not be at her side so often. She would need to be able to handle these things on her own. Michelle took a deep breath. "Okay, let's start with you, Jeremy. What isn't working between you and Summer?"

"I think I've said it. She hasn't pulled her weight from the start. She shows up at meetings late, I call her and she doesn't call back, I explain things to her 20 times—"

BORROW YOURSELF RICH

As a real estate investor, you are trying to solve two basic problems:

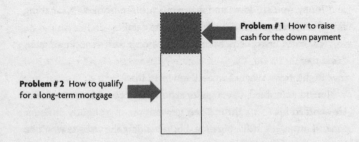

Problem #1 How to raise cash for the down payment

Problem #2 How to qualify for a long-term mortgage

If you have plenty of cash, excellent credit, and so on, then you have no problem. If you lack any of the four C's—credit, cash, cash flow, or collateral—you'll need to rely on OPR: Other People's Resources. "But," you ask, "why would a financially 'strong' investor agree to help a financially 'weak' investor?" Because you will show them how they can win by doing so. Within a 50-mile radius of you, thousands of investors are looking to invest millions of dollars at higher rates of return. These investors don't have the time, the inclination, or the expertise to ferret out great real estate deals. They'll be happy to bring you in as a junior partner for as much as 50% of the deal just for finding the property and managing the details. If the deal is good enough, they won't even look at your financial circumstances. In essence, you become a bird dog. It's how we got started. It's how most real estate investors get started.

There are nine kinds of potential partners close to every real estate deal, who can be "educated" to the benefits of participating in the deal with you:

"That's so unfair!" Summer burst out.

Michelle jumped in. "I know it's difficult, but I'm going to ask both of you not to interrupt each other. Actually, though, Summer, it is your turn. But try to stick to the facts and keep the accusations out of it."

"Huh," Summer grunted. Then, after a pause, she responded to what Jeremy had said. "What's a fact is that Mr. Big Shot loves to show off what he knows. He drops big terms like HTML and RAM and ROM and REEM and then when I ask him for an explanation, he acts like I'm a dumb blonde who can't understand anything. As for not being on time, I have been late once or twice. But not by more than a few minutes and not any more often than he is. He just always assumes that what he's doing is important and worth me waiting for, and what I'm doing is my 'freaking nails,' as he so charmingly put it."

Inwardly, Michelle thought that both Summer and Jeremy had valid complaints against each other. Jeremy had an arrogant side, an attitude that might well have been behind his failure to back up his original data. The positive side of his arrogance was that he was able to think big, something that she had come to more slowly, with Sam's encouragement. As for Summer, she was easily distracted, and Michelle suspected that she had been late more than once or twice. But when she was late it was probably because she was helping a Golden House resident with *her* manicure, not waiting for her own nail polish to dry. Summer was as conscientious and caring a person as Michelle had ever known.

"Here's something I want to say to both of you," Michelle said. "Do you all remember a discussion Sam had with us early on about the definition of marketing?"

Renee and Courtney nodded, but they knew that the question was directed at Jeremy and Summer. It was Jeremy who answered. "I was the one who asked Sam that. She said, 'The definition of marketing is building relationships.'"

The Seller
The Realtor®
The Creditors
The Renters
The Hard-Money Lenders
The Mortgage Holders
The Property
Private Individuals
The Buyer

On the next few pages, we'll teach you several specific Nothing Down techniques involving each of the preceding partners. We'll show you win/win ways for both of you to profit.

THE TOP NOTHING DOWN TECHNIQUES

Ninety-five percent of the sellers are resistant to any kind of creative financing. Ninety-five percent of Realtors® will tell you that you can't buy real estate with nothing down. Ninety-five percent of the time they are right.

As an investor, you are searching for the 1% to 5% of the sellers who need to sell NOW—and are willing to accept unconventional solutions. Then the following techniques can be very useful.

"That's right," Sam said.

Summer chimed in, probably wanting to show that she had been paying attention at the discussion, too. "Sam, you said unless you build relationships with your clientele, you'll only have one interaction with them. To be successful you need multiple interactions."

"I think you have that word for word." Sam smiled.

"Very good," Michelle agreed. "Now let me ask you, what do you think the definition of communication is?" She glanced very quickly at Sam. At a recent session at the Rock she had discussed the issue with her mentor.

Jeremy shifted from foot to foot. "Isn't it . . . I mean, it has to be telling somebody to do something."

"You're good at that," Summer said.

"Jeremy, I can see why you're getting into trouble. Here is a better definition. Communication is the response you get."

Jeremy wrinkled his brow as if he didn't understand.

"So," continued Michelle, "it follows that if you don't get the response you want, you haven't communicated properly. What response *do* you want from Summer?"

"I want her to be a strong member of our team. That means being here when I need her. I want her to learn more about computers and not mess up. I want her to come up with her own ideas, not just wait for me to give her instructions."

"You see how he—" Summer started, but Michelle took over.

"Jeremy, let's start with that last communication. Summer isn't your employee, let alone your slave. She's your partner, but that's not how you're treating her."

"Huh," Jeremy grunted, just as Summer had a moment before.

"So how do you think you can get the response you want from her?"

Jeremy thought a moment before he answered. "I can be more patient about explaining things."

"And not so smug?" Summer asked, but her tone was lighter now.

SELLER AS PARTNER

Nothing Down Technique #1: Raise the Price, Lower the Terms

Suppose the seller has a property worth $100,000 with an underlying loan of $90,000 and an equity of $10,000. He is desperate to sell. If he lists the property with a Realtor®, he will have to pay most of his equity in commissions and closing costs—leaving little or no money for the seller. Here is the dialogue you would have with the seller:

> *"Mr. Seller, I'd like to make you two separate offers for your property. The first offer is for a price of $95,000. I'll assume your first mortgage and give you $5,000 cash for your equity. The second offer is for a purchase price of $101,000—a thousand dollars above your asking price. Instead of cash, I'll give you a note for $11,000 bearing an interest rate of 10%. Let's compare both offers as if they were investments.*
>
> *"Five thousand dollars cash in a safe bank CD bearing 5% interest would grow to $8,144 in 10 years. An $11,000 secured note bearing 10% would grow to $28,531 in 10 years.*
>
> *"In fact, it would take 17 years of compound growing for the first offer just to equal what I'm willing to give you today with Offer #2. I encourage you to take Offer #2 because we both can win."*

Often the seller can be "educated" to the advantages of a Nothing Down deal.

Nothing Down Technique #2: Using Talents, Not Money

A buyer will often have professional expertise that can be "traded" in lieu of down-payment funds. Contractors, painters, landscapers, health-care professionals, lawyers, Realtors®, insurance agents, car dealers, merchants—all of these can provide valuable services or discounts that could be used in place of down payments. Sometimes a supply of plain elbow grease can help swing a deal in the absence of funds.

"And not so smug," Jeremy agreed. "See, I'm proud of the stuff I know about computers, and I guess that was my way of showing it off. And I can ask you for your input." He was talking directly to Summer now.

"This sounds very promising," Michelle said "But Summer, it works both ways. What response do you want from Jeremy?"

"I want him to treat me with respect. And I want him to include me in what's supposed to be *our* team."

"And how do you get that response?"

"Well . . . when I don't understand something, I don't need to be ashamed to ask for more clarification. We're all learning here. And I can take initiative, without waiting for his approval."

"That's right," Michelle agreed. "I think one of the reasons that you've been getting this unwanted response from Jeremy is that you have communicated to him that you're the dumb blonde waiting for her orders. If I may be so blunt."

For the first time since Michelle's mediation had begun, Summer and Jeremy looked at each other. They both seemed a little wary, but then Jeremy ventured, "One response I always want from you, Summer, is to see you smile."

"I think I can pull that off," Summer replied, and she bestowed on all of them one of her radiant, ingenuous smiles.

"I have faith in both of you," Michelle said.

"Okay, eaglets," Sam said. "Looks like we're ready to get back to work."

"And there's plenty of that to do," Courtney said, but she sounded as relieved and happy as Michelle knew everyone was.

They could all bask in that for a while and forget that the website had crashed. That one-third of their streams of income had dried up, at least for now.

REALTOR® AS PARTNER

Nothing Down Technique #3: Raise the Commission, Reduce the Cash

Let's assume the same facts as in the previous example—except, this time, the property has already been listed with a Realtor®. After closing costs and a $6,000 real estate commission, the seller effectively has zero equity. In reality, the Realtor® has the most to gain from the sale. Here is your dialogue with the Realtor®:

> "Ms. Realtor®, the seller is going to walk away with little or nothing from this sale, and the longer this property remains on the market, the further the seller goes in the hole. So here is what I propose. I'll assume the first mortgage. I'll pay closing costs for title transfer, and so on, so the seller can walk away from this deal clean. As for the commissions, instead of $6,000 in cash, I propose to give you a note for $8,000 bearing an interest rate of 6% secured by the property. I'll also give you a guaranteed listing when I sell the property anytime in the future. I'm prepared to close immediately."

This technique has a greater probability of success if the Realtor® involved is also the listing broker, so there is no need to split commissions with other agents or brokers.

CREDITOR AS PARTNER

Nothing Down Technique #4: Assume the Seller's Obligations

When negotiating, you need to ask a sensitive question: "Mr. Seller, I know this is none of my business, but it might help me solve your problem if I know what you're planning on doing with the proceeds of this sale." You're hoping to hear that the seller is planning to pay off some debts with the money he gets from the sale. If you can arrange to assume

67 Days . . .

Michelle entered the main lobby of Golden House, anxiously looking for Tilly, who had left an urgent message saying she needed to see Michelle immediately. Michelle was dreading the news, wondering if the toy deal was dead.

She walked into the lounge where she had first met Tilly. She remembered how crazy she thought the old woman had been, babbling on about being a president. Now she had actually been with Tilly to the offices of one of the largest companies in the world. Not only had Tilly not been crazy, but she turned out to have one of the sharpest minds Michelle had ever encountered.

Tilly rolled into the lounge, a somber look on her face. But her eyes gave her away. The corners of her mouth were lifting. Like a little child, she could not hide her delight.

"My dear," said Tilly, breaking into a smile. "We did it."

"What do you mean, Tilly?"

"We did the impossible. They're going to do the toy."

"What happened, Tilly? The last time I talked to you they had rejected it."

"As soon as the higher-ups at Hasbro got wind that another company might get involved, they met again in committee. Just as I thought, they've decided to 'fast-track' it. Of course, the call I made to the CEO didn't hurt."

"What happens now?"

"They're drawing up the contracts as we speak. We should have our advance within 14 days."

"Advance?"

"We get an advance on our future royalties. In the old days, I used to regularly receive advances of $100,000, $200,000, sometimes $250,000. That's changed a little bit lately with the tightening of the economy. But because of the rivalry with the other company, and because of my history with Hasbro, the CEO didn't

these debts and then pay for them over time, you can avoid having to come up with the down payment all at once.

In our example, suppose the seller has $10,000 of medical bills. He is selling his home because he wants to get out of debt. You could approach the hospital and arrange to take over the seller's obligation by agreeing to a monthly payment plan. In essence, you take the seller's debt and put it on your shoulders. The seller is relieved of the debt, you get the house for nothing down, and the hospital gets a steady stream of cash.

Everyone wins.

RENTER AS PARTNER

Nothing Down Technique #5: Using the Rents and Deposits

Deposits: Usually a landlord requires a tenant to pay first and last month's rent as a security deposit. If a property is sold, these deposits are passed along to the new buyer. Unless local laws prohibit, the buyer can use the deposit funds given to him at closing as an offset to the cash down payment obligation.

Other types of security deposits can be used toward a down payment. In one instance an investor in Tampa, Florida, needed an additional $7,000 for a down payment on a small commercial property. He discovered the previous owner had been required to deposit a $7,000 security deposit to insure the payment of the utility bill. The new buyer convinced the utility company to replace the cash deposit with a surety bond—an insurance policy that pays the utility bill in the event the bill goes unpaid. The bond cost less than $500. The $7,000 was released and used as part of the down payment at closing.

Rents: Since rents are paid in advance, a buyer who closes on the first of the month when rents are due stands to receive the gross rental income for that month. The first mortgage payment is generally not due until 30 days after closing, so the buyer has a 30-day breather. His cash down payment obligation has therefore been offset by an amount equal to the rents.

skip a beat when I told him on the phone that we wanted a $300,000 advance."

This was the first time that Michelle had heard any numbers and it took her breath away. *Three hundred thousand dollars!*

"I gave him a little room to negotiate. He countered back almost immediately—which was very uncharacteristic of him—and agreed to pay $250,000. I went ahead and made the decision without consulting you. I hope you don't mind."

Michelle had to sit down on the couch to absorb this news.

"If this toy is as successful as I think it will be, it's going to make us both millions of dollars. Hasbro wouldn't have made this decision if they hadn't felt strongly about it."

"Oh, Tilly, I just can't tell you how excited I am." Michelle was already calculating in her mind what she was going to do with her half of the advance. "I want you to know that I had made a commitment to give away 10% of my half of the money to charity."

Tilly said, "And I have just the place for you to put it—Hasbro Children's Hospital. It's located in Providence, Rhode Island. It's one of their favorite charities. I'll match your gift. That'll make the CEO happy."

"Forgive me for asking, but after this first check, how soon will other checks begin arriving?" Michelle was trying to figure out how much she could count on toward the million dollars for Ericksen.

"Oh, we won't see any more money until the middle of next year. But if my predictions come true, there will be steady royalty checks each quarter for many years to come."

This pronouncement was devastating to Michelle. The initial news had thrilled her, but now she wondered how she could have been so naïve. "How can we parlay this into the million dollars, Tilly? This isn't even close to what I need."

"Don't you worry, dear. I've negotiated to sell Hasbro only a portion of the master license—the mass-merchandising rights. Hasbro can sell to the big chains, but I've retained the rights to sell directly

When you combine these advance rents and security deposits, there can be thousands of dollars the new buyer can use toward the down payment. Bob once bought a large apartment building where these rents and deposits amounted to $16,000—exactly the amount needed for the down payment. In essence, the renters bought the property for him.

Nothing Down Technique #6: Lease/Option

When you read the classified ads in your local newspaper, be sure to check the Homes for Lease section and look for ads that indicate that the seller might be willing to lease the home with an option to buy. These are excellent sources for Nothing Down deals. Why? When you find an owner who is willing to rent the home and/or lease it with an option to buy, it indicates that the seller may not need a large cash down payment. In many instances, the seller is just trying to find a tenant to help pay the monthly payment. Often, the seller will consider a purchase with little or no money down instead of a lease.

Sometimes you should lease a home with an option to buy instead of buying. Suppose you locate this lease/option situation: An owner is willing to rent his vacant $150,000 home for $1,200 a month with an option to buy it in three years for $160,000. It might be cheaper to lease it than buy it. You get the upside potential without the ownership responsibility. If the property appreciates to $200,000 in three years, then you exercise your option, buy the property, and make the profit. If not, you move out and find another lease/option scenario.

HARD-MONEY LENDERS AS PARTNERS

Nothing Down Technique #7: At All Costs

Hard money refers to funds borrowed from banks and lending institutions under strict conditions of qualifying and repayment, generally at market interest rates. Soft money from sources like sellers comes more cheaply with terms that are generally much more flexible. For that reason creative

to the 'gift market.' There are thousands of smaller stores and gift shops across the country where we can sell the Always Together Bear."

"I know," said Michelle. "My friend Courtney has a store and goes to the gift shows every single year. I'm sure she'll know exactly what we need to do to market our bear. But how can we sell something we don't have?"

"Hasbro has agreed to include our toys with their order so we can get the lowest possible volume price. We get to pick up our toys and pay for them when they land here in America."

"How do we pay for them?" Michelle sat forward, interested.

"We plow our advance back in. With that amount we can buy approximately 60,000 toys. If we sell them to the gift market, and I'm confident that 60,000 is just a start, we can earn a profit of about $10 a toy."

$600,000 was a huge sum, but even if everything went off without a hitch, Michelle was still going to be short. She knew she had to rely on her other streams of income: her own real estate dealings and Jeremy's Internet ambitions. She had, at least, growing confidence in the former.

"What's our next step, Tilly?"

Tilly proceeded to give her a more detailed description of how a toy goes from an idea in someone's head to a physical product on the shelf at a store like Toys "R" Us. Tilly was having a fine old time, reliving past glories and demonstrating her expertise, but most of the words were unfamiliar to Michelle. *Production patterns. Counter samples. Gross units.*

Tilly concluded with a final comment. "You don't know how lucky you are, dear. This only happens once in a million years. Frankly, I honestly don't know if it's me or if there are some forces in the Universe that are combining to make this happen."

"I'd say it's both," Michelle said.

"Well, I never take less credit than what's my due, but still, you'd better say your prayers tonight."

buyers tend to exhaust soft-money sources before turning to the banking industry. Nevertheless, hard-money lenders are an important source of down payment capital to which buyers, sooner or later, must turn.

Credit Cards: It may cost 20% interest but if the deal is good enough, it could warrant pulling part of the down payment in cash advances from one or several credit cards. Or you can use your credit card to buy the seller what he needs—such as an airline ticket—for part of the down payment.

Home Equity Loans: Even in tight-money times, there are mortgage and finance companies willing to make second-mortgage loans secured by the equity in a buyer's home. Often the beginning investor will get his or her start in this way. One Arizona couple used a $20,000 home equity loan to acquire two single-family rental homes and get their investment ball rolling. They even came out with a modest positive cash flow.

Refinance Boat, Car, Stereo, or Other Personal Property: Hard-money lenders are often willing to loan money secured against valuable personal property. One buyer needed an extra $2,000 to buy an excellent condo. He had no family, no partners to turn to, and no more money in savings, but he did own a new pickup truck free and clear. He borrowed the money using his truck for collateral.

The Hardest of Hard Money: In your newspaper classifieds there is most likely a section entitled Money to Lend. These ads are placed by private individuals or small lending institutions that specialize in lending money at high rates of interest. They usually don't care about the borrower's credit—only the collateral for the loan. Suppose you locate a super bargain home valued at $100,000 that you can buy for $67,500 cash. You call the hard-money lenders and find out that they are willing to lend up to 75% of the value of a property. But the money is expensive—14% interest PLUS 10 points. (A point is 1% of the amount of the loan.) In this case, they'll lend you $75,000 but they'll deduct 10 points (or $7,500) from the amount they give you—you'll have to pay back $75,000 at 14% but you only receive $67,500. (We told you it was expensive!) But wait! Let's look at the bright side. You were able to buy a $100,000 property with OPM and you only have a $75,000 loan to pay back. You could put the property on the market and sell it for $90,000 and pocket a

63 Days . . .

Michelle and Renee tracked down their third property as they were driving along a tree-lined avenue in one of Riverdale's wealthier neighborhoods, a community with its own golf course, where million-dollar homes were the norm.

Actually, it would be fairer to say that Michelle tracked it down, since Renee was opposed to the purchase from that first day.

Michelle now had radar that seemed to detect "For Sale" signs a block away. When she saw this one, she quickly pulled over.

"Why are you stopping?" Renee asked. "This neighborhood is way out of our price range, Michelle."

This "For Sale" sign had a little box underneath containing information flyers. Michelle grabbed a sheet for herself and one for Renee, who had rather grudgingly joined her on the lawn.

"We can't afford a house like this," Renee reiterated as she looked at the sheet again. "Mickey, may I draw attention to the fact that the monthly payments on this would be astronomical? We'd be out of money in just a few months. Don't forget I have *some* experience here. Properties like this can stay on the market longer than you might think. You have to remember that rich people can afford to build their own dream homes, and they prefer to do that rather than moving into someone else's. Besides, look at this place."

Michelle knew what Renee was talking about. Given the neighborhood, it was surprising that the community would allow the house to get so run-down. The yard was overgrown with weeds, the paint was peeling from a bad paint job, and the front entry was piled with old newspapers. Obviously the house not only was vacant, it had been for many months.

But Michelle countered, "Isn't this exactly what we're looking for, the worst house in the best neighborhood? And if I've learned anything from Sam, it's that when you have a situation where other

short-term profit of $15,000. You don't care how much it costs you to borrow the money as long as you can flip the property for a quick sale. The only way this technique will work is if you negotiate a SUPER deal. But it's nice to know that if you do find a super deal, there are ways to raise the cash to fund it.

THE MORTGAGE HOLDER AS PARTNER

Nothing Down Technique #8: Discount Yourself Rich

In researching a property there are two vital questions: How much are the loans against the property? Who holds them? Most mortgage holders are banks or lending institutions that are rarely flexible or creative. But from time to time the mortgage holder is a private individual. And then the green lights start to flash!

Private mortgage holders are generally sellers who accepted a note for part of their equity when they sold the property. Now they are receiving payments over time, sometimes at below market interest rates. Some are willing to sell their notes at a discount for cash. Better to get a chunk of cash now than a trickle over many years.

The strategy is to convince a private mortgage holder to discount his mortgage for cash and then arrange for a new loan against the property that pays off the discounted mortgage. For instance, a $100,000 home has a first mortgage of $20,000 and a second mortgage of $60,000. The seller wants his equity of $20,000 paid in cash. You contact the second mortgage holder and agree to pay him $40,000 cash for his $60,000 note. He agrees in writing. You then refinance the property with a new $80,000 first mortgage. The old loan of $20,000 is paid off. The second mortgage of $60,000 is paid off with $40,000 cash. And the remaining $20,000 is paid to the seller. You end up with a home worth $100,000 and a new mortgage of $80,000. Everyone wins and you make $20,000.

A variation on this technique is to find a property with a lot of equity, create a note against it, and then sell the new note at a discount to a private investor. Suppose you find a $100,000 house with a $40,000 first

people see problems, then what you need are problems solvers. That's us."

"Okay," Renee said reluctantly, "but it looks to me like you'd be spending all of your profit fixing this place up. It has 'money pit' written all over it."

"But Renee," Michelle insisted, "I've got a *hunch* about this one." She tapped her chest. "A strong hunch."

"Huh," was Renee's bemused response. "Well, you *are* the Queen of Hunches now."

From the front lawn—"the front weed patch," Renee called it, still a bit grumpy—they called the Realtor® whose name was on the sign. The call was forwarded to her cell phone, and it turned out that she was in her car, just a few blocks away.

"See?" Michelle beamed. "It's falling into place."

A few moments later the Realtor® pulled up in a black BMW. She was about 50 and stylish in an understated way, with a tailored black suit and short salt-and-pepper hair. After cursory introductions, she let them in. The inside turned out to be much worse than Michelle had expected. Whoever had decorated it had done so with a misguided notion of saving money, or extremely bad taste. The living room and hallway colors ran to hospital green, while the kitchen cabinetry was painted a shade of yellow that clashed hideously with the avocado appliances.

Deferred maintenance was too nice an expression for the condition of the poorly kept interior. There were stains on the wall from a leak in the roof. Tile was cracked and chipped and the toilets looked like they were from the Truman administration.

With each room she inspected, Renee shook her head more and more impatiently, and each time Michelle insisted on continuing, she sighed. At the end of the tour she took Michelle aside to insist that the property was truly not worth considering.

"But doesn't that depend on the financial background?" Michelle whispered. "You'd buy it for a dollar, wouldn't you?"

mortgage against it. The seller indicates that she would be willing to sell for $80,000 for an immediate sale. This means you need to come up with a $40,000 cash down payment. You create a new $60,000 second mortgage against the property bearing an interest rate of 10% and sell this new note at a discount to a private investor. The note has a face value of $60,000 with yearly interest payments of $6,000 but it only costs the investor $40,000. Therefore, the yield on his investment is 15%—not counting the extra $20,000 built into the note. The seller gets $40,000 cash, the investor gets a note bearing 15% plus. And you buy a property with no money down.

Win/win/win.

THE PROPERTY AS PARTNER

Nothing Down Technique #9: Split Yourself Rich Using Hidden Assets

Buyers who are on their toes learn to recognize any surplus assets attached to a property that might be sold off to raise funds for the purchase. The variations are endless—everything from fixtures to parts of the land itself.

Splitting Off Furniture: One creative investor needed an extra $30,000 in down payment to buy an apartment building. During his inspection, he noticed that the units were furnished with dozens of antique-quality pieces. He made arrangements with an antiques dealer to lend him the money. Upon closing, the furniture was removed, refinished, and sold to pay off the loan. Another investor bought a commercial building and the grocery store that was the major tenant. He discovered that all of the commercial fixtures—the cash registers, the freezers, the coolers—were all paid for. He arranged for a leasing company to buy the fixtures and lease them back to the grocery store. The money raised from the lease was used to buy the entire building.

Splitting Off Other Assets: Another creative investor in Florida was $5,000 short of funds needed to purchase an option on a valuable tract of land near Orlando. While wandering over the property one day pondering

"I'm not sure about that," Renee whispered under her breath, but Michelle ignored her and turned back to the Realtor® to ask for details that weren't on the flyer.

The Realtor® reviewed the circumstances. "The owner has bought and moved to another property in Riverdale and has kept this property for over a year. It's been vacant that whole time. She's had many different offers on it but has turned them down. They just weren't quite enough. The property has recently been appraised at $1.2 million. The mortgage balance is approximately $800,000. She's a wealthy woman, so the $8,000-a-month payment doesn't seem to bother her that much. She's just waiting for the price that she wants."

Renee smiled. "That's just what I told my friend here: the payments would be too high. Sorry to take up your time." She held out her hand.

But Michelle gently pushed it down. "Not so fast," she said cheerfully. Then, back to the Realtor®, "Tell me about the mortgage."

The Realtor® referred to the flyer. "We think it's possible for a new buyer to be able to assume it."

"I would like to make an offer," Michelle said, remembering her training from Sam. "We're real estate investors. If the deal is right, we could move very quickly. My offer is $805,000. I'd like for you to write that up right here on the kitchen table and I'd be happy to sign it and give you an earnest-money check."

Renee gasped. She tugged at Michelle's sleeve, but Michelle shook her off.

The Realtor® didn't seem all that eager to pursue the offer either. "Well, $805,000—that's certainly not going to be enough to cover the mortgage, my commission, the closing costs—and there'll be other fees."

"You know," Michelle reminded her politely but firmly, "you're legally obligated to present any and all offers on a property. So I'd like to make a firm offer of $805,000. I'd be happy to give you a check for $1,000 for earnest money."

how he might come up with the necessary capital, he noticed a large area overgrown with beautiful ferns of the type one finds offered for sale in florist shops. Since problems often lead to creative solutions, he put two and two together and arranged to split off the ferns to raise enough money to bring the deal together. Today, the property is being developed into a multimillion-dollar recreational park—all because of a patch of ferns and a creative mind.

Splitting Off Part of the Property: In some cases a given property is structured so that parts of it—extra lots or individual buildings—can be split off and sold to raise funds for the acquisition. An investor in West Bend, Wisconsin, located an attractive single-family home on a large lot with a price of $99,000. Since he needed to come up with a hefty down payment, he resurveyed the property and established two lots on either side of the house. By the time of closing, one lot had sold for $15,000 and the other for $10,000, contributing the bulk of the down payment to acquire the entire property in the first place. It was all taken care of in a simultaneous closing.

PRIVATE INDIVIDUALS AS PARTNERS

Nothing Down Technique #10: If You Don't Have It, Somebody Does

Borrow Partner's Financial Statement: If the deal requires partnership support, successful investors will add to their team the strength they need and go into the marketplace with confidence. For example, a creative buyer in Albuquerque induced a seller to discount an 11-plex by over 20% and carry most of his equity on a wraparound mortgage, largely on the strength of his partners' financial statements. Both of the buyer's partners happened to be millionaires, not bad company to keep when facing an experienced seller.

Borrow Partner's Money for Down Payment: Frequently an investment partner can be persuaded to loan the buyer all or part of a down payment. The loan may or may not be secured by a trust deed on the property. In

"That won't be enough," said the Realtor®.

"We'll let the seller determine whether she wants more earnest money or not. If she'll accept my price, perhaps we might be willing to increase our earnest money to give the seller more reason to believe that we're serious about this offer. We would be happy to give you three days to check with the seller to see if that would be something she might be willing to accept."

Three days later the Realtor® called Michelle back on the phone. There was an icy undertone to her voice as she informed Michelle that the woman who owned the home had finally grown tired of carrying it and recently decided that the best option was to sell it to the next person who made her an offer. Between property taxes and the uncertainty of the market, she might just lose more if she waited longer.

"I don't understand," the Realtor® said, sounding more as if she were speaking to herself. "I have taken three other offers to the same woman, all in excess of $900,000, and she turned them down flat. And yet with hardly a second thought, she accepted your offer, knowing she would have to come up with money out of her own pocket just to be able to close this transaction and move on with her life. If I would have known she would be willing to accept this kind of price, I myself might have been willing to buy it."

This is what happens when you have intuition on your side, Michelle congratulated herself. Of the Realtor®, she thought, *Maybe if you weren't so busy waltzing with your Yabuts you would have thought of buying the property before I did.*

The closing happened a week later and true to the Realtor®'s calculation, the seller had to write a large check to be able to buy her way out of the transaction. While Michelle walked away with $400,000 in equity.

any case, the buyer who is just short on funds for the down payment is probably better off to avoid giving the partner an equity position in the property unless absolutely necessary. Equity-sharing partnerships are costly when calculated over the entire life of the investment.

Your Cash Flow/My Equity or Some Combination: Often the partner provides something other than cash to make the deal come together. An investor in Florida involved a partner to help him buy a large motel. The partner used his stock portfolio as collateral in order to borrow the $20,000 essential to the deal.

You Put Up the Cash; I Put Up the Time and Expertise: This is the most common partnership arrangement: In exchange for cash needed at the front end, and sometimes cash to offset negative cash flows, the partner receives an equity position in the property.

A beginning investor in Atlanta with only $100 rent money in his pocket was able to close his first deal using $2,000 from a partner. A father-and-son team in San Diego located a partner with the $7,000 needed to get into a condo. A Los Angeles investor lined up several partners to provide the cash needed ($148,000) to close on a 72-unit property. Regardless of the amount invested by partners, the principles are always the same.

BUYERS AS PARTNERS

Nothing Down Technique #11: Flip Yourself Rich

Whenever you make an offer to purchase a property at X price in X number of days, you sign a legal document called an Offer to Purchase. In essence, an Offer to Purchase is a short-term option. It is a legally binding agreement that obligates the seller to sell to you within a specific time frame. For example, suppose you offer to buy a $100,000 home with a closing date 60 days in the future. In essence, you have a 60-day option on this property with a locked-in price of $100,000. What if someone approaches you DURING this 60-day period BEFORE you have actually taken title to the property and offers you $110,000 for your position?

That's when the problems began. According to more than one contractor's estimate, it was going to take over $50,000 of repairs and
renovations to bring the house up to market standards. And if Michelle
used all of the Millionaire Eagles' money from the Jasko deal, she
would certainly be putting the group's profits at risk.

But that wasn't the worst of it. As Michelle got into the fix-up,
she discovered that $50,000 wasn't going to be nearly enough. And
after about a month, she was short in her construction estimate to the
tune of at least $20,000. What had seemed to Michelle to be a slam-
dunk way to make some fast cash had now indeed turned into a
money pit. Michelle made a call to one of the private lenders she had
become acquainted with in her real estate wanderings and was able to
attain an additional $25,000 at an exorbitant rate of interest to com-
plete the work. Now with the clock ticking toward her showdown
with Ericksen, Michelle was sitting on a beautifully renovated home
in an upscale neighborhood with a loan balance of about $800,000
and an appraised value of at least $1.2 million. But now the mortgage
payments had kicked in, and Michelle could see herself quickly
becoming one of those "highly motivated" sellers with $8,000/month
payments leaking out of her bank account. Jeremy did the math and
told her that she was losing about $300 a day. For some reason, the
daily rate made it all the more real, and therefore terrifying.

50 Days . . .

For two weeks, it seemed to Michelle as if every single waking
moment was spent either negotiating or signing Hasbro contracts.
The negotiations could be stressful—for after Tilly's initial verbal
agreement there were dozens of details to iron out—but they filled
Michelle with excitement, too.

Could you flip your contract to this new buyer and pocket the $10,000 profit? The answer is yes. The new buyer completes the purchase in your place. To strengthen your legal position, always include these three words after your name in the purchase offer: *and/or assigns*. This gives you the right to purchase a property AND/OR to assign your contract to someone else. (Check with your attorney about the details.)

One creative investor named John began buying HUD foreclosures using a unique strategy. Rather than buying and holding each property, he immediately flipped each one. Here was a typical deal: A home valued at $80,000 was purchased in foreclosure for $60,000 with a small down payment. He then ran an ad in the newspaper offering to resell the home for $80,000 with only $900 down. This attracted many calls. John's profit came in the form of payments made on a second mortgage that John would carry back. This may not seem like much of a profit until you learn that John was buying and flipping four to five houses A MONTH! The last time we talked to him, he had purchased and flipped over 800 homes in this manner. His accumulated equities in the second mortgages totaled millions of dollars with a cash flow of tens of thousands of dollars a month.

One investor and his spouse were on a ski vacation at a famous Colorado ski resort. To be able to get a partial tax deduction for the ski trip, he spent several hours searching through real estate listings and found what we call "the worst house in the best neighborhood." It was priced at $1,250,000 while other properties nearby were priced in the $2,000,000 to $5,000,000 range. He offered $800,000 cash. His offer was countered at $900,000. The offer was signed by both parties with a 90-day closing date. During this 90-day period, he remarketed the property and received an offer for $1,150,000—a full $250,000 higher than his contracted purchase price.

Because he had included the phrase *and/or assigns* he was able to flip the property to the new buyer and reap over $200,000 as cash profit in a few short months. He made a substantial amount of money without ever having owned the property.

That's the advantage of the flipping technique.

Once that was accomplished, Michelle and Courtney began to focus on preselling the inventory they knew they would have, 60,000 units, to the customers left to them by their share of the license. Over the next few weeks, armed with some newly created knockout prototypes, they traveled to every gift show they could get to across the country, and trekked down aisle after aisle, looking for retailers who would buy a minimum of 100. The so-called gift market was potentially enormous, but they were in a difficult bind. Although Courtney herself was looking forward to carrying the Always Together Bear in her own store, most mom-and-pop operations would not be in a position to order so many, and given her deadline as well the shipping time, it wasn't practical for Michelle to sell the toy in smaller amounts.

It was a labor-intensive process. Courtney called in a few favors from some other shop owners and gift catalog companies she worked with, and managed to move a few thousand that way, but even at $10 profit per unit, it would make only a small contribution to Michelle's million. Courtney also had the idea of approaching small chains of airport gift shops that would fall under the protection of their license, but that was also proving to be a tough challenge.

The greatest obstacle they faced was the timing. Most retailers plan their Christmas inventory six months or more in advance and the gift shows were really geared for toys that would be sold the following spring. But the gift shows did give Michelle and Courtney an opportunity to meet face-to-face with buyers and see whether they were looking for any additional merchandise or were having any problems with merchandise in the pipeline—possible manufacturer recalls or company bankruptcies. They would present their product as the perfect solution to the merchandising problem.

Their absolute favorite way to sell the bear was simply to give their pitch a personal touch. With the new professionally made prototype in hand, complete with electronics, Michelle and Courtney would present themselves as working moms traveling to the gift

THE PART-TIME JOB THAT PAYS
$120 PER HOUR

Buying real estate is a numbers game.

You may need to scan through 200 properties to find 20 that show promise. Of these, maybe 10 warrant an on-site inspection. And of these, only two or three warrant writing an offer. Then it may take 10 written offers before one seller agrees to your terms. Don't get discouraged. Look at the possible return on the hours you invest. Suppose you spend 100 hours researching and negotiating to buy one excellent real estate deal below market that nets you a $10,000 equity profit. That's like earning $100 an hour. Would you be willing to invest some of your spare time if you knew it would eventually be worth $100 an hour to you? Absolutely!

Well, the numbers get better. Suppose you spend an additional 50 hours in sweat equity to clean up the property; you could potentially increase the value of the property another $10,000. That's $200 per hour for your effort.

Then suppose you spend two hours a week on that property—or about 100 hours a year—and the property appreciates in value $10,000. That's another $100 per hour for your effort.

All told, you invest 250 hours to find, buy, fix up, and manage this one investment property. It now has an equity profit of $30,000. In one year, it is feasible to turn that one property into a money machine that nets you $120 per hour for every hour invested.

Suppose you had two like that? Or three? And all of this can be done right from your own kitchen table!

That's why we say, *Don't wait to buy real estate. Buy real estate and wait.*

shows on business and away from their kids. They would take turns playing the recorded messages for potential buyers—parents and grandparents among them. Often it made such a powerful impression on the buyer that he or she would decide somehow to make room on the shelf, even if it meant building a new shelf.

The sell-in was exhausting, but soon Michelle and Courtney were writing hundreds of orders for the bear. Tilly had been right—it was a hit, and hanging on to the gift market license had been pure genius, Michelle realized.

Back in Deer Creek, some of the residents at Golden House, especially friends of Tilly's who were excited to be part of her worthwhile project, had been on the phone successfully contacting their own networks—grown children (and sometimes grown grandchildren), children's friends, and friends of friends—to find anybody they could think of who might want to buy 100 or more of the toy.

Michelle also discovered a win-win opportunity in making arrangements with several charities. There were over 50,000 charities and charitable foundations and organizations around the country, all of whom had a need to raise money, all of whom might enjoy this particular toy. "It's perfect for grandparents," she pitched them. "It's perfect for mothers and fathers. Baby showers." If Michelle were to agree to split this profit with the charity, she could end up with a profit of as much as five dollars a toy.

After weeks of exhausting work they had managed to sell 50,000 Always Together Bears. Tilly's projections had been close—they'd moved most of their inventory. The orders were in hand. That would mean half a million in net profits for Michelle. But she wouldn't be paid until her customers took delivery, and she had 10,000 extra bears she'd eventually need to sell.

There was nothing to do but wait. Michelle was going crazy.

Tilly kept trying to reassure her. The toy was being produced in mainland China and when that was done, they would put it on

ONE MINUTE REVIEW OF THE REAL ESTATE SYSTEM

1. **To be a successful investor, you must either find value or create value.** Here is what you're looking for:
   - Discount situations
   - Distressed properties
   - Conversion opportunities
2. **Being successful as a real estate investor boils down to mastering three specific skills:**
   - Finding deals: How to find real estate bargains
   - Funding deals: Qualifying for mortgages and finding down payments
   - Flipping deals: Marketing properties quickly and profitably

There are the seven steps to this process:

Step One. Only buy residential property within a 50-mile radius of your home. Single family homes, apartment buildings, condominiums and town homes are easier to sell, easier to finance, and easier to fill. Stay away from everything else.

Step Two. Pick a target territory about one mile square and become an expert there. Within these boundaries there will be 3 to 10 excellent bargains per year. Be there first. Focus on this target territory but consider any property in the broader 50-mile radius.

Step Three. Use one of nine methods to locate motivated sellers. There are numerous reasons why people become flexible in the selling of their property.

Step Four. Analyze each potential deal by asking five key questions: What is the price? What is the property condition? What are the terms? How about the location? Is the seller highly motivated to sell?

Step Five. Determine which Nothing Down technique to use.

Step Six. Write offers on all properties that score 12 or more.

Step Seven. Buy it! Keep it or flip it.

container ships bound for the United States. "I know it's hard to wait. When you're marketing, you're busy. From what you tell me, you have plenty of other things to do. But I know how you feel. Don't you think I wish I could come help you paint one of those properties you're fixing up? The fact is, there's not much else we can do to speed up this process. Our little bear is now part of the big machinery of the toy industry."

Less than three weeks later Tilly called her to let her know that the toys were finished. Even as they spoke the bears were being prepared for shipping. The boat was scheduled to leave the next morning. There were going to be several stops along the way, and about 21 days later the container ship would be unloaded on the docks of Los Angeles.

The toys would have to be shipped via ground to the various different outlets that had made arrangements to pay for the toys upon delivery. Given two or three or four days leeway, Michelle would be receiving payment for the sale of her toys most likely a week before her deadline with Anthony Ericksen. That was if everything went smoothly.

Sam and Michelle had spent so many hours discussing the necessity for having Multiple Streams of Income,[p. 262] and now the wisdom of that philosophy was hitting home. The Millionaire Eagles hadn't made as much money as they thought they would in real estate, and all Internet profits were still hypothetical.

At the Rock the morning after the ship had left China, Sam repeated to Michelle a dictum that she had shared over two months ago. "If I had a sawmill, I'd sell sawdust as well as lumber." One could only assure one's success with Multiple Streams of Income.

"We planned on this," Sam said. "We knew that there would be failures. That's why we do Multiple Streams of Income. You never can tell where one mine shaft hits gold and the other mine shaft hits salt. So you sink as many mine shafts as you can, because eventually they are all going to produce something."

BUSINESS

Michelle counted the days in her head. By the time the boat docked, she would have scarcely less than 10 days before the challenge was up.

33 Days . . .

It had been almost two months since she'd made her bet with Anthony. Now Michelle sat in Sam's conference room alone. It was early in the morning, and none of the other team members had yet arrived. Michelle surveyed the walls where their original brainstorming pages were stilling hanging on the walls. She remembered how eager they had all been to learn, how full of hope, how naïve. She recalled how many of their initial ideas had never been implemented, how many deals had fallen through, how many leads had dead-ended in disappointment.

There were a few bright spots: Michelle smiled when thinking about Tilly and the Always Together Bear. Unfortunately, all of their profits were now sitting on a slow-moving boat. They had flipped two real estate deals for nice cash profits but had rolled these profits into a large single-family home with a huge mortgage. She'd like to take that decision back. Jeremy kept assuring her that he was preparing for a huge Internet launch that was going to generate an enormous amount of money. She'd listened to his projections and had nothing but skepticism at this point. He always seemed to overpromise and underdeliver. It was his pattern. Perhaps she had chosen the wrong man after all to be on their team. It didn't help matters when Jeremy called to say that the one Internet toy company he had been working with to buy 10,000 Always Together Bears had gone belly up.

If it's not one thing, it's another, Michelle thought. But what worried her most was the vacant property with its huge monthly payment.

In the middle of Michelle's mental review, Sam came strolling into her office to find Michelle sitting there alone. Michelle asked

MARKETING YOUR WAY TO MILLIONS

One of the fastest ways to create wealth is in climbing the Business Mountain. If you want to reach the summit of this mountain quickly—a million-dollar profit in a year or less—you need three things.

Dream: A clear vision and a definite "Why"
Team: A network of expert mastermind partners
Theme: A million-dollar product, service, or idea

Where can you find a "killer" product to market? Actually, they exist all around you right now. At this very instant you are standing in the middle of millions.

Russell H. Conwell, in his famous speech "Acres of Diamonds," said,

"Oh, my friends, if you will just take only four blocks around you, and find out what the people want and what you ought to supply and set them down with your pencil, and figure up the profits you would make if you did supply them, you would very soon see it. There is wealth right within the sound of your voice."

Within the sound of your own voice? Sounds too simple, doesn't it? Yet every great Fortune 500 business started out as an idea in someone's head. One great, brilliantly insane idea like Mickey Mouse or the Apple Computer. Or one terribly simple, boringly mundane idea like Arm & Hammer Baking Soda or Kellogg's Corn Flakes. Why couldn't you come up with an idea like that? Have you ever had an idea for a new product or service flash through your head . . . and then a few months later, you saw someone else had executed the same idea? Have you ever said to yourself, "Hey, that's *my* idea . . . I was going to do that"?

Sam what they were going to do with this large home with the even larger monthly payment. Sam pursed her lips. "You know I was quite against you buying that particular property, Butterfly."

"Were you really?" Michelle asked, her voice quavering.

Sam looked sober. "Always surprises me, how our memories work. Let me get yours going again. I was afraid we'd use up our capital and have nothing but a big fat monthly payment to show for it. Sounds like about where we are."

Michelle hung her head. Finally she asked, "What are our options at this point?"

"Well," Sam said, "we could put an ad in the paper and lease option it. I'm sure you could get rid of it fairly quickly that way, and frankly, that might be your best option."

"But that doesn't give me the cash I need," said Michelle.

"Missy, at this point, you're losing cash at about $8,000 a month. You may run out of money to be able to make the next mortgage payment and then you're going to be in the same situation as all the people you've been buying property from."

"How does that work—a lease option?"[p. 294] Michelle asked.

"You put an ad in the paper that says 'Lease option—Lease this home with an option to buy it.' You're right, it doesn't give you the cash, but it stops the bleeding."

Michelle still didn't quite understand. "Who'd go for something like that?" she asked despairingly. "If they can afford that payment, why not buy their own house?"

"There are people out there who have the cash flow, but not the lump sum for a down payment, and they don't want to go about it our way. What you're more likely to find is a fairly wealthy person or couple or family who's just moved to town—maybe one of them has been transferred—and they want to rent for a while while they check out the neighborhood. If they do buy the house, you'll eventually get your cash. The most important thing is that it preserves your equity."

Well, now it's your turn to execute your own million-dollar idea—to do it—to manifest your idea into reality.

As you go about your day today, ask yourself these "what if" questions:

What million-dollar business idea is floating around in my head right now?

What if I could notice a need in my own neighborhood that could turn into a profitable business?

What if I knew someone who already had a fabulous business idea but wasn't executing it?

Don't concern yourself with how you would pull it together or where you would get the money to do it or even how would you find the people who might want to buy it. First, just incubate the idea.

Imagine what it could be like to own a multimillion-dollar business.

TOP 10 MILLIONAIRE TRACKS
FOR ENTREPRENEURS

There are more than six million businesses in North America. Of these businesses, 98% have fewer than 100 employees and have average annual gross incomes of less than a million dollars. We want to show you how to be in the top 2%—with only a handful of employees while earning as much as a million dollars net income per year. Interested?

To do this, you'll have to polish your entrepreneurial skills. At the turn of the last century, over 90% of us were small-business entrepreneurs. During the Industrial Revolution, we came off the farms and into the cities

"Is there *any* way I could get some cash out of this situation sooner?" Michelle asked, still focusing on the Ericksen bet. "I mean, especially if we got down to the last few days?"

"Well, no bank is going to lend you more than about 75% or 80% of the property's value. So in this particular case, you'd probably not be able to get a second mortgage for more than $100,000."

"At least that would give me $100,000 in cash that could go toward the amount of money that I need."

"I wish you hadn't told your daddy-in-law you were going to make a million in cash," Sam said, grinning for the first time since their conversation had begun. "The next time you do something like this, make sure you can be a paper millionaire instead of a cash millionaire. It would have made it a whole lot easier on all of us."

Michelle forced a grim smile in response. "I guess I will put that lease option ad in the paper. We haven't had a nibble in three weeks of showing it."

"Time to try something new," Sam agreed. "Offer some good terms. Put in there that you might be willing to carry some financing or you might be willing to exchange for something else. 'Beautiful home, best neighborhood, totally renovated, ready to move into. Do you have something you'd like to exchange for it? Or a lease option?' Let's throw some flexibility out there. Let's see if we can exchange for something."

"Exchange for something? Why would I do that?" Michelle asked. "What I need is cash."

"So you keep saying, and so I'm well aware. Time to face facts, missy. You have a property that you can't sell. And you can't convert to cash. You can't borrow against it because there's not enough equity there. What we need at this point is something else that might be more easily sold."

"But we're running out of time, Sam."

"I understand. But we don't have any other options at this point. Just put the feelers out there. Let the networks—including

to find work. We gave up our independence for a steady, secure paycheck. So much for that pipe dream! Now we're being forced back to the farms, so to speak—back to individual financial responsibility.

The world is desperate to have more entrepreneurs. According to Warren Buffett, there are only two ways to create wealth: find value or create value. Entrepreneurs find and create massive value for other people at a profit. Entrepreneurs create jobs, foster excitement, and basically make the system work. They see possibilities where others see only problems. Entrepreneurs think to grow rich. As they do they inevitably enrich the lives of others. Our objective is to awaken the entrepreneur that is hidden inside you. As you awaken your moneymaking possibilities, you will make everyone better off and no one worse off.

Most people are acquainted with a few entrepreneurial business models but there are literally dozens of them. Following are 10 of the most basic models. One of these models will work for you.

1. B to C Model: Businesses selling to individual Customers (like Wal-Mart, McDonald's)

2. B to B Model: Businesses selling to other Businesses (OfficeMax or Sisco Foods)

3. B to G Model: Businesses selling to Governments/government agencies (Fedco)

4. B to P Model: Businesses selling to Philanthropies and charities (Chicken Soup & Red Cross)

5. B–B Model: Buying out (–) your Boss and becoming owner

6. B to C^2 Model: Business to Customer Joint Venture (Network marketing, Avon, USANA, etc.)

7. B to B^2 Model: Business to Business Joint Venture (Partnership between two companies)

8. I to CBGP Model: Intrapreneur to C, B, G, or P as a commissioned employee (3M)

9. L to CBGP Model: License your ideas to C, B, G, or P (Duracell battery)

10. C to CBGP Model: Consult your ideas to C, B, G, or P

the Infinite Network—start to work. The Universe can't help you if you're not doing anything. You have to be moving. What we need at this point is movement. We've been standing still for so long. Move! Get it going. Get something happening. That's what it's going to take."

Michelle sighed.

"Something else, Michelle." Sam's serious tone immediately got Michelle's attention. "I've done my best to help you learn to use your intuition. Ever since you told me about this property you've been saying that it has to be right because your intuition told you so. But it's not quite that simple. Intuition is a tender flame. It can be influenced by a lot of things, but there are two factors you have to watch out for. One is greed, and one is fear. They're like two bullies. The bully of fear can cause you to not do something that you ought to do. But the bully of greed can influence you to do something that you ought not to do. I can't see into your heart, though I know you think I can sometimes, but it seems to me in hindsight—"

"Yeah, hindsight," Michelle said.

"It seems to me," repeated Sam, "that the bully of greed might have been talking into your ear during this one. I remember in the early days of my own investing, I got kind of cocky. And it's easy to get cocky when the deals seem to be going your way. But this was necessary, too. The only way an investor can become a great investor is to lose on a couple and to realize that there is no safety net. That when you lose, you lose, and it can cost you an awful lot of money. So I hope that you're at least learning that from this process. You get that ad in, but don't just wait for the phone to ring. Put the word out. Let people know that you have a beautiful home here that you might be willing to exchange for something else. Like, if they have a smaller home that's free and clear. Say, somebody who has a $400,000 home—same as your equity in this alligator—who is just dying to move up and to get into the right neighborhood,

THE ONE MINUTE MARKETING PLAN*

Complete this four-step marketing plan before you launch your new business. Review it one minute each day. It will amaze you.

ONE. THE BIG PICTURE: WHAT EXTERNAL CONDITIONS WILL AFFECT MY BUSINESS THIS YEAR?

Research the six major trends in your industry. Identify one opportunity (+) and one challenge (–) facing your business in the next year:

Economy:	(+)_____	(–)_____
Main competitors:	(+)_____	(–)_____
Technology:	(+)_____	(–)_____
Ecology:	(+)_____	(–)_____
Social/Cultural:	(+)_____	(–)_____
Legal/Political:	(+)_____	(–)_____

---

*© The One Minute Marketing Plan was created by Mark Victor Hansen, Robert G. Allen, and John Robert Eggen.

with the right golf course. That's a kind of home that we could crank."

"Crank?" Michelle echoed.

"Oh, that's just slang for refinancing your equity. See, if we could trade your large home for a smaller home that's free and clear of mortgages, we could refinance the new home and pull some cash out. Do you follow me?"

"Yeah," Michelle said tentatively.

Sam cocked her head. "Michelle, one minute you're steeped in the gravity of the situation, and then the next minute you don't get it at all. You've got to be willing to do whatever it takes. So get busy."

"All right," Michelle said.

As she headed out of Sam's office, Sam called after her, "Put the ad in first. We want it in tomorrow's newspaper."

It was in. Michelle merely revised what Sam had spoken aloud:

Exquisite home
Exclusive neighborhood
Perfect move-in condition
Looking for exchange or lease option
Extremely flexible

Michelle was walking up to the front door of Sam's bungalow when her cell phone rang. It was Stephanie from Sam's office. "Michelle, the phone here has been ringing off the hook with response to your ad. People seem to be really interested in the terms you've been offering. I haven't known what to tell them, so I've just taken a list of numbers down here. At least 12 people have called."

"Can you fax me the names and numbers of those people?"

TWO. MY DESTINATION: WHAT ARE MY BUSINESS GOALS FOR THE NEXT YEAR?

Financial goals:

What is my first year sales goal?
$_____

Minus how much for product costs?
$_____

Minus how much for marketing?
$_____

Minus how much for overhead?
$_____

What is my estimated profit/loss?
$_____

Additional marketing goals:

Total # of units sold?
_____

Total # of customers in database?
_____

To improve product quality?
_____

To improve costs per sale?
_____

Total amount donated to charity?
_____

THREE. MY CUSTOMERS: WHO ARE MY CUSTOMERS AND WHAT DO THEY WANT?

Interview successful people in your industry who are not your competitors and uncover the following information:

What does my perfect customer look like? Age _____ Sex _____
Occupation _____ Income _____ Location _____
What does my perfect customer want? _____
Which of my product benefits does my perfect customer value most? _____

FOUR. MY MARKETING SYSTEMS: HOW WILL I FIND AND SERVE MY CUSTOMERS EFFECTIVELY?

Product: Given my customers' wants and my competitors' products, how can I position my product to be superior? What's my USP?

What's my **U**ltimate Advantage? _____
What's my **S**ensational Offer? _____
What's my **P**owerful Promise? _____

"Sure thing. Are you at Sam's house now? I can fax everything over."

"Thank you, Stephanie. And forward any more calls to my cell phone." Michelle hung up. She walked into the house, into the familiar place where all this had begun not that long ago. She looked in on the small bedroom where she had awakened on that very first morning when Sam had pulled her out of bed for a jog to the Rock. In the past two months, she couldn't remember a single morning that she'd missed her run except for her day of rest, which was on Sunday. She had a few near misses, but it was a firmly ingrained habit for her now. She could feel the surge of energy that flowed through her whenever she finished her exercise, and she knew that this extra flow of energy could last her late into the night. When she had been younger, she used to get tired about a half an hour after supper and was usually in bed and asleep well before 9:30. Of course, having two children close together had put some stress on her energy levels. But she could see now that it was more than that.

Maybe it was the deadline that was pushing her to stay up longer hours. She thought constantly of Nicky and Hannah—and Gideon. Gideon's spirit seemed to be with her at all hours, energizing her to move forward and get their family back together.

In spite of the risk she was facing, she couldn't remember a time in her life when she was more excited to be alive. Maybe it was the way that she was exercising. Maybe it was just the flow of exciting ideas that were constantly pumping through her head. She found herself easily awake well past 11:00 at night and rarely slept past 5:45, up and ready to tackle another day.

There was something that she actually loved about living on the razor's edge, walking the tightrope of life. She looked at people differently now, the people in their cubicles at work plugging their umbilical cords into the mother ship and sacrificing some of their freedom for a little more security. She remembered a moment at the Rock when Sam had told her, "There are only two doors in life:

Pricing: How will I profitably package my products to be perceived as a "super value" compared with those of my competitors?

_____

Distribution: How will I profitably and promptly deliver my products to my customers (directly and through intermediaries)?

1. _____ 2. _____ 3. _____

Advertising and Publicity: Rank the order in which you will test various channels of paid and free media to attract qualified leads:

Radio _____ TV _____ Newspaper _____ Direct Mail _____ Internet _____

Free PR _____ Other _____

(As you test each approach, determine your cost per lead [CPL = ad cost divided by the # of people who respond]. The goal is to discover which media mix gives you the lowest CPL.)

Personal selling: Rank the order of the methods you will test to convert your qualified leads into paid customers:

Inbound phone _____ Outbound telemarketing _____ Internet _____

Face-to-face _____ Groups _____ Direct mail _____ Wholesalers _____

Other _____

(As you test each selling approach, determine your cost per sale [CPS = ad costs plus sales costs divided by # of sales]. The goal is to discover which sales mix gives you the lowest CPS.)

Sales promotions: What special offers will I test to stimulate first-time trials of my products? _____

_____

Marketing information: How will I track and analyze my weekly marketing activities to measure progress toward my one-year goals? _____

_____

Marketing experts: Which experts will I consult to help me maximize my marketing? _____

the door marked 'Security' and the door marked 'Freedom.' If you choose the door marked 'Security,' you lose both."

When Sam had said that, Michelle had thought she was crazy. Back then, the thing that she wanted most in her life was security. She wanted to be able to come home, to a home that she owned, and most of all, to a family that she loved. She wanted to be able to feel like there was nothing that could harm her or her children. She wanted to be in a cocoon. And yet, she now knew, having lived both sides of the equation, that no other life would ever be able to compare to the aliveness that she felt, to the clarity of her thinking, to the quickness of her step. It was a lifestyle that she wouldn't have chosen unless she had been forced to experience it. But now, having been forced, she understood what Sam was talking about.

She would never choose the door marked "Security" again. "Freedom" was the only option left. She rushed to the fax machine to find the list that Stephanie had sent her, and just as she was sitting down at the kitchen table with a cup of hot chocolate, her cell phone rang.

"Hello, this is Michelle."

"Are you the lady who wants to trade the home for something?"

"Yes, I am. Do you have something you'd like to exchange for a beautiful home in an exclusive neighborhood?"

"Well, I just might be able to offer you something that's a possibility. I've got some very valuable rubies from South America that I'd like to trade for the equity in your home."

"Uh, thank you very much. It just doesn't seem to be what I need right now. I need something that I can turn into cash."

"These stones can be sold."

"Then why don't you sell them yourself?"

"I'm just looking for a place where I can take the entire inventory that I have and exchange them. I'm looking for a home to live in."

"I have to say, sir, that I hadn't considered taking gemstones for the property."

ONE MINUTE MARKETING MAGIC

Marketing is the oxygen of your new business. Dan Kennedy, the great marketing guru, illustrates the power of marketing with the results of two almost identical ad headlines. Guess which of the following ads out-pulled the other by a factor of eight to one.

> **Headline #1: Put Music into Your Life**
> **Headline #2: Puts Music into Your Life**

They look similar. But if the first headline generated $10,000, the second one would have generated $80,000. It's the difference between survival and enormous success. On this page we'll teach you the essentials of marketing success in three simple steps.

Step #1: Look for Addicts. No, we're not talking about drug addicts, but addicts in the positive sense. Every one of us is positively addicted to something—exercise, weight lifting, golf, sports, Beanie Babies, food, hobbies, dieting, Häagen-Dazs, chocolate, money, prayer, pregnant mothers, video games, Starbucks. Addicts make the best customers. Addicts buy quickly and more often. Addicts talk to other addicts. Your motto: Addicts R US.

Step #2: Make Your Ads Addicting. You've heard about USP—Unique Selling Proposition. Here's how to make your USP positively addicting.

▲ *Ultimate Advantage.* What one benefit does your customer "get" that they won't get from a competitor? Gold prospectors in the 1870s bought Levi Strauss jeans because their jeans were reinforced with a patented copper rivet. Nobody else could compete, so Levi's became the standard for toughness in men's work clothing. What's the "copper rivet" for your product? You must find it and flaunt it.

"Think about it and I'll call you back."

"Tell you what, if you want to put your proposal in writing, I might be willing to consider it. I've got to bounce it off of my associates."

As she hung up the phone, Michelle shook her head. Rubies from South America. What next—the Brooklyn Bridge? "Maybe he'd trade the rubies for 10,000 stuffed bears," she chuckled to herself. At least there was a little comic relief in all this.

Michelle spent the next two hours returning the messages that Stephanie had sent her. She was about to make her final call when her call waiting beeped. She flipped over to the other line.

"Michelle here."

"I think you're the lady I'm looking for," said the male voice on the other end. "Is your name Michelle Ericksen?"

"Yes, this is Michelle Ericksen."

"My name is Fred Tandy. I received a letter from you about 30 days ago regarding your interest in an apartment building that I own in the Branson area of Riverdale." Michelle racked her brains and tried to remember which letter he was referring to. She had sent at least 500 letters in the previous six weeks to all different kinds of people around the country.

"You'll have to be a little more specific. Exactly what street is it on?"

"It's on Parkinship Road." Michelle had a faint image of a fairly run-down apartment building, and then it came back, so vividly that she was surprised she had ever forgotten. She had made inquiries of a shirtless apartment manager who smelled of beer and marijuana and who complacently shared that the owner, being from out of state, never checked on his building.

"Yes, I do have a recollection of that building now. How can I help you?"

"I've actually been out of the country. My mail has piled up and so, several weeks later, I'm finally getting through to all of the various

▲ *Sensational Offer.* Do you recognize a good deal when you see it? Eight music CDs for only 1 cent! Now, that's a good deal! It made Columbia House a fortune. What bonuses could you offer to "sweeten" your deal? An extended warranty? A discount coupon? A valuable special report? A free CD-ROM? Something that doesn't cost much but gives high perceived value. Build into your price enough room to offer "surprise" bonuses.

▲ *Powerful Promise.* Offer a clear, unmistakable, no-questions-asked guarantee. Then supercharge it. Marriott Hotels promises: "Your meal in 30 minutes or it's free." Now, that's a promise with teeth! Make powerful promises that you can keep.

Step #3. Leverage Your Efforts with Joint Venture Partners. Hook yourself up with people who already have relationships with existing groups of positive addicts. Get their endorsement to introduce your product to their clients/customers for a split of the profit. Rather than competition, think cooperation.

Look for addicts. Make your marketing addicting with a powerful USP. Leverage yourself with partners. Reviewing this list for one minute each day will put you ahead of 99% of all businesses in the world. We promise.

people who sent me letters. I'm interested in what you wanted to know about the apartment building."

"At the time I was interested to find out if you might be willing to sell it. I'm a real estate investor. I like to buy properties at the best prices I possibly can. I don't know what your circumstances are or whether you might be willing to consider a sale or an exchange."

"Exchange. That's an interesting option. Actually I hadn't considered selling it, but just recently discovered that my apartment manager has been skimming money off the top of the rents and has not been paying a lot of utilities, or making the repairs he's responsible for overseeing. I found this out when one of my tenants had his electricity cut off, and since we're on a centralized meter, he called me in a panic, trying to determine what happened. Supposedly, the manager's apartment has been vacant and we do not know where he is at this point. The building has really gone to seed and it's frankly been a pain in the neck."

Michelle appreciated his candor but decided there was nothing to be gained by commenting further, now that the owner clearly understood the circumstances.

"My wife and I have owned the building for many years while we've been out of the area, but now we're planning on coming back. My wife has been begging me to return, but my work has kept us on the road. I finally decided to go into business for myself. What's the good of a good job if your family life is suffering?"

Michelle's pulse quickened. This time she really could trust her intuition, because she and this man could help each other. A fair, win-win deal. "Mr. Tandy, it just so happens that I have a beautiful home that has been completely renovated. It's on a golf course in a very fine neighborhood. It has three appraisals on it at $1.2 million. And the mortgage on it is about $800,000 at this point. I was looking for an older, dilapidated apartment building that I could trade it for."

Mr. Tandy chuckled at her bluntness. "The house sounds about exactly like what we might be looking for, and the building we own

ANTIMARKETING:
ATTRACTING PERFECT CUSTOMERS

Previously, we've learned the principles of manifesting abundance. Now let's apply these principles to marketing. The techniques of traditional marketing (advertising, promotion, and PR) are very left-brained—numbers, quotas, databases, closing ratios, CPM, and so on. What you are about to learn is right-brain marketing. It's beyond permission marketing, beyond relationship marketing, beyond guerrilla marketing. In fact, it's so revolutionary, we call it *antimarketing*.

Stacy Hall and Jan Brogniez, in their powerful new book *Attracting Perfect Customers*, say that the main reason why so many businesses fail is precisely *because* they waste so much money on traditional marketing in finding or "targeting" customers.

Hall and Brogniez propose that it is time for us to question those who say "it is difficult to find good customers, that we have to steal them from our competitors, and that we have to keep meeting our customers' ever-increasing and outrageous demands in order to keep them as our customers." Instead, they recommend applying the principles of attraction "to envision perfect customers easily flocking to your doors on a regular basis."

What!? Does this mean cutting ad budgets and scrapping direct mail campaigns? Yes! Hall and Brogniez have amassed impressive success stories with companies large and small to prove their point. "There is a long-held adage that 20% of a business' customers account for 50 to 80% of the profits. If these 20% account for the vast majority of profits, why does the company need the other 80%? Is it possible to build a business where every customer is 'the best' or, as we would say, the 'most perfect'?"

Yes. "It's the difference between working hard to find customers and having them attracted to your organization as if 'by magic.'"

most certainly needs a little TLC, as they say in your business. I'm sure the deal would depend on whether my wife would like the home or not. We're not planning on being in Riverdale for another two or three months, but your proposal is one we might consider once we move back."

Michelle's heart sank. "Could we make arrangements for it to happen a lot sooner? I have personal reasons for needing to move on this right away."

"My current employment contract doesn't expire for another two or three months, so I just can't see how I could do it any quicker than that."

"You mentioned that your wife's opinion was the deal-maker or -breaker anyway. Why don't you bounce it off of your wife, and see whether or not she might consider coming to look at it? Frankly, my phone has been ringing off the hook with calls from people who are interested in this particular property, and I just put the ad in yesterday. I've received 13 calls already on it, but my gut tells me that you're the one."

"Ms. Ericksen, you're a very interesting young lady, and I like your straightforward manner. All right, I'll bounce it off of my wife and get back to you as quickly as I can."

Michelle hung up the phone, hoping that she had turned the direction of her precession from negative to positive. She went back to her list of calls, then made herself a salad and fell asleep in front of the fireplace, suddenly too exhausted either to eat her light dinner or to change out of her clothes.

She slept fitfully at first and then fell into a deep dream. It was as if she had drifted upward through the ceiling of her simple bedroom and floated freely out into the night air. Below her was Sam's cottage, surrounded by the twinkling lights of the sleeping city. Drifting farther skyward, she noticed the surrounding cities sparkling together in the darkness. Up and up, until the lights of a hundred cities, a thousand small towns, flickered in the patchwork of the

So, how do you do it? You begin by asking four critical questions of your business:

1. What does my perfect customer look like? (Imagine your ideal customer.)
2. What makes my perfect customer tick? (What inner values drive him or her?)
3. What do *I want* my perfect customer to expect of me? (Rather than doing market research to discover what your customers want, this question is to help you get clear about what YOU want to provide! In other words, if you want to take Fridays off, you want to attract customers who will expect that of you.)
4. What do I need to improve about my business to attract more perfect customers?

According to Hall and Brogniez: "The clearer you become in what *you want* your perfect customers to expect from you, the more of them will appear—quickly and easily."

We encourage you to use both traditional "left-brained" finding strategies combined with these new "right-brained" attracting strategies to maximize your marketing efforts.

night below, linked by ribbons of flowing lights. Up and up again until the entire earth came into view—a blue ship sailing on the vast ocean of stars.

She wanted to linger there, but she found herself being drawn farther out into space, beyond the sun and its circling planets, speeding through the milky stream of stars. Even farther into space, past the flat spiral of the Andromeda galaxy with its two trillion suns. So far out that every patch of light she saw—up, down, and all around her—was not a star but the light from a galaxy of stars.

Michelle had seen pictures of galaxies in magazines but had never experienced time-traveling through them before—not like this—floating in the mind of God. As her mind expanded to this new dimension, her own problems and pressures shrank to subatomic proportions.

She couldn't remember the journey back. She found herself observing a woman sleeping peacefully on her bed just before daybreak. She felt intense love for this woman, whoever she was—so vulnerable, yet so strong. So insignificant and so magnificent at the same time. And then she realized that the woman was herself.

When she woke it was morning. Her eyes were moist. But she felt more at peace than she had felt in months.

23 Days . . .

Over the next several days, Michelle made a few attempts to contact Mr. Tandy, but he and his wife seemed to be on the move again, since the number he had given her was no longer in service.

No matter, she thought at first, as many more promising leads came her way. Yet as she pursued them, one by one, they went cold. Now she was days away from yet another $8,000 mortgage payment. She remembered hearing a folktale as a child about a man who loads up his boat with treasure. The treasure sinks the boat and the man drowns. Would this "treasure" of a house sink her boat, and her with it?

INFO-PRENEURING—A MILLION-DOLLAR BUSINESS FOR EVERYONE

There is no better way to make millions than being an info-preneur. This strange word is a twenty-first century hybrid of *information* entre*preneur*. In simple language, you market and sell information—either yours or someone else's.

In the process you get to share:

- ▲ knowledge
- ▲ entertainment
- ▲ adventure
- ▲ how-to-do
- ▲ how-to-be
- ▲ inspiration
- ▲ little-known secrets
- ▲ your life or the life of another
- ▲ special interests
- ▲ hobbies
- ▲ work habits
- ▲ observations
- ▲ successes or failures
- ▲ imagination
- ▲ spirit
- ▲ soul
- ▲ love
- ▲ enthusiasm
- ▲ humor or sadness (as we have done for many years) with others
- ▲ ways to make millions and love life to its fullest at the same time!

Why did I do that deal? she asked herself nearly every minute. *Why? Why? Why? If I had just kept doing what I was doing. If I could have just bought smaller properties. I was comfortable there. I knew what I was doing.*

As she sat in Sam's conference room one afternoon, alternately reproaching herself and pondering her next move, Stephanie brought her a message. Michelle looked at it carefully, then fairly grabbed the nearest phone. "Mr. Tandy?"

"Yes, hello, Mrs. Ericksen. My wife is especially anxious to take a look at the house since she's quite familiar with the neighborhood, as it turns out. We've made arrangements to fly in over the weekend. If it's what we have in mind, then you just might have a deal."

As he spoke, Sam walked into the conference room. Michelle covered the receiver and whispered, "It looks like that guy with the apartment building might consider taking our home in exchange." Sam nodded her approval.

"Mr. Tandy, I'm pleased to hear that. When are you coming in? Well, then, I'll pick you up at the airport the day after tomorrow. 9:30 in the morning? Excellent. We can go straight to the house if that will work for you. Is there a way I could take a look at the apartment building before you get here?"

"Yes," Mr. Tandy said. "I made arrangements to have the new apartment manager take you through some of the units tomorrow. We actually have three vacancies right now—we're lucky not to have more, so that will give you a good idea what the units look like."

"What will your asking price be?"

"Well, just like you, I figure we'll get a professional appraisal. We can go from there."

"And what kind of mortgage is on it?"

"Oh, it's free and clear. All paid for."

That's my guy. "Thank you, Mr. Tandy. I'll see you at 9:30 in the morning, the day after tomorrow."

Michelle hung up the phone and looked over at Sam, who was now perched on the edge of the conference table. "What do you

By being an info-preneur you change, not just your immediate sur-roundings and people with whom you have direct contact, but the world.

You Make a Difference! In return the world pays you handsomely for sharing.

There is not an easier or less costly business in the world to engage in. Think of it: You manufacture from your mind or the mind of another and harvest it without huge tooling, production, and manufacturing costs.

Let's face it, today you can produce a book for nothing except time. How is that possible? Simply write a book, and sell it electronically as an e-book. No print costs, no delivery costs! The money you earn for doing this can be automatically deposited in your bank account. Yes, this new twenty-first-century system is in place and operational, right now, and many authors are discovering the rewards of being their own publishers.

Furthermore . . . You can use the revolutionary print-on-demand printing system. It is remarkable. All you do is write the book, lay it out so it looks like a book, and send it by e-mail to the printer. Within two weeks, you have your book delivered to your doorstep or delivered to your customers, automatically. You can print as few as 25 books for as little as a penny a page and about a $1.50 for the cover. Today, anyone can be a published author.

More Revolutionary . . . You don't even have to write your book. You can talk it. There are several voice-activated programs that will place those words hidden in your brain onto the computer screen via voice, not fingers.

More Wonders Still . . . There are simple systems that will guide you through writing your book in a weekend, a week, or a month.

On the next pages, you'll find the seven-step system for turning infor-mation into cash.

think?" Sam asked, having picked up the relevant portions of the conversation.

"I'm afraid to say it sounds good—not what I once thought was good, but anyway . . . It's a 20-unit apartment building that's across the street from where the new mall is going in. It's an old building, and as apartments, they're marginal, from what I could tell from the manager's unit. He might not be the best representative, though," she said ruefully, remembering the stink of alcohol and drugs.

"If it could be converted into office space, it could be substantially more valuable," she continued. "But I need to look at it, which I'm going to do tomorrow afternoon."

"Good plan," Sam said, and even this mild expression of approval did a lot to erase the pain of her earlier reprimands.

20 Days . . .

When Michelle walked out of the closing of the apartment building, she felt both extreme relief and total dread. The house was gone, along with its $8,000 per month payments. And Michelle was now the proud owner of a 20-unit apartment building that needed a bare minimum of $100,000 in work to bring it back up to speed.

According to the appraisals, the building was worth about just under $1 million. Michelle's equity in her house was $400,000. She used this as the down payment, and the seller financed the deal, giving her a loan for $600,000. This left Michelle with a small positive cash flow after the rents and mortgages were paid. Michelle was almost panicked to think about the hundreds of hidden problems that could suddenly appear. She had stopped her deal from becoming a catastrophe. Could she still turn it into a success?

THE BOOK WITHIN:
THERE IS A BOOK IN YOU

We firmly believe that all people—including you—have at least one good book in them. You have enough information and experience in your head *right now* to turn into a lifetime stream of income. With some proper positioning, your book can become the cornerstone of an information empire. An information empire? Well, at the very least, a modest stream of income that could support you and your family.

Almost all success books start off with a miserable failure. The author tells how he or she used to be fat, poor, ugly, unhappy, lonely, addicted, or dead and through some miracle, willpower, or newfound knowledge was able to overcome failure and rise to the heights of success. Many authors now produce books, seminars, newsletters, tape programs, video courses, speeches, consulting relationships, and infomercials. They turned their "failure-to-success" story into a fortune.

What is your story? Everything in your life has value. The failures. The successes. It's all part of the equation. One mediocre idea with some good marketing can generate a lifetime stream of cash flow. And with some luck can turn into millions. So figure out how to turn your life around now and then tell the rest of us how you did it.

There are three essential skills of the successful info-preneur.

▲ **Skill #1: Targeting: Finding Schools of Hungry Fish.** Think of your market as a school of fish. Does your market contain enough fish? Is it a growing or declining school of fish? Is it easy to find where they are and what their feeding pattern is? Are they really hungry? Is the weather cooperating? Does a certain bait make them go into a "feeding frenzy"? Are they willing to come out of the safe, dark depths to fight for this new bait? Can you catch them?

Michelle anxiously sat in the passenger seat of Sam's Mercedes as they headed for the building on Parkinship Road.

"Well, Butterfly, you've come a long way in two months. You're the owner of an apartment building with $400,000 in equity that I don't think half the people this side of town would want. But let's go have a look at it. Let's go see what we've got to play with here."

They pulled up in front of the building. Michelle glanced across the street to see where the construction work had already begun on the mall. Most of the surrounding homes had been vacated and would soon be torn down or moved, and ultimately her acquisition would be a prime piece of commercial property. Whether she would be able to capitalize in a short period of time was still to be seen.

Sam got out of the car and strolled up and down the block in front of the building. "I want to go inside in a minute," she said. "But this is what I would do if I were you, Michelle. Obviously the building is going to take a lot of work and frankly, you don't have the time to do it. What I suggest is that you get a hold of the owners of the mall and talk to their real estate arm. They might be looking for properties around the mall to acquire on spec, since the values are sure to take a big leap with the rezoning. They can convert it to office space and make a bundle. But what *we* want to do is flip this property as quickly as we can. And that's what it's going to take. It's another win-win."

"I don't entirely follow."

"Right now this apartment building is worth about a million. But as office space—which it can become now that the street is rezoned—this same property will probably be worth $1.5 to $2 million. Maybe you can get somebody to pay you $1.5 million. Essentially what you're doing is splitting the future profits in exchange for getting your share out *now*."

"What if the person I approach won't go for it?"

Sam regarded her sharply. "What do you think?"

"I think . . . I think I need to see if I can find another developer who sees the same potential. And fast."

- ▲ **Skill #2: Baiting: Creating Irresistible Bait.** Find a way to offer your expertise in such a way that the fish "rise to bite in a feeding frenzy." Basically, there are no real new or totally unique human needs or wants. They have been the same for millennia. Sex, money, self-esteem, health, God, relationships, beauty. Your information should tap into one of these universal wants/needs with just the right bait at just the right time.

- ▲ **Skill #3: Lifetiming: Landing Lifetime Customers.** With just a few thousand loyal customers, you can create a powerful information business. If each customer spends just $100 a year for your information, you can make $100,000 a year with as few as a thousand customers. If you can find a thousand customers to spend $1,000 a year, you can create a million-dollar-a-year business. The secret is to take care of your "fish" once you've landed them, and they'll be with you for life.

SEVEN-STEP GETTING-STARTED
ACTION PLAN FOR INFO-PRENEURS

1. **Select a subject that matches your passion/expertise.**

Weight loss	Management	Addictions
Nutrition	Sales	Hobbies
Relationships	Marketing	Languages
Sports	Advertising, PR	Fear
Investments	Asset protection	Emotional issues
Stocks	The Internet	Entertainment
Real estate	Computers	Public speaking
Business	Time management	

Sam nodded. "We need to be canvassing all the properties on this side, and the ones across the street, and find out if there happens to be a developer who might be interested in converting this to office space."

"All right, Sam. That's what I'll do."

Michelle started with the mall developers but didn't wait to hear back from the big corporation. She went on to spend the rest of the day calling every high-end Realtor® in the city. And after placing at least 15 voicemail messages and reaching another 25 Realtors®, she finally connected with somebody who knew somebody who knew a real estate developer who had been looking for a project of exactly the magnitude that Michelle possessed at this point.

A meeting was set up for the next day and Michelle arrived at the developer's office. When the numbers were finally negotiated, and with a quick closing scheduled 10 days away, Michelle would walk away from the property, after commissions and costs, with a check for $550,000.

It wasn't what she wanted. It wasn't what she needed. But in another lifetime, that kind of figure would have astounded her. In a short period of time, Sam had turned her into a marketing maven.

The 10 days would just allow time for approvals and inspections to be done. $550,000. Now if she could just get something else to happen on her other various different streams. In 10 days her time with Ericksen would be up.

10 Days . . .

As Michelle walked into the foyer of Sam's offices, Stephanie handed her a telephone message. "Michelle, I think you need to read this now."

2. **Find the hungriest fish in the lake.** Do research online and with mailing list brokers to find groups of hungry fish.
3. **Discover the kind of bait your fish have been biting on.** This is called market research. Study what bait other fishermen have been successfully using. Or talk to the fish yourself. Just what do your potential customers want? Call them up. Ask. Ask. Ask. Find out what information is vital to them and how they want that information.
4. **Design your own unique bait.** Ask your target fish what they don't like about your competitor's product. Ask them what they would add to your competitor's product to make it perfect. Ask them what they would delete from your competitor's product that is not necessary. Ask them to design it *exactly* the way they want it.
5. **Test your bait.** As we said before, marketing is the key. Having determined your USP, you have to create advertising that causes people to ACT!
6. **Roll out your campaign.** Not only can you roll out a single information product, but you can launch multiple versions of the same information: tapes, videos, seminars, newsletters, infomercials, home study courses, manuals, CDs and DVDs, etc. Your hungry fish will want to buy your information in a myriad of ways.
7. **Enjoy the lifestyle of an info-preneur.** Work from home or from anywhere in the world.

Still euphoric after a particularly exhilarating session of exercise and meditation at the Rock earlier that morning, Michelle took a moment and glanced at the message from Tilly. *Call Hasbro immediately. There has been a complication with the Always Together Bear.*

She rushed into the conference room and made the dreaded telephone call. "Oh, Michelle," said Ira Schwinn, the Vice President of Production at Hasbro. "We've had a snag with the container boat. A huge storm front moved south of Taiwan with hurricane-force winds. We just got word that the container ship had to take a longer route to avoid the storm. It looks like the shipment is going to be delayed at least three, maybe four days."

Michelle's heart sank again as she realized that the deadline with Anthony would come and go with the merchandise sitting in a boat in the middle of the Pacific Ocean.

We're not going to make it in time, she thought to herself. *All of this effort for nothing.*

Michelle burst into Sam's corner office. Sam was on the phone with her chair swiveled so that she was facing the huge plate-glass windows that overlooked the park. She turned to acknowledge Michelle, then held her hand over the receiver and mouthed the words *Just a minute.*

Michelle paced back and forth in front of Sam's desk impatiently. As soon as Sam hung up, Michelle launched in.

"Sam, it's all falling apart."

Sam took a deep breath. "Michelle, it's just like one of those school plays. Complete chaos until opening night, and then things fall into place."

Michelle was shaking her head. "No more pep talks. I just got a call from Hasbro. There's been a hurricane off of Taiwan and the container ship has been delayed. It's not going to make it in time."

Sam sat thoughtfully as she heard this latest bad news.

MONEY FOR NOTHING

Cindy Cashman took an old idea and added a twist to it and made a fortune in the information business. Cindy was able to purchase a huge mansion on a lake in Texas, having made over a million dollars from marketing her specialty book, which she published with a partner. You might have seen her book, *Everything Men Know About Women*, by Dr. Alan Francis (her pseudonym). But here's the real amazing part: Cindy's book is totally blank! There isn't a single word printed on any of the 128 pages of this paperback! And yet women bought this book by the caseload. A hundred books at a time to give to their friends! Cindy made enough to retire.

Stan Miller loved to collect quotes. He started when he was 16 and continued until after he was married. For Christmas, he and his new wife, Sharon, decided that a compiled collection of all his quotes and stories would be a good Christmas gift. So he went to a printer to ask how much it would cost to have a hundred copies printed and bound. She said it would be cheaper to have a thousand copies made. She quoted him $1,000 for 1,000 copies. Stan thought that sounded like a good price so he ordered a thousand copies. Unfortunately, when the bill came, it was $10,000 instead of $1,000! The secretary had misplaced a ZERO!

Stan and Sharon were devastated. In desperation Stan took a few copies to the local university bookstore, but the bookstore didn't want them. But they did agree to let him leave a few dozen copies on consignment. When Stan came back a week later the books were all gone . . . much to everyone's surprise. The book took off like hotcakes, and now more than a million copies of several versions of this book have been sold. That was over 25 years ago and the checks are still flowing. That secretary's silly mistake had turned into a million-dollar godsend. By the way, the name of Stan's book is *Especially for Mormons*. There are now six volumes of quotes, stories, and thoughts all designed to inspire and warm the heart.

Michelle began again, this time more plaintively. "Sam, I can't lose my kids. Couldn't you lend me the money?"

"But your contract specifically states that you can't borrow the money. You have to earn it. . . ."

"We've got to do *something*. Maybe you could sell me one of your buildings at a huge discount. I'd agree—under the table—to sell it back to you as soon as I got my children back. Ericksen would never have to know."

"But *I* would know. . . ."

"Sam, we're talking about my children. . . . I'm willing to do whatever it takes. Even beat Ericksen at his own game, if I have to."

Sam lowered her head and shook it slightly. "Michelle, I can't imagine what you're going through. In your place, I honestly don't know what I'd do. But what you're proposing is immoral."

"Yeah, but hasn't Erickson done immoral things to steal my children from me?"

"Yes," said Sam, "he has. And he's going to pay the negative precessional consequences."

"What are you talking about, Sam?"

"It's one of the first things I taught you—the spiral of the Enlightened Millionaire.[p. xv] There's upward precession and downward precession. . . ."

"Yes, I remember. But it was just a *theory*."

"It's not a theory. It's the way the world works . . . or doesn't work. Integrity isn't just a *nice* way to live. It's the only way. If you're dishonest, the weight of your actions compound to eventually pull you down. Like ice that forms on an airplane's wings, until it just can't fly anymore. That's why you can't even tell a *little* lie. Because it starts you on a negative spiral—as Darth Vader would say, down to the dark side. There is only one approach that can lift you—the enlightened approach—which requires that you be impeccably honest, impeccably fair. Even when people are hurtful and harmful, your only choice is the upward path."

You, too, can turn your expertise/passion/hobby into lifetime streams of cash flow. There is a book inside you. And there is an audience for that book. You can create an endless variety of products from the same information. The income is residual. You produce it once, and it keeps paying you back, sometimes for decades.

YOU ARE ONE CLASSIFIED AD AWAY FROM A FORTUNE!

Bob graduated in 1974 from Brigham Young University with a master's degree in business administration (MBA). Don't let that impress you. He graduated in the one-third of his class that made the top two-thirds possible. It was during a major recession and jobs were scarce. He sent resumes to 30 of the top companies in America: General Foods, General Electric, General Motors (generally, anybody that he could think of). He received 30 rejection letters. Bob was running out of money. He had no job prospects. He was desperate.

He had always had an interest in real estate investment since reading William Nickerson's classic book, *How I Turned $1000 into $1,000,000 in Real Estate in My Spare Time*. Rather than going for the secure paycheck (since nobody was offering him one), Bob asked a local multimillionaire real estate developer to take him under his wing and teach him the ropes. Bob was single at the time. His financial needs were minimal. He would do anything the developer asked. The fellow gave Bob a job. Working for him, Bob found and bought his first property . . . a small duplex apartment in Provo, Utah. The down payment? $1,500. It was everything he had. This led to other successful purchases and a few notable failures.

Michelle shook her head, refusing to listen.

"When I was a little girl . . . ," Sam began, "my four brothers and I made kites from scratch."

Michelle rolled her eyes. *Not another one of Sam's analogies.*

Sam didn't seem to notice. "It took us the better part of a day to make a kite. For the frame, we split long, thin pieces of wood from fence posts. For the body, we used brown grocery bags. For glue, we mixed flour and water. We tore up old rags for the tail. In the late afternoon when the breezes started to blow, we ran through the fields as fast as we could. . . ."

"Could you please get to the point," Michelle said impatiently.

Sam paid no attention. "When that kite would catch a breeze and soar up the wind, it was the most beautiful, the most exhilarating feeling . . . tugging hard against the stick in your hand. But the kite wouldn't fly unless there was a wind. Missy, every time you have a problem, you come running here as if it's the end of the world. Problems don't drag you down. They're like the wind. You can't fly without them."

Sam looked directly into Michelle's eyes until Michelle lowered her gaze. "The wind might cause a kite to rise, but what keeps it up there is the fact that somebody on the ground has a steady hand. You have to hold steady to your values—your integrity. It's your anchor. You let go of that . . . well, it isn't long before your kite comes crashing down."

Michelle was getting angry. "Sam, I've already lost a husband. If I lose my kids, I don't think I'd want to go on living."

Sam matched Michelle's anger. "That's the most selfish thing I've ever heard you say!"

They glared at each other for several seconds.

"It's true, Sam. I don't care what you say. If I came this close and lost them, I would want to die." She sat down in one of the overstuffed chairs in Sam's office and put her face in her hands.

Sam took a deep breath, and sat down beside her. "One of my

Within a few short years and some massaging of the numbers, Bob was a "paper" millionaire.

Bob decided to share his systems with a few of his close associates, who also profited. He wondered if anyone else might be interested and ran a small classified ad in his local newspaper. It offered to teach "How to Buy Real Estate with Little or No Money Down." The next day Bob's phone rang off the hook. Within weeks he was making up to $10,000 a day in the information business. Within months, he was pulling down up to *six figures a month.* It was crazy!

Then Bob licensed his name and ideas to a national seminar company that agreed to train people how to use his systems and to pay him a nice royalty for every student they taught. The timing was perfect. Within a year, his royalty checks had grown to between $25,000 and $50,000 a week! This went on for six years! These residual streams gave Bob the time to write and promote two #1 bestselling books, *Nothing Down* and *Creating Wealth.* When his licensing royalties dried up in 1985, Bob launched a new training business that took in another $100,000,000 from many of *the same loyal customers.*

The concept of real estate investing was as old as the hills. What Bob added to the equation was to take old techniques and to repackage them under the banner of a single, sexy concept, "Nothing Down." In the last 20 years, he has marketed over $200,000,000 worth of information products. Over $200,000,000 from one silly idea!

During his lifetime, between Bob and his copycat competitors, over a billion dollars is going to be dug out of the mine shaft called Nothing Down real estate. It was A BILLION-DOLLAR IDEA!

What is your billion-dollar idea?

spiritual guides was a fellow by the name of Buckminster Fuller. I never met him. But some of my mentors studied under him. He was an amazing man. The creator of the geodesic dome. Never earned a doctorate degree but received over 20 honorary doctorates. Wrote 40 books. Owned about 500 different patents. He was a genius."

Michelle looked over at Sam. *Where is she going with this?*

"But as a young man, he was a complete failure—kicked out of Harvard twice. He married a woman who had money, but he squandered it all. When his young daughter died in his arms of an illness, he went into a depression that caused him to contemplate suicide. Standing on the shores of Lake Michigan, he decided to swim out until he had no more strength and would sink beneath the waves and die. As he was standing there, he had an epiphany. As he later described it, it was almost as if God was talking to him. Even 50 years later, he could remember every word."

"What happened?" asked Michelle, who had suddenly forgotten her own problems.

"This was the message he heard: 'Bucky'—which was his nickname—'You don't belong to you. You belong to the Universe. You can rest assured that if you devote your time and attention to the highest advantage of others, then the Universe will support you, always and only in the nick of time.'

"He went back home and refused to speak for the next two years. For two years he just thought and meditated. And then he spent the remaining 50 years of his life in a frenzy of creative productivity. He called himself *Guinea Pig B*. The *B* was for 'Bucky.' Guinea Pig B decided that he would devote his life to helping the world. The income he earned from his many patents he immediately donated to charity. He balanced his books so there wasn't a single cent in his bank account at the end of every month. Some months, he would give away a million dollars. To the end of his days, he never lacked for anything. He knew the Universe would always support him, always and only in the nick of time."

HOW TO MAKE A
MILLION DOLLARS IN ONE MINUTE

One minute. One million dollars. That's a lot of money in a very short period of time. There is only one business vehicle in the world fast enough to generate that kind of income—the Internet. So let's explore how to achieve the impossible. Hold on to your hat.

The Internet is the ultimate 24-hour-a-day money machine. While you eat, while you sleep, while you play, money is pouring into your life—and from all over the world.

Bob's friend David first showed him how to make instant cash flow from the Internet. Sitting at the computer in Bob's office, David sent an e-mail broadcast to a list of 1,500 subscribers for David's opt-in e-mail newsletter. David offered to sell them one of Bob's tape programs at a 50% discount. It took only 61 seconds for the first order to bounce back. In the next hour they received about 15 orders—or a 1% response. The cost of sending this e-mail broadcast was zero. Bob was flabbergasted. *Hmmm.*

Then the lightbulb went on. He started to play "what if?" What if there had been 150,000 e-mails instead of 1,500. It could bring in thousands of dollars—no marketing costs, no mailing costs, no printing costs—in pure profit. *Hmmm.*

Inspired by this, Bob immediately launched his own website and e-zine. Within a few short months, he had gathered over 11,000 e-mail subscribers. Then, while planning for a TV infomercial, the producers asked him to come up with some dramatic demonstration of his money-making techniques. He instantly thought of David and his 1,500 e-mails. Bob told the producer that he thought he could make $24,000 in only 24 hours on the Internet. The producer arranged to film Bob as he sat at his computer and sent off a message to his 11,516 subscribers. At the end of

Sam paused. "Michelle, you've done everything you could do. Work. Prayer. Intuition. Tithing. You've applied every form of leverage I've taught you. There's only one thing left to do."

Michelle looked up to hear her mentor.

"Stop doubting, Butterfly."

The Last Day:
Two Hours . . .

Most of our lives change imperceptibly, day to day. A marriage deteriorates, a degree is earned, children go from infancy to adolescence.

But sometimes our lives change in a moment. A car accident, an unexpected inheritance, being fired from a job.

Michelle's marriage, her husband's death, and the moment when the judge awarded temporary custody to her in-laws stood out to her as turning points from the Universe.

And the next few minutes promised to contain just such a sudden change. Michelle and Jeremy were alone in the conference room. The others, even Sam, had decided that their presence would add nothing but pressure, though they eagerly—"eagle-ly," Summer joked—were awaiting news of the results.

Sam was right, as usual. Not just about the pressure of having her mentor watch her triumph or crash but about Michelle's use of her intuition. Early on Sam had told her that she needed to stay open and to tune in to where the Infinite Network might lead her. That she might well get the results she wanted, but at a path perpendicular to the one she had expected to take.

Michelle would certainly be a rich woman from the Always Together Bear by this time next year. She would very likely have amassed a small fortune in real estate, given her quickly garnered experience and her developing network of contacts. Earlier this morning, she'd pocketed a check for $550,000, after closing on her apartment building.

the 24 hours, he had received $94,532.44 in cash orders—almost all pure profit. Once again, he was flabbergasted. *Hmmmm.*

Then along came this book—*The One Minute Millionaire.* We already knew that the right offer to the right list could generate a huge profit in 24 hours—but could we make a million in a minute? Only if we had access to a huge number of legitimate e-mail addresses—at least a million. Now, here is where Mark came into the picture. His *Chicken Soup for the Soul* e-mail list delivers 800,000 *Chicken Soup* stories PER DAY to his list of subscribers. Our two lists combined equal over a million e-mail names.

"What if" we blasted a million e-mails with an irresistible offer for a $100 package of information delivered over the Internet—a package of digitized special reports, streaming video and audio, some digital audio books—with a strong money-back guarantee? "What if" we could get 1% of the people to respond almost immediately—that would be 10,000 orders times $100. Hey, that's a million dollars!

"What if" we offered a $1,000 One Minute Millionaire seminar. We'd only need $\frac{1}{10}$ of 1% response to find our 1,000 people. *Hmmm.*

Now it gets interesting. Let's play "what if" again. "What if" we went on a national TV show—*Oprah, Larry King, Good Morning America, 20/20*—and offered to demonstrate how to make a million dollars in one minute? "What if" we agreed to donate the entire million to the host's favorite charity? *Hmmm.*

What if we didn't do just one show, but all of them. *Hmmmmmm!*

Is it possible to make a million dollars in only one minute? Through the vehicle of the Internet: absolutely! As we said at the beginning of this book, every 60 seconds someone in North America becomes a millionaire. Whether it takes you sixty years or sixty seconds, we hope we've provided the inspiration to encourage you to bcome an enlightened millionaire as soon as possible. Good luck, good leverage and God speed.

But that still left her $450,000 short of one million.

She had not counted on Jeremy's Internet activities to provide her with a very large percentage of the final amount. His schemes had always seemed a little grandiose; the problems with Summer had not boded well; and then the website had crashed.

But now it turned out that her entire future—for what future did she have without her children? —would pivot on a few clicks of a mouse.

Jeremy assured her that all would be well. For the previous 21 days, he and Summer had been working feverishly around the clock to set up systems for selling Enlightened Millionaire Coaching at the appointed time.

Jeremy, the self-proclaimed computer whiz, said that he had learned as much about computers over the past 90 days as Michelle had learned about toys and real estate. He had learned a lesson in humility as well. He now had backed up all of his data and had four or five servers ready to be redundant in case of a system failure.

He and Summer were getting along better. Summer had found her role as the people person—dealing one-to-one with the people behind the bits and bytes and making up for Jeremy's sometimes-brusque personality.

Their code name for the project was Operation Hungry Fish, and Hungry Fish Day—the day they would sell Enlightened Millionaire Coaching in real time—was set for 10 A.M. on December 6. Michelle had pressed Jeremy to set it up for at least a day sooner, but with the various problems they had encountered it had proved to be impossible. So now, with barely two hours to go before their deadline, they faced timing as precise as a NASA launch.

Jeremy had checked and double-checked all their systems. The credit card companies were ready. Of crucial importance was the fact that Jeremy had negotiated with their joint-venture partners that, in exchange for a higher overall commission, Michelle would receive the first million dollars of profit. This part of the deal might

ONE MINUTE REVIEW OF MARKETING

1. **Million-dollar ideas are floating around you every day.** You just have to recognize them and act on them.
2. **Discover which of the 10 basic business models fits you and your circumstances.** Do you want to sell to customers, businesses, government agencies, or charities?
3. **Create your One Minute Marketing Plan.** Review your plan for at least one minute daily. It will put you ahead of 99% of businesses.
4. **Use the three essentials of marketing success:**

    Step #1.   Look for positive addicts.

    Step #2.   Make your ads addicting, with an ultimate advantage, a sensational offer, and a powerful promise.

    Step #3.   Leverage your efforts with joint venture partners.
5. **Use antimarketing strategies.** Attract perfect customers by focusing on and specifically attracting the 20% of your customers who give you 80% of your profits.
6. **Become an info-preneur.** Learn to market information products where the profit margins are up to 95%.
7. **Make up to a million dollars in a minute on the Internet.** Information that is digitized can be marketed and sold 24 hours a day online.

substantially reduce the time it took to break the $1 million mark. By "substantially," they meant half an hour. And half an hour was just as close as they were going to cut it.

Jeremy tilted back his swivel chair and rubbed his hands together. It was a gesture of his that she had seen before, but suddenly it reminded her of Uriah Heep. Then he began cracking his knuckles as if he had all the time in the world. "Jeremy, I'm sorry," she burst out, "but I'm already so nervous—"

"Michelle, relax. We have a few minutes before 10. This ones and zeros dude has learned how to rely on his intuition, and my intuition tells me that we're going to be just fine."

"You really think so?" Michelle looked anxiously at the computer.

"Hey, I learned that from you and Sam. Trusting this, I mean." He tapped his chest.

"I just wish things weren't so close." She looked at her digital watch. "In just a little over two hours I have to be at my former father-in-law's house with a briefcase full of a million dollars in cash—and as we speak I've got just a little over $500,000."

Jeremy's e-mail blast would go out to 100,000 peoplep. 350—the people who had sent for their free PDF-format book, *Money Loves You*. According to Jeremy, if just 1% of them were willing to pay $1,000 for a weekend seminar with Sam, the Millionaire Eagles would have money to spare. Some of their customers would choose a yearlong mentoring program with Sam that, at $5,000, would generate even more income. Many more would probably sign up for the year after taking the weekend, but that income would come in later.

Now Jeremy seemed to hesitate a moment.

"What are you waiting for?" Michelle was concerned.

Jeremy cracked his knuckles again. He pursed his lips. "There's something I've been meaning to tell you."

Michelle looked at him sharply.

Jeremy tilted the chair back even farther as if to avoid her. "My name isn't Jeremy Cavalieri. It's Jeremy Stuyvesant. I was an

THE ENLIGHTENED WAY TO WEALTH

AFTERWORD

Money: The Last Taboo!

Almost nothing is sacred anymore. But money is the last taboo. People go on major talk shows and brag about the kinkiest kind of sex. Yet when the host asks how much money they make, they clam up like it's the dirtiest of secrets.

Why are people so hung up about money? It's time we came out of the closet and learned to be comfortable with the idea of prosperity. Russell H. Conwell spoke about this over a hundred years ago. He said,

> "I say that you ought to get rich, and it is your duty to get rich." How many of my pious brethren say to me, "Do you, a Christian minister, spend your time going up and down the country advising young people to get rich, to get money?" "Yes, of course I do."
>
> They say, "Isn't that awful! Why don't you preach the gospel instead of preaching about man's making money?" Because to make money honestly is to preach the gospel. That is the reason. The men who get rich may be the most honest men you find in the community.
>
> "Oh," but says some young man here tonight, "I have been told all my life that if a person has money he is very dishonest and dishonorable and mean and contemptible." My friend, that is the reason why you have none, because you have that idea of people. The foundation of your faith is altogether false. Let me say here clearly . . . ninety-eight out of one hundred of the rich men (and women) of America are honest. That is why they are rich. That is why they are trusted with money. That is why they carry on great enterprises and find plenty of people to work with them.
>
> Says another young man, "I hear sometimes of men that get millions of dollars dishonestly." Yes, of course you do, and so do I. But they are so rare a thing in fact that the newspapers talk about them all the time as a matter of news until you get the idea that all the other rich men got rich dishonestly.

out-of-work actor until I was hired by your father-in-law to keep an eye on you."

Michelle put her hand to her mouth. "But you look so . . ."

"Italian? My mother was Italian. Her maiden name was Cavalieri. All the rest of my background, I made up."

Michelle looked over at the computer, where the screen saver had just come on. Toasters were flying at her. Could she push him aside and send out the e-mail blast herself? She didn't know enough about how he had set it up. She could click on an icon that would save her—or destroy her last hope of ever seeing her children again. *I'm like the mother whose child is trapped underneath a car*, she thought. *I'm strong enough to lift it, but I don't know where the car is.*

One Hour and 58 Minutes . . .

It was 10:02 A.M.

Jeremy went on rocking in the chair. Michelle's heart pounded in her ears like the percussion section of a heavy metal band. "I'm sorry, Michelle, but didn't you ever wonder why a loser like me would be so eager to join your team and work so hard?

"For the first month, I reported your every move to Ericksen. You should be pretty proud of those first two deals you flipped, because you would have had even more leads if Ericksen hadn't been working behind the scenes to get as many people as possible to stay away from you." Jeremy swiveled his chair to face Michelle directly.

"Even then, though, I was getting caught up in the excitement of what we were doing. I was watching how you were turning your life around. You risked it all. You've done things in three months that very few people do in a lifetime. And I saw how you were doing it—by listening to your mentor, by dedicating yourself to others. Like that old lady you helped—what was her name, Jasko?—I saw that you were putting her ahead of your profits even

My friend, you . . . drive me . . . out into the suburbs of Philadelphia, and introduce me to the people who own their homes around this great city, those beautiful homes with gardens and flowers, those magnificent homes so lovely in their art, and I will introduce you to the very best people in character as well as in enterprise in our city. . . . They that own their homes are made more honorable and honest and pure, and true and economical and careful, by owning the(m).

We preach against covetousness . . . in the pulpit . . . and use the terms . . . "filthy lucre" so extremely that Christians get the idea that . . . it is wicked for any man to have money. Money is power, and you ought to be reasonably ambitious to have it! You ought because you can do more good with it than you could do without it. Money printed your Bibles, money builds your churches, money sends your missionaries, and money pays your preachers. . . . I say, then, you ought to have money. If you can honestly attain unto riches . . . it is your . . . godly duty to do so. It is an awful mistake of these pious people to think you must be awfully poor in order to be pious.

Russell H. Conwell, *Acres of Diamonds*

though you needed those profits so badly. I saw how you were tithing from the beginning, even though you could have so easily said, 'I'll do that later.'

"You lived on the edge. You lived from faith. The Universe was supporting you. You were in what Sam calls a positive precession. Your star was rising. And mine, well . . . I had a harder and harder time looking at myself in the mirror every day."

Michelle still couldn't believe what she was hearing.

Jeremy shifted in his chair. "I kept playing both sides of the fence. Then one day when we were all together Sam talked about negative precession. It was like—it was like Saul on the road to Damascus. Suddenly I saw that all the bad things that had happened in my life—there is no Jeremy Jr., but there *is* a broken marriage I'll always regret—were things I had created, not bad luck or evil people persecuting me. *I* was the one persecuting me."

Michelle closed her eyes. She thought she could hear her watch ticking. *Battery-operated watches don't tick.*

"So that's the real story," he finished. "What does your intuition say about me now?" He grinned at her slyly, a grin that was familiar to her and yet now held new meaning.

Michelle took a deep, slow breath. For several moments she didn't speak. And then she had her answer. "I think . . . ," she began, as a smile spread slowly across her face ". . . that my original hunch was right."

Jeremy began to nod. "I was hoping you'd say that. About 30 days ago I began to provide Ericksen with false information. I wanted you to know . . . before I send this e-mail . . . that you've converted me to your way—the enlightened way. After we pull this off, I want to join with you in this company."

He stuck out his hand. She didn't take it immediately. Intuition or no, he had betrayed her original trust. *What would Sam do?*

She clasped his hand. "Welcome to the Millionaire Eagles . . . Mr. Stuyvesant?"

NO MORE EXCUSES?

Self-doubt drowns your dreams. Hesitation holds you hostage. Skepticism scares away your success. You wonder, "What will they think? I don't have a degree or a diploma. I don't have the qualifications. I don't have the experience or the credentials."

Here's a list of billionaires and multimillionaires who never graduated from college. They didn't let their lack of degrees or diplomas hold them back.

Bill Gates Microsoft	**Peter Jennings** ABC News
Paul Allen Microsoft	**Walter Cronkite** CBS News
Michael Dell Dell Computer	**Harry S. Truman** U.S. president
Larry Ellison Oracle	**Debra Fields** Mrs. Fields Cookies
Jay Van Andel Amway	**Stephen Spielberg** Movie director
Richard DeVos Amway	**Ralph Lauren** Clothing designer
Steve Jobs Apple Computer	**Rosie O'Donnell** Actress/talk-show host
Thomas Monaghan Domino's Pizza	**Ted Turner** Turner Networks
Jim Jannard Oakley Sunglasses	**Wayne Huizenga** Blockbuster Video

Here is a list of hugely successful authors who self-published their first major book. They didn't let their lack of a traditional publisher hold them back.

Tom Peters In Search of Excellence	**James Redfield** The Celestine Prophecy
John Grisham A Time to Kill	**Richard Paul Evans** The Christmas Box
Ken Blanchard & Spencer Johnson One Minute Manager	

"Let's stick with Cavalieri." He held her hand a moment longer. "Okay, it's showtime."

Earlier she and Jeremy had both carefully set each of their watches to the correct time. Now Michelle held her wrist in front of her face. In spite of what had just passed between them, a tremor ran through her. Jeremy sat calmly, his chair still tilted back, his fingers forming a steeple now.

"Ten," Michelle announced. "Nine, eight, seven . . ."

Will he click on the right button? Will he click on the button at all?

". . . three, two . . ."

"One!"

Jeremy touched the mouse. The screen saver disappeared. He moved the arrow to the left-hand side of the screen and clicked on a gray button marked Send.

A dialog box appeared in the middle of the monitor. It tallied the number of e-mails as they went out: 5,000, 10,000, 15,000, 20,000, 25,000. . . . Would they land in the right places? Were there people at the other end who had been praying for an answer for their particular challenges in life? She didn't know. She just turned it over to the Universe.

For the next five minutes they sat in silence. Then the computer dinged. The first order had come back. *There's the first $1,000.* Would there be any more?

Michelle and Jeremy watched, mesmerized, as the number of responses piled into their "inbox"—each returning e-mail was worth at least a thousand dollars: 11 . . . 27 . . . 42 . . . 55 . . . 87 . . . 92 . . . 123 . . .

7 Minutes . . .

The week before, with Sam's help, Michelle had optimistically made arrangements with her bank to have a million dollars in cash ready that morning, and they had agreed to provide it—*if* she had that

Other well-known self-publishers include:

William Blake	James Joyce	Carl Sandburg
Edgar Rice Burroughs	Rudyard Kipling	Gertrude Stein
Deepak Chopra	D. H. Lawrence	Henry David Thoreau
e.e. cummings	Thomas Paine	Mark Twain
Benjamin Franklin	Edgar Allan Poe	Walt Whitman
Zane Grey	George Bernard Shaw	Virginia Woolf

The only diploma that counts is a million-dollar idea. The only qualification needed is a burning desire. The only credential required is fearless action. Everything else can be borrowed or bought. You can hire people with multiple degrees and diplomas. You can buy experience from mentors and consultants. You can assemble a team of people who possess all of the money, skills, and experience you lack.

All of these people are waiting for someone to say, "Follow me. This is the way."

much money in her account. She did. Immediately upon ordering the seminar, the client's credit card was charged, and then her own bank account was credited.

She brought her own briefcase, and two rather impressed tellers along with the operations officer helped her fill it with stacks of $100 bills—100 stacks of $100 bills. The brown briefcase was filled— and to her, filled with joy.

Sam drove Michelle and Jeremy, who sat in the backseat. They parked right outside the gate of the mansion. Michelle, who preferred to walk up to the front door rather than be chauffered in Sam's Mercedes, had been holding the briefcase in her lap. "It's not as heavy as I thought it would be," she said cheerfully, as she got out of the car.

Jeremy got out at the same time, according to plan, while Sam, cutting the engine, stayed put. "Blessings of the Universe on you, my children," she said.

Michelle unexpectedly found she couldn't speak, but she was confident that Sam would know what she was feeling. *I wouldn't be here without you.*

After Estella buzzed them in, Michelle and Jeremy hiked up the drive. At the door, Estella greeted them with surprising warmth and led them up to the library. Even as they walked, Michelle looked at her watch every two seconds. They only had a few minutes to spare. Could something still go wrong?

1 Minute . . .

Anthony was waiting for them, with Natalie, who wore a lilac shantung pantsuit, at his side. Michelle knew why he looked so smug, and why he gave Jeremy a knowing look. After the orders for Enlightened Millionaire Coaching had put them over the top, Jeremy had made one last call to Ericksen, telling him that Michelle was going to appear at the appointed hour, show him

WILLING TO PAY THE PRICE

We'd like to close with a true story by an entrepreneur named John McCormack, who found a mentor—and a true Enlightened Millionaire—in a local shopping mall:

When my wife, Maryanne, and I were building our Greenspoint Mall hair salon 13 years ago, a Vietnamese fellow would stop by each day to sell us doughnuts. He spoke hardly any English, but he was always friendly and through smiles and sign language, we got to know each other. His name was Le Van Vu.

During the day Le worked in a bakery, and at night he and his wife listened to audiotapes to learn English. I later learned that they slept on sacks full of sawdust on the floor of the back room of the bakery.

In Vietnam the Van Vu family had been one of the wealthiest in Southeast Asia. They owned almost one-third of North Vietnam, including huge holdings in industry and real estate. However, after his father was brutally murdered, Le moved to South Vietnam with his mother, where he went to school and eventually became a lawyer.

Like his father before him, Le prospered. He saw an opportunity to construct buildings to accommodate the ever-expanding American presence in South Vietnam and soon became one of the most successful builders in the country. On a trip to the North, however, Le was captured by the North Vietnamese and thrown into prison for three years. He escaped by killing five soldiers and made his way back to South Vietnam, where he was arrested again. The South Vietnamese government had assumed he was a "plant" from the North.

After serving time in prison, Le got out and started a fishing company, eventually becoming the largest canner in South Vietnam.

When Le learned that the U.S. troops and embassy personnel were about to pull out of his country, he made a life-changing decision.

He took all of the gold he had hoarded, loaded it aboard one of his fishing vessels, and sailed with his wife out to the American ships in the

the $500,000 she had managed to amass, and beg him for an extension.

"I already know what you have to ask, Michelle," said Anthony as they walked in, "and the answer is no."

Jeremy's watch began to sound its alarm. It was noon.

Michelle hefted the briefcase on Anthony's desk, as she did knocking over a statuette of a baseball player swinging his bat. She quickly pressed the appropriate numbers on the combination lock keypad, then flipped open the case. She turned it to face the Ericksens, so that they could see the layers of stacked $100 bills. "There's my million. You can count it."

"How . . . how did you do this?" Anthony was too shocked to be angry for the moment. "Wait . . . It must be fake." He rose from his seat and began pawing through the money, tossing stacks of bills to one side. Natalie bit the corner of her lip.

"Whoa, there, Anthony," Michelle said. "I hope you're planning on putting that back."

"Is it all there?" Natalie asked, leaning over the briefcase.

"It's all there," Michelle said sharply.

Ericksen threw a pile of $100s back into the briefcase and slammed it shut. He glared at Jeremy. "You betrayed me!"

Jeremy shrugged and looked up at the ceiling. "I'll consider that a compliment. But meanwhile, I don't see what you can do, Mr. Ericksen, but give this young mother her children." From under his arm he took out a copy of the contract that Michelle had signed with her father-in-law 90 days before.

Before anyone could respond to this, there was a shriek, the happiest shriek that Michelle had ever heard. Before she could stop herself, she shrieked, too.

Nicky and Hannah were rushing into the room, with Estella behind them.

"Mommy!"

"Mommy!"

harbor. He then exchanged all his riches for safe passage out of Vietnam to the Philippines, where he and his wife were taken into a refugee camp.

After gaining access to the president of the Philippines, Le convinced him to make one of his boats available for fishing and Le was back in business again. Before he left the Philippines two years later en route for America (his ultimate dream), Le had been a major figure in helping to develop the fishing industry in the Philippines.

But en route to America, Le became distraught and depressed about having to start over again with nothing. His wife tells of how she found him near the railing of the ship, about to jump overboard.

"Le," she told him, "if you do jump, whatever will become of me? We've been together for so long and through so much. We can do this together." It was all the encouragement that Le Van Vu needed.

When he and his wife arrived in Houston in 1972, they were flat broke and spoke no English. In Vietnam, family takes care of family, and Le and his wife found themselves ensconced in the back room of his cousin's bakery in the Greenspoint Mall. We were building our salon just a couple of hundred feet away.

Now, as they say, here comes the "message" part of this story: Le's cousin offered both Le and his wife jobs in the bakery. After taxes, Le would take home $175 per week, his wife $125. Their total annual income, in other words, was $15,600. Further, his cousin offered to sell them the bakery whenever they could come up with a $30,000 down payment. The cousin would finance the remainder with a note for $90,000.

Here's what Le and his wife did: Even with a weekly income of $300, they decided to continue living in the back room. For two years they kept clean by taking sponge baths in the mall's restrooms. For two years their diet consisted almost entirely of bakery goods. Each year, for two years, they lived on a total—that's right a total—of $600, saving $30,000 for the down payment.

Le later explained his reasoning: "If we got ourselves an apartment, which we could afford on $300 per week, we'd have to pay the rent. Then, of course, we'd have to buy furniture. Then we'd have to have transportation to and from work, so that meant we'd have to buy a car. Then we'd

They both grabbed her tightly, hanging on to Michelle as if they were trying to stop her from going away. Weeping, she hugged them back, burying her face in their hair.

"We were outside the door," Michelle heard Estella say.

Then Ericksen's voice, cold as winter. "Get out of my house. All of you."

It was Natalie who gave a final, surprising demonstration of genuine emotion. "Children," she asked, "do you really want to leave us?"

"I'm sorry, Grandma," Nicky said politely. "But we'll be back to visit." Hannah nodded but held even tighter to Michelle.

Michelle let Jeremy take the job of re-collecting the money and bringing the briefcase out. She barely looked over her shoulder to say good-bye to the Ericksens, only dimly registered that they were frozen in place. She was too busy gripping Nicky's and Hannah's hands, with occasional breaks to pat their backs and ruffle their hair. She had been starved for their touch, and clearly, without saying so, they felt the same. Michelle was so overcome with emotion that all she could manage was small talk—how much they'd grown, what they were doing in school, who their new friends were. She knew there would be plenty of time for the more important conversations very soon. The nightmare was finally over.

Outside, Michelle saw Sam leaning against her Mercedes, waiting for them. "Well, hello," she greeted the children. "Your mama does nothing but talk about you. I feel like I know you already."

They were about to bundle into the car when Michelle heard an unexpected voice call out, "Wait!"

Estella was practically running down the drive. She held something in her hand that Michelle didn't dare recognize.

"What do you want?" Michelle asked suspiciously as she gripped Nicky's and Hannah's hands protectively. Estella stopped in front of her, not speaking as she caught her breath. Hannah's face lit up. "Mr. Moo-Moo!" She let go of Michelle's hand. "Thank you," she

have to buy gasoline for the car, as well as insurance. Then we'd probably want to go places in the car, so that meant we'd need to buy clothes and toiletries. So I knew that if we got that apartment, we'd never get our $30,000 together."

Now, if you think you've heard everything about Le, let me tell you, there's more: After he and his wife saved the $30,000 and bought the bakery, Le once again sat down with his wife for a serious chat. They still owed $90,000 to his cousin, he said, and as difficult as the past two years had been, they had to remain living in that back room for one more year.

I'm proud to tell you that in one year, my friend and mentor Le Van Vu and his wife, saving virtually every nickel of profit from the business, paid off the $90,000 note and, in just three years, owned an extremely profitable business free and clear.

Then, and only then, the Van Vus went out and got their first apartment. To this day, they continue to save on a regular basis, live on an extremely small percentage of their income, and, of course, always pay cash for any of their purchases.

Do you think that Le Van Vu is a millionaire today? I am happy to tell you, many times over.

said, her eyes shining as she took the pink-trimmed yellow blanket and buried her face in it. "I'll miss you, Estella," Hannah said.

"Me, too," Nicky said.

"Estella was really nice to us," Nicky told Michelle. "She used to sneak Hannah extra food. And she never told Grandma about the pillows."

Michelle stood back as a teary-eyed but smiling Estella gave the children one last hug. *I completely misjudged her,* she realized. "You don't know how much this means," Michelle said, feeling the ice now melted forever.

"Yes, I do," Estella said. "I loved Gideon like a son. I'm sorry I ever doubted how much you loved these kids. I did my best to watch out for them, and I prayed you'd get them back."

"Thanks for being their guardian angel," Michelle said. "If there's ever anything I can do—"

"Well . . . ," Estella hesitated, looking back at the Ericksens' mansion, "I might be looking for a new job tomorrow."

Michelle looked over at Sam, who raised her eyebrows. Michelle took a card out of her purse. "Here's my card. Call me."

Estella took it and stared at their company logo—an eagle. Then she kissed the tops of the children's heads and smiled one last time.

As Sam got behind the wheel, Jeremy held the front passenger door open for Michelle. "I'll sit in the back with the kids," he offered.

Michelle laughed. Somehow she had gotten a hold of Nicky's and Hannah's hands again, and she held them up now. "I don't think so. The three of us are *way* behind on our snuggle time."

Grinning, Jeremy opened the rear door for them. Michelle got in between her two children and made sure they were both buckled in.

"Where are we going, Mom?" Nicky asked.

"To a party," Michelle said.

"For us?" Hannah wanted to know.

"Well . . . not exactly, sweetheart. It's for all of us, but especially for a good, good friend of mine—of ours." She nodded toward Sam

and Jeremy. "Her name is Tilly and we're having a special party for her at the place where she lives. Tilly did a lot of work to help me get you back." Michelle blinked back bittersweet tears, vowing not to dwell on her last year of mothering but instead on the life she would begin to rebuild with her precious children.

"She sounds nice," Nicky said.

"She is. And she'll be very happy to meet you."

"Will there be cake?" Hannah asked.

"Three different kinds and you can have as much as you want. Isn't that right, Sam, that you really *can* have as much as you want?" she asked, catching Sam's eye in the rearview mirror.

"Yes, Butterfly, you can," Sam said, as she started the engine.

EPILOGUE:
FULL CIRCLE, SIX MONTHS LATER

It was 7:15 P.M. at the Mariposa Plaza. Anna Muñiz, a newly hired waitress, had been assigned to serve at a private dinner in the boardroom. As she came through the swinging doors into the softly lit meeting space, she observed what looked like a group of well-dressed businesspeople, seated around the table. At the far end at the head of the table sat an African-American woman in a cranberry-and-white African robe with matching headscarf. Next to her was a striking brunette who looked to be in her mid-30s.

Anna watched as the woman in the African robe suggested to the group that they begin their meal with a prayer. They all joined hands in a ring and the woman offered up a prayer that they might be able to share their blessings with those less fortunate.

How unusual, the young waitress thought.

Following the prayer, Anna began to deliver the salads—*always from the left side,* she reminded herself. She kept her eyes down-cast; she was trying to be subservient, yet pleasant, the way they'd taught her. She glanced up briefly to see who hadn't yet received a salad and noticed that the brunette was looking at her. Directly at her. *Have I done something wrong?* The woman was dressed simply, yet elegantly. Her only touch of color came from a silk scarf, patterned with brilliant monarch butterflies, tied loosely around her neck. Anna felt embarrassed. She glanced back down and as she did, she noticed the head of the serpent tattoo on her own forearm, peeking out from the end of her sleeve. Evidence of a former life. But now she was a single mother, with a young son to take care of. She adjusted her apron and stood straighter. She wasn't going to be intimidated by these people.

She had her dignity, too. Still, she wondered how they all had gotten here.

After the main course had been served, Anna began to refill the water glasses. She glanced up. *Is she looking at me again?* Anna quickly finished her rounds and disappeared into the kitchen to prepare to deliver the dessert.

After dessert, for some reason, Anna felt compelled to linger near the door as the brunette rose to address the group.

"Hi, my name is Michelle," she began. "I used to be a waitress here."

Impossible, thought Anna, feeling guilty to be eavesdropping. But as she listened to the story of how the woman named Michelle had become a millionaire, an expectant hope began to build in her.

"I'm looking to repay my debt to Samantha," the woman continued, absently fingering the butterfly scarf, "by finding someone to mentor just as Sam mentored me."

The young waitress had been listening intently, her head down, staring at her drab waitress shoes. When she heard this last statement, she looked up suddenly.

The two women made eye contact.

A FINAL WORD...

You Can Be a Millionaire

We have given you the techniques, the technology, the mind-set, the principles, and the ways to effectively apply them to manifest *leveraged* results now. You came here to learn and vastly increase your earnings. We are cheering you on to your finest hour yet.

When we started, we had a dream **to create a million millionaires in this decade.** To do that, we must have over 10 million readers. That's one of our goals. We will only achieve it with your help. We want you to encourage three of your friends, relatives, and loved ones to read, absorb, discuss with you, and apply the wisdom and insights of this book.

The toy that started out as fiction took on life and became a reality with the Hasbro Toy Company. We want you to see that toy, called The Always Together Bear. Please visit our website (www.oneminutemillionaire.com) and we'll share with you the story of how this toy was "manifested" into reality using the principles taught in this book. The book and the toy demonstrate as proof positive that what we teach and practice is true.

We want to stay in touch with you and help you achieve all your hopes, dreams, and desires. We also want you to share with us your success stories and let you read others at our website.

Additionally, if you visit our website, we will invite you *free* to a future, live teleseminar taught by "Mark and Bob."

We eagerly look forward to meeting and greeting **YOU.**

Mark Victor Hansen & Robert G. Allen

ACKNOWLEDGMENTS

We dreamed the impossible dream, conceived an outrageous title, and got together a team that would support it and help us make it happen, for which we are humbly and deeply thankful and eternally appreciative.

Great books happen because Dream Teams are assembled to make them happen. We are deeply thankful to everyone who has helped, whether they are known and unknown to us, and we apologize if we inadvertently missed someone.

We have the agent of agents, Jillian Manus. We love, like, respect, appreciate, and admire her. Jillian went the extra mile for us at every turn. As James Bond said: "Nobody does it better." As neophytes at fiction writing we were introduced to the perfect coach and helper in Donna Levin. Donna guided, guarded, edited, and taught us how to improve and perfect our treasurable story. Donna, you are a true master. We couldn't have done it without you.

Our lifelong friend and colleague Marshall Thurber worked ceaselessly with us to ensure that readers would have a predictable system to become millionaires, if they would but work the system. Marshall's brilliant and creative thinking was enormously helpful and totally appreciated. Thanks a million, Marshall!

We love and thank our wives, who supported a book task that constantly expressed as leaky margins due to our breakthrough thinking. We deeply appreciate Patty Hansen and Daryl Allen for understanding, love, encouragement, and helpful ideas and thoughts—through each iteration— of this book. We respectfully thank Patty Hansen for her tireless assistance with legal accounting and permissions and for her brilliant business insights.

Wow! How did we get so blessed as to have the world's best and most caring editor, Becky Cabaza, at the crème de la crème of publishers, Harmony Books?

Our respective staffs have raised us on their shoulders and done their jobs better than ever to free our time so we could deliver this project, which we believe will change the economic future of the world. Our deepest thanks go to Mark's staff: Lisa Williams, Trudy Marschall, Michelle Adams, Dee Dee Romanella, Dave Coleman, Shanna Vieyra, Jody Emme, Mary McKay, Carly Baird, and Laurie Hartman. Bob's working staff smiled and helped throughout the process. We thank Joyce Edlebrock, Maria Carter, Trulene Hutchings, Jan Stephan, Phyllis Martell, Annie Taylor, Kurt Mortensen, Mike Ray, Steve Waters, Tad Lignell, Lisa Taylor, Dan Brink, Jared Severe, Emily Spencer, Jake Simpson, Dan Micheli, Dave Williams, Curtis Holder, Denise Michaels, and Matt Jensen.

Our deepest gratitude goes to Janet and Chris Attwood, who worked with us to create the Millionaire Eagles program to test, teach, and perfect these principles, strategies, and techniques. Their colleague Pat Burns worked relentlessly on our Millionaire Summit to help make millionaires into billionaires and supergivers. Tom Painter gave us incredible marketing support through the Multiple Streams of Income. Tom is a true marketing genius and we couldn't get our message to the world without him. You all impressed us and the world by taking pure imagination and turning it into dramatic proof of positive realization.

We wrote about a toy that our fictional shero Michelle used to make a million in 90 days. To our amazement, Mike Fry owned the patent to the real toy and shared it with us. Better yet, Mike introduced us to the world's most profitable and famous toy creator, Joan Kaplan, who quickly and effectively created our masterpiece called The Always Together Bear. Joan sold the concept and idea to the toy company of toy companies Hasbro, and they said: "Congratulations, you are 'One Minute Millionaires,' you have the next 'Cabbage Patch Dolls,' and we're doing the impossible for you and bringing it out this Christmas." We love the Hasbro team, Joan, and Mike for believing in the impossible and making it possible.

Several people provided content for the Millionaire Minutes. We would like to thank John Eggen for his brilliant insight in brainstorming the One Minute Marketing Plan and the magnet analogy (Aha #19). Thanks to Al Fahden and Linda Chandler for much of the unique material in the section on teams. The HOTS model is their proprietary content and they have graciously allowed us to share it with you. Also, Frank Wagner provided excellent material on networks. Thanks, Frank. Thanks to Patrick Chisholm for his sharp researching skills. Thanks to Cindy Cashman and Paul Hartunian for their excellent advice and examples. Thanks to Stacy Hall and Jan Brogniez for the material on Attracting Perfect Customers from their excellent book by the same name. Thanks to Don Wolfe for the material on Transformational Learning. Thanks to all the dozens of others who helped in a myriad of ways.

Obviously, we are profoundly thankful that the principles work that we wrote about in our book. We used what we teach to deliver these extraordinary results. These principles manifested all of the preceding individuals and companies and made the impossible possible. We hope these ideas and principles will do the same or more for you.

We also want to thank the thousands of our students in dozens of cities in North America who served as the true "guinea pigs" for this book. Specifically, to Karen Nelson Bell and her husband Duncan Guertin. All of the fictional properties that Michelle bought were patterned after actual real estate deals that Karen and Duncan did on their way to becoming real Enlightened Millionaires. Thanks, guys! The names of our Millionaire Eagles are printed on the following pages. You can read their incredible true stories on the One Minute Millionaire website.

We appreciate you, our fans and readers, for reading, absorbing, and using the principles in the book and sharing them with those whom you love and care about. We hope this book makes your wallet grow and your soul glow as you philanthropically share with others. Again, thank you for reading us.

Mark Victor Hansen

and

Robert Allen

Linda Kreplick Anita Kugler Tim & Preeta Kuhlman Dan Kuschell Carol Kwek Joe LaCount Liz Lafferty Dr. Gilles Lamarche Michael Lang Paul Langstaff Elaine Larson Guy & Lisa Larson Julie Larson Carrie Lauer She'lah La'Voyn Donald Lawrence Tom Lee Sharon D. LeFlore Bruce Len Tom Lenahan Mary Ann Leslie Lawrence Levin Stewart Levine Jasun Light Michael Lim Sue Lindequist Ralph Linzmeier Albert Litto Wayne Livingood Debora Logan Liza Lomboy John Lonczynski Keith & Gini Lovell Jenny & Curt Lovins Susan Lowes Edward Lubrano Ryan & Caroline Luelf Paul Luskin Scott Lynch Sue-Ann MacGreggor Susanna MacGregor Lori Mackey Carleen MacNeil Judy & Roland Madden Mark Madison Carlos Magana Michael J. Maggio Tim Mai Aliah MaJon Cheryl & Greg Malcham Marianne Manning Michael Manning Karmen Marasovich Art Marchand James Markey Brian & Deborah Marling Jared Eric Marshall Carolann Martin Kevin Martin Greg Mascaro Rance Masheck Bruce Mason David Massar Matt & Grace Masterson Vera Matovina Steven Mattos Trevor McAlpine Shar McBee Bobbi McKenna Dave McKibben Denise & Frank McKinley Ken McLachlan Jorli McLain Kathleen McNamara Darren & Donna McNees Jackie McReynolds Ivy Meadors Carol Merlo Denise Michaels Kathleen Mierswa Eleanor Milinusic Dan Miller Fred Miller Melanie Mills Ann Mincey Amanda Misasi Cynthia Mitton Michelle Mitton Potheri Mohan Sarah Mondol Brook Montagna Ples & Betty Montgomery Gerry Moore Michael Moore Keith & Lynn Morales Sally A. Moran Sheevaun O'Connor Moran Julia Moses Betty Muegge Laura Mullaly Carla Myers Sharon Myers Beverly & Denise Nadler Rao Narra Lacy Nathan Louisa Nedkov Anastasiya Nesterenko Jacob & Robyn Nielsen Eduardo Nieto Shirley Norway Linda M Nowell Jerrie Noyes Dawn Oakes Cheryl Oaks Ikechukwu (Ike) Odum Diane Ogden K. J. Ogden Dr. Michael O'Halleran Dr. Drew Oliphant Kim Ortloff Bill & Joan Ortman Michelle Ota Bob Paeth Gary Page Kevin Page Tom Painter Ruben Palacios Tim Parent C. Olivia Parr-Rud Angele Patenaude Mark Paton Doris Payne Tim & Helen Peak Collynn Pearl Marsha Pederson Janet & Brooks Peek Suze Penton David Perkins Julie & John Pfister Gregory Phillips Vivian Phillips Jim & Mary Piccolo Sandy Pichitpai Lynn Pierce Pepper Pierson Jo Ann Pina, Ph.D. Jerry Piper Paul Pittana Ray & Christine Pizinger Hector & Florence Placencia Sylvia Poareo Donna Poisl Tina Polk Elena Popp Aimee Poquette Alison Porter Carol Porter Joan Portman Valorie Prahl Rev. Margaret Price James Proetz Lisa Provenza Kelly Pryde Steven Pybrum Max & Marla Quintana Esperanza Rader Edie Raether Aubrey Rankin Alexis Ray Ellen Reach Tim & Tammy Reading Susan Redfern Audrey Reed Don Reed Georgia Hanes Reed Linda Reeder Peter Reichert Ellen Reid Paula M. Reid Sara & John Reid Rebecca Rengo David & Carol Renner Roger Resnick Paul Ricard Dr. CC Rice Debbie Ringchop Michael Rivait Don Roach Ray Robbins Wendy Robbins Mark Roberts Virginia Rocha Charmaine M & Frank Rosales Jana Rosenblatt Pamela Roskin Jay Rothstein Julie & Don Roy Allen Rubin Kathy Ryan Robin Ryan Phyllis Ryser N. Leina Santana Anne Saylor Lorna Schauseil Bob Scheinfeld Dan Schmidt Steven E. Schmitt Terry & Joni Schneider Ruth Schuckard Pat Schuler Flora & Peter Schupp Marilyn Schwader Radhika Schwartz David & Alicia Sciortino David & Chari Scott Ryan Scotting Irene Segal Steven Selig Mary Sell David & Sonja Selley Craig Senior Samantha Servey Lance Shaw Wesley & Dottie Sheader Tatiana Shevchuk David Shihadeh Marci Shimoff Harold Shore Terry Shreeve Stuart Silverberg Charnetta Simmons Dawn & Pete Simon James R. Sinclair David Slettum Linda Slocum Paul Sloop Jr Pamela & Wayne Slowick Gary Smiley Bill Smith Brian Smith Carol Smith Paul K. Smith Peggyanne Smith Robert Smith Lynn Sokolov Angela Solis John & Theresa Sorflaten Judy Sorrells Dr. Minta Spain John Speer Rose Spurrier Priscilla Staffl Scott Stanglin Rich Starr Jan & Randy Steinman Michael Stephenson Paul & Rise' Stokstad Gail Stolzenburg David & Bobbie Stratman Suzanne Struble Michael & Ann Marie Stuart Judy Suke Joy Sullivan Bill & Abby Swartz Peggy Swords Russell Sydney Fred Talisman Pilar Tan John D. Tasa Richard Taylor Rosann Taylor Olga Teleguina Steve Tenney Sean Terry Bonnie E. Thompson Debra Thompson Ken Thompson Ric & Liz Thompson Robin Thompson Victor Tichy Patrick Tierney Donna Tighe James Tjulander Steve & Cheryl Tochterman Danny Torak Brian Tracy Anjalie Trice Manuel & Candie Trujillo Rose Tubati Bob Tubridy Penelope Tzougros Dr. James Underwood D.C. Elizabeth Updike Dan & Lorraine Urbina Bob Uyeda Tommy Vadell Olga & Andre Vainberg Sona van der Hoop Mary & Richard Van Dyke John Verkley Greg & Judy Verkuilen David & Judy Vigil Ouida Vincent MD John Visser Arti Pramod Vora Norma Vranken Mark Wakeman Kay Walburger Kevin Walls Patty Walters Janet Smith Warfield Kitty Watkins Timothy Watson Fran Weiland Skip Weisman Gabrielle Weiss Kim Whalen Vashti Whelan Maggie White Nancy Marie White Sarah White Susie Wild Joe & Lori Wilkinson Lisa Williams Del Metri Williams Lisa Williamson Elise Wilson Mark Wilson Mary Anne Wilson Ray Wilson Lou Ann Winchester Rachel Wolcott Mary Wood Debbie Wood Andrew Wozniewicz Randy Wright Mary Wylie Lonnie Yanda Bonita Joy Yoder Sandra Young Jolanta Zakrzeloska Arlina Zaplutus Alicia Zavala Larry Zogby John James Zoltek

INDEX

commitment (*cont.*):
  second step, xx
  signing up, xix, xx
computers, 118
Confucius, 140
congruence, 74, 76, 94
connectors, 196, 198
control, 240
conversion opportunities, 276
Conwell, Russell H., 98, 100, 314, 356, 358
Cosby, Bill, 100
Coué, Emile, 64
Council of Light, 142
Covey, Stephen R., 94, 132
Creating Wealth (Allen), 348
credit cards, 296
cross-pollination, xxiii
customer service, 322, 324

D
Daniels, Peter J., 84
decision, 8
DeGreen, Keith, 114
Deming, W. Edwards, ix–x, 252
desire, 74, 94
destiny, 58, 60
destruction, 90, 92
Diana, Princess of Wales, 140
discounting real estate, 274, 298
Disney, Walt and Roy, 168
distressed properties, 276
drawbacks, 186
dream, 48, 50
Dream Team:
  characteristics of, 162
  creation of, 172, 174
  leverage of, 162
  manifestation, 188
  maximum benefits from, 184, 186
  organizing, 178, 180, 182
  speed of, 182, 184
  your own, 164, 166, 168
Dyer, Wayne, 220

E
earnings, 240
Eat That Frog (Tracy), 246
Eddy, Mary Baker, 140
Edison, Thomas A., 166
education, 360
emergency funds, 240
Emerson, Ralph Waldo, ix, 130
endarkened Millionaire, xiv
energy, zero, 262
engineers vs. artists, iv
Enlightened Millionaire, iii
  commitment, xxvi–xx

decision of, xi
diagnostic, 1
DNA of, xv
  Manifesto, xiii–xiv
  moment of, xii
  paradoxes of, 30
  pattern of, xii
  principles of, xvi–xvii
  to sign up, xix
  technique of, xii
  threshold of, xii
enough, 96
entrepreneurship, 70, 316, 318
exercise, 246

F
Fahden, Allen, 176
Feldman, Ben, 68
financial goals, 54
flipping techniques, 278, 304, 306
focus, 244
Ford, Henry, 92, 166
Fox, Betty, 232
Free Agent Nation (Pink), 230
freedom, 44, 46
free will, 26
FTF (Feared Things First), 244
fulcrum, 108
Fuller, R. Buckminster, xiii, 132, 140, 216
furniture, splitting off, 300

G
Gardner, Howard, 46
Gates, Bill, 28, 56, 166
Gates, Melinda, 28
genius, tapping into, 56, 58, 60
giving, 22, 30, 32, 82, 84, 86, 224
Gladwell, Malcolm, 196
Gleick, James, ix
goals, 54, 56, 246, 322
Golf My Way (Nicklaus), 50, 52
Graham, Benjamin, 128, 130
Graham, Katharine, 140

H
Hall, Stacy, 330, 332
Hansen, Mark Victor, 114, 132, 148, 168
Hares, 176, 178
Hasbro Toy Company, 375
Hawthorne/Stone Real Estate and Investments, 190
Herbert, Frank, 218
heroes/sheroes, 140, 142
Hill, Napoleon, 78
Hippocratic oath, xvii
home equity loans, 296
Hotchner, A. E., xvi